The PHOTO SHOP WOW! BOOK

The PHOTOSHOP WOW! BOOK

Tips, Tricks, & Techniques for Adobe Photoshop

Windows Edition

Linnea Dayton & Jack Davis

The Photoshop Wow! Book, Windows edition

Linnea Dayton and Jack Davis

Peachpit Press, Inc.
2414 Sixth St.
Berkeley, CA 94710
(510) 548-4393
(510) 548-5991 (fax)

ISBN 1-56609-070-9

0 9 8 7 6 5 4 3 2 1
Printed by Penn & Ink through Colorcraft, Ltd., Hong Kong

To Joe and Betty Brown, Laura, Kathy, and Sandy Z.

— Linnea Dayton

To the artists and designers exploring the new mediums of creative communication; to our family and friends; and, to The Source of all creativity, who graciously allows us to participate in the act of creation.

— Jack and Jill Davis

ACKNOWLEDGMENTS

This book would not have been possible without a great deal of support. First, we would like to thank the Photoshop artists who have allowed us to include their work and describe their techniques in this book; their names are listed in the Appendix. We are also grateful to many Photoshop artists whose work does not appear in the book but who have passed along some of their Photoshop knowledge and experience; among them are Russell Brown, Daniel Clark, Robert Schwarzbach, Michael Ulrich, and Mark Siprut. We appreciate the support of Adobe Systems, Inc., particularly Steve Guttman, Jeff Parker, Rita Amladi, LaVon Peck, Eric Thomas, Brian Lamkin, and the technical support group, who kept us up to date on the development of the program, supplied us with software, and answered our technical questions.

We are grateful to Lisa King and Matthew Rantanen, who helped us with research and production and to John Odam, who made the resources of his studio available when our work expanded beyond the capabilities of our equipment. Thanks also to our service bureau, Laser Express of San Diego, whose principals were delighted to take on the task of outputting our PageMaker 4.2 files through Aldus PrePrint from their Select Set 5000 imagesetter, and whose operators worked like champs to get the job done.

We'd like to thank the friends, family, colleagues, and co-workers who supported us throughout this endeavor, and who only occasionally told us to "get a life."

And finally, our heartfelt thanks to Jill Davis, the third member of our team and one of the most positive and competent human beings we've ever had the pleasure to know. She designed the book and managed the production, from rough layouts to finished film, and we simply couldn't have done it without her.

CONTENTS

WELCOME TO *THE PHOTOSHOP WOW! BOOK*

ADOBE PHOTOSHOP IS ONE OF THE MOST POWERFUL visual communication tools ever to appear on the desktop. The program has expanded the visual vocabulary of designers and illustrators to include color photo imagery, making photos the "raw material" for creative expression. It also lets photographers do their magic in the light, without chemicals! And it makes it much easier to do the resizing, cropping, and basic color correction of production work. Beyond that, it provides a laboratory for synthesizing textures, patterns, and special effects that can be applied to photos, graphics, or video.

As our time spent using the program began to exceed 90 percent of the work day, as we watched others experiment, and as we saw the near miraculous transformations that appeared on-screen, the tools the program provided, the shortcuts for carrying out complicated changes, and the ways people combined the things Photoshop could do, the response we continuously heard was "Wow!" So when we needed a title for this book we were planning, it just sort of came naturally — *The Photoshop Wow! Book.*

HOW TO USE THIS BOOK

You'll find five kinds of information in the body of this book: (1) basic information about how Photoshop's tools and functions work, (2) short tips for making your work quicker and easier, (3) step-by-step techniques for particular kinds of projects, (4) galleries of work done by experienced Photoshop artists, and (5) illustrated lists of resources — the images and other products that can make Photoshop even more valuable and easy to use.

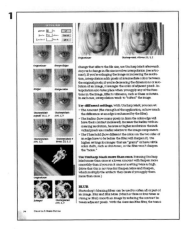

1 The **Basics** sections tell how Photoshop's functions work. *The Photoshop Wow! Book* wasn't designed to be a substitute for the *Adobe Photoshop User Guide,* which is an excellent reference manual. Instead we've gathered and condensed some of the most important of the basics, and in some cases explained a little further, with the idea that understanding how something works can make it easier to remember and to apply in new ways. Our goal is to provide an "under-the-hood" look at Photoshop that will help you maximize the program's performance and your own productivity with it.

2 To collect the kind of hands-on information that can make you instantly more efficient, flip through the book and scan the **Tips.** You can easily identify them by the title bar on top. The tips are a kind of hypertext — linked bits of information that we've positioned alongside the basics and techniques wherever we thought they'd be most useful. But you can pick up a lot of useful information quickly by reading the tips on their own.

3 Each **Technique,** presented in 1 to 4 pages, is designed to give you enough step-by-step information so you can carry it out in Photoshop. Our goal was to provide enough written and pictorial instructions so you wouldn't have to hunt through the manual to follow the steps. But to spare you a lot of repetition, we've assumed you know the basic Macintosh interface — how to open and save files, for instance — and we've focused on specific techniques in some cases, rather than explaining every technique used in a particular project. Some techniques are presented using artwork created specifically for the demonstration. Other techniques are descriptions of the methods artists used to create particular illustrations or parts of illustrations. Since Photoshop 2.5 is the first version of the program that's available on the Windows platform, many of the examples shown in the book were done on the Macintosh, some of them in earlier versions than 2.5. However, we've updated the techniques for the current version and for the Windows platform.

The step-by-step techniques consist of numbered, illustrated instructions. The first step of each technique tells, briefly, how to get to the starting point. If you need to know more about some process described in step 1, check the index for references to other sections of the book.

4

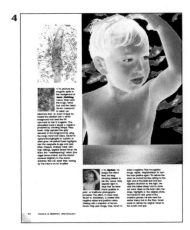

5

4 The **Galleries** are there for inspiration. Each gallery piece includes a description of how it was produced. Many of the techniques mentioned in the Galleries are described more fully elsewhere in the book. Again, check the index if you need help finding a particular technique.

5 Throughout the book, and especially in Chapter 5, "Using Filters," and in the Appendix at the back, is information you can use to locate the kinds of **Resources** Photoshop users need to know about, such as stock photo images, and plug-in filters.

Experiment! The techniques and examples presented in this book are there to get you started using the tools if you're new at it, and to give you some new insight and ideas if you're an old hand. As you read the book and try out the tips and techniques presented here, we hope you'll use them as a jumping off place for your own fearless experimentation.

Linnea Dayton
Jack Davis

December 1993

PHOTOSHOP BASICS

THIS CHAPTER IS DESIGNED TO GIVE YOU some general pointers on using Photoshop more easily and efficiently. But it won't replace the *Adobe Photoshop User Guide* or the *Tutorial* as a comprehensive source of basic information.

CPU, RAM, AND ACCELERATION

Photoshop files tend to be large — a lot of information has to be stored to record the color of each of the thousands or millions of dots that make up an image. So it can take quite a bit of computer processing just to open a file (which brings that information into the computer's memory, or RAM) or to apply a special effect (which can involve complicated calculations that change the color of every dot in the image). Photoshop needs a lot of RAM to hold an image while it works on it. Although you can do a lot of good Photoshop work on a smaller, slower, less powerful computer system, the program works best if you have a fast computer, a great deal of RAM, full photorealistic color, and a very large, fast hard disk.

The minimum system that the Photoshop packaging says will run the Windows version of Photoshop 2.5 is an 80386 or faster PC with 4 MB available for running the program (that doesn't include RAM required for supporting the system), MS-DOS 5.0, Windows 3.1, a VGA monitor and adapter, and a mouse or a stylus and pressure-sensitive tablet. For decent Photoshop performance, though, Adobe recommends using an 80486 processor running in 386 Enhanced mode (rather than Standard mode) and more than 8 MB of RAM. To work comfortably with photorealistic color, you'll also need a 24-bit graphics card suited for the size of your color monitor, and, as they become available for Windows machines, accelerator products designed specifically to support some of Photoshop's calculation-intensive functions, such as running filters or resizing images.

If Photoshop doesn't have enough room to handle a file entirely in RAM, it can use hard disk space instead. In that case, the amount of empty hard disk space (you'll want three to five times the size of any file you work on) and the transfer rate of the disk drive (the speed at which data can be read off a disk)

continued on page 6

UPDATING DRIVERS

Adobe's Technical Support team reports that the difficulties most commonly encountered by new users of Photoshop for Windows are problems that result from incompatible drivers, the programs that interface between Photoshop and the video system, a scanner, a digitizing tablet, or a printer, for example. These drivers are made not by Adobe but by the manufacturers of the equipment they drive. You'll need to check with the manufacturers to get the latest versions of the drivers.

Resetting the amount of virtual memory for a system with 16MB of RAM, so that it's double the amount of RAM.

REDUCING THE DISK CACHE

To gain more RAM for Photoshop to use, you can reduce the disk cache (the amount of RAM that the Windows SmartDrive application reserves to hold program code that has been loaded from the disk recently and that it therefore assumes may be needed again soon). The "Getting Started" booklet suggests reducing the disk cache to 512K. You can do that by using the Windows Notepad to open the autoexec.bat file and typing some memory specifications into the default SmartDrv command line.

Working at low resolution saves time and disk space. Several designs for the Healthy Traveler book cover were worked out at 72 dpi so that a design direction could be chosen for development at high resolution, as described in Chapter 9.

become important. One way to gain disk space is to cut down on the amount used by Windows, although you don't want to reduce it so much that it interferes with the operation of the system. The "Getting Started" booklet that comes with Photoshop suggests setting the Windows program's own Virtual Memory reserve to the equivalent of RAM if you have 20 MB of RAM or more, or to twice the amount of RAM if you have less than 20 MB. You can change the Virtual Memory setting by double-clicking the Main icon in the Program Manager, then double-clicking the Control Panel icon and then the 386 Enhanced icon. Then click the Virtual Memory button and the Change button and set the Drive (fastest hard drive), Type (Temporary), and New Size.

WORKING SMART

Once your system is set up with lots of RAM, a fast hard disk drive, and a 24-bit graphics card, here are some other things you can do to reduce the time you spend in "hourglass land":

- **Starting out in low resolution.** For some images you can do your planning and "sketching" on a lower-resolu-

KEEPING PALETTES HANDY

The control palettes for Paths (the pen tool), Info, Colors, Brushes, and Channels can be kept available and ready to use without taking up much space on your screen. Click the small box in the upper right corner of each palette to collapse it, and then store the palettes along the edges of the screen. (Option-click the box to collapse a palette even further, to its title bar alone.) When you click the box again to expand the palette so you can use it, it will pop up into the window.

A set-up for working efficiently in Photoshop, with most of the palettes available, a second window open for close-up work, and rulers to indicate size.

Alpha channels can be saved separately from their original file in order to reduce file size. As long as the main image stays the same size, the channels can be loaded as selections through the Image, Calculate, Duplicate command.

tion file than you will ultimately need for output. (See "Resolution" later in the chapter for a discussion of how to determine the resolution you need.) Working at low resolution will reduce processing time for changes you make to the image. Although you may have to make some of the changes again when you begin work on the higher-res file, certain of the changes can be saved as dialog box settings and then loaded and applied to the bigger file with a click of the mouse. For instance, settings for the four most useful functions of the Image, Adjust submenu — Levels, Curves, Hue/Saturation, and Variations — can be saved.

- **Building a file in stages.** If you're planning to modify and combine images, do the modifications on the separate, smaller parts first, and then combine them into a larger file.

- **Saving selections as you work.** If you're making a complex selection, save it periodically to an *alpha channel,* a permanent, stored selection mask. (Making selections and using alpha channels are discussed in Chapter 2.) With some version of the selection saved, if you accidentally drop the selection, you won't have to start over completely. And be sure to save the selection as an alpha channel when it's finished, so you can reselect exactly the same area if you need to later. (If you're using the pen tool to create a selection outline, save the selection as a path rather than as an alpha channel, because it takes much less disk space.)

- **Saving alpha channels as separate files.** To cut down on the amount of space a file occupies when you store it or send it for output, or to eliminate extra channels that will prevent placing the image in a page layout, you can save the alpha channels as a separate Multichannel file. Do this by running the Image, Calculate, Duplicate function to make a second copy of the file. Then delete the alpha channels from one of the files and delete the RGB channel from the other. That way the finished file is free of excess baggage, but you can use Image, Calculate, Duplicate to load the alpha channel back into the main image as a selection.

- **"Emptying" the clipboard.** If you cut or copy something to the clipboard, it's retained in RAM even after you paste a copy in place. Since some of Photoshop's commands can be carried out only in RAM (not in virtual memory) and since Photoshop doesn't have a Clear command to empty the clipboard, the best strategy for releasing the RAM from a large clipboard selection you no longer need is to replace the clipboard contents with something really small. Select a small area (just a few pixels) and choose Edit, Copy. Or

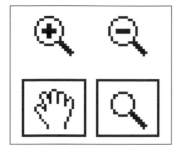

You can use these magnifier tools or use keyboard shortcuts. To zoom in while using another tool, press Ctrl-spacebar; to zoom out, press Alt-spacebar.

KEEPING TRACK OF SIZE

Use Rulers (Window, Show Rulers, or Ctrl-R) if you need a reminder of how much of your image you're looking at (see the illustration at the bottom of page 6). In showing the dimensions, the Rulers display takes into account the resolution of the image.

OPENING TWO WINDOWS

When you're doing close-up work, it's a good idea to keep a second window open with a 1:1 view. Sometimes changes that look smooth close-up are very obvious when you zoom out, or vice versa. To open a second window on the same file (as shown on page 6) so that each window reflects the changes you make in the other, choose Window, New Window.

launch the clipboard viewer from the Main group and delete the clipboard through the Edit menu.

- **Cleaning up virtual memory.** If Photoshop tells you it can't complete an operation because there isn't enough space in virtual memory, simply closing another file that's open on-screen may not release the space you need. After you close the files, save a document in Photoshop 2.5 format to get the hard disk to clean up its virtual memory allocation. If that doesn't do the trick, you can Exit the program and start up again. Or go to the Windows Program Manager, Main, File Manager and search for and delete "*.tmp" files (any temporary files, which will have the .tmp suffix).

- **Closing other applications.** When you want to work in Photoshop, open Photoshop first, before opening any additional applications (other than Windows). If you find that you need more RAM, close any other programs you have open. Even if you aren't doing anything with them, open applications reserve their assigned amount of RAM, which may cut down on the amount available to Photoshop.

- **Taking advantage of on-line help.** The Windows version of Photoshop provides a handy reference through the Help selection in the main menu. In addition, many dialog boxes have a Help button along with OK, Cancel, and others. Though not as complete a guide as the printed manual, on-line help puts a great deal of useful information at your fingertips.

CHANGING YOUR VIEW

As you work with Photoshop, you'll want to change your view:

- From close-up views (so you can work in fine detail),

- To 1:1 view, which shows the image at your monitor's resolution and shows editing most accurately,

- To zoomed-out views (for making an image small, so you can get it out of the way, for example, or so you can get an overview of a large image).

Zooming in. There are several ways to get a close-up view:

- For an enlarged view centered on the click point, click with the magnifier tool. The window size stays the same, but the view doubles or halves with each click, so the magnifications you get are 2, 4, 8, and 16 times the 1:1 view.

- **To enlarge a particular area,** drag the magnifier across the area you want to view. It will enlarge to fill the window.

- **To increase both window size and image size in steps** from 1:1 to 2:1 to 3:1 to 4:1, press Ctrl-+ (really Ctrl-=

To have several windows open and available on-screen without stacking them on top of one another, choose Tile (rather than Cascade) from Photoshop's Window menu.

Holding down the Alt key makes the eraser operate in Revert mode (right), restoring the last saved version of the image.

Define Pattern
Take Snapshot
Composite Controls...

Rubber Stamp Options

Option: From Snapshot   UK

Stylus Pressure

Vary: ☐ Size   Cancel

☐ Opacity   Help

Storing a current image or selection in a Snapshot buffer (found under Edit) makes it possible to restore it later with the rubber stamp tool.

RESETTING DIALOG BOXES

You can cancel the settings you've made in a dialog box by clicking Cancel to close the box. But if you want to reset the box to its defaults without closing it, hold down the Alt key to turn Cancel into Reset.

because you don't need the Shift key, but Ctrl-+ is an easier way to remember it), or choose Window, Zoom In. The window stops getting bigger when you run out of room, but the image continues to enlarge up to 16:1.

- **To get a close-up view while working with another tool,** press Ctrl-spacebar and click; then release the keys to go right on using the original tool.

Zooming out. There are also several ways to "back away" from the image to get a broader view:

- **To reduce the view,** Alt-click the magnifier tool; the reductions are 1/2, 1/4, 1/8, and 1/16.
- **To reduce both the size and the magnification** of the window from 1:1 to 1:2 to 1:3 and so on, press Ctrl-minus (that's Ctrl-hyphen) or choose Window, Zoom Out. This is a good way to have several windows open and available on-screen without stacking them on top of each other.
- **To zoom out while working with another tool,** press Alt-spacebar and click.

Here are some other view-changing shortcuts:

- **To return to the 1:1 view,** double-click the magnifier.
- **To make the entire image fit in the window,** double-click the hand tool.
- **To center an image on a black screen,** click the right-hand window control at the bottom of the tool palette. This automatically closes the menu bar. To close the palettes as well, press Tab. You can reopen the palettes by pressing Tab again.

RECOVERING

Photoshop 2.5 provides only one level of Undo — you can use the familiar Windows Ctrl-Z (Undo) command only to undo your last instruction to Photoshop. However, the program provides several other very useful options that will allow you to work backwards if you need to. Here are some suggestions:

- **Saving As.** By using the Save As function, you can retain several intermediate versions of a file under different file names. Save As before you start work, and then Save As often during the editing process. Then if you decide to change something that you did halfway through the development of the file, you can open one of the saved files.
- **Reverting to the last saved version.** Choose File, Revert to eliminate all the changes you've made to the file since you last saved it. To restore only part of the image, use the magic eraser, which is the eraser tool with the Alt key held down. Or use the rubber stamp tool in From Saved mode; this method gives hand-held control of the restora-

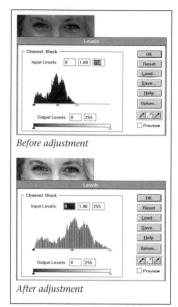

Before adjustment

After adjustment

Increasing contrast in the highlights with the Levels dialog box by moving the Input white point inward

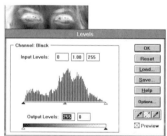

Inverting the image map with the Levels dialog box by moving the Output sliders to opposite ends of the bar

tion process, as does the magic eraser, but with the added control of the mode and brush type.

- **Taking Snapshots.** The Snapshot is a buffer, or storage space, in which you can store one intermediate stage of an image — either the entire image or a selected part of it. Choose Edit, Take Snapshot to store the current image or selection in the buffer. Then you can use the rubber stamp tool in From Snapshot mode to restore the selected area later. (You can make the selection with any selection tool; the buffer will save a rectangular area that includes your entire selection.) Keep in mind that, like the clipboard, the Snapshot ties up RAM. To clear the Snapshot buffer and thus release most of its RAM, in your main Photoshop window select a few pixels with a selection tool and choose Edit, Take Snapshot.

- **Using Levels.** One way to get the most out of a single level of Undo is to use the dialog boxes available through the Image, Adjust submenu — especially the Levels box. With their Preview boxes selected, these dialogs allow you to make and view several changes to an image without leaving the dialog box, so that if you decide you don't want to keep the changes you've made, you can undo all of them at once. And you can save the settings at any point by clicking the Save button, so it's possible to save several intermediate settings before clicking the OK button to finalize changes. Then, if you need to press Ctrl-Z, you can restore an intermediate version of the changes by loading a particular set of saved settings, and go on from there.

Here are some of the changes you can make without leaving the Levels dialog box, and then you can undo them all with Ctrl-Z if you need to:

- By moving the input sliders, you can **increase the contrast** in the highlights, midtones, or shadows independently, for the entire image or for an individual color channel or alpha channel. (For a channel's name to appear in the pop-out menu at the top of the Levels dialog box, the channel must be active for writing — that is, the pencil icon must be showing next to its name in the Channels palette, opened by choosing Window, Show Channels.)

- You can **decrease the contrast** (by using the Output sliders) while lightening or darkening a selected area or an entire image.

- You can use the black (or white) eyedropper to **set the black (or white) point,** pushing to black (or white) all colors darker (or lighter) than the color you select.

SCANNING IN 3D

By placing a small object on a flatbed scanner, you may be able to capture its dimensionality. One or more sides of the object may show, depending on where on the bed you place it.

AVOIDING RAINBOWS

To reduce the rainbow sheen that can appear when you scan a 3D object, select the area and use Image, Adjust, Hue/Saturation to desaturate. In the column of colors at the left edge of the box, sequentially adjust only the red, green, and blue colors (not the cyan, magenta, or yellow) by moving the Saturation slider. The color will remain but the rainbow glare will be lessened. Or scan in Grayscale mode and colorize the image afterwards.

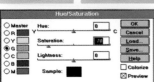

- You can **get rid of a color cast** by clicking the gray eyedropper on a neutral area.
- You can even **make a negative** (accomplishing an Image, Map, Invert) by switching the positions of the black and white sliders on the Output Levels bar.

IMAGE INPUT

Scanners — desktop, mid-range and high-end — can turn photos into image files that can be manipulated in Photoshop. An inexpensive desktop flatbed scanner can capture photographic prints, other hardcopy, and even small three-dimensional objects to make files you can use for photo-illustration. In addition, desktop slide scanners make it possible to capture images from 35 mm transparencies. Many of the images used in this book were scanned on the desktop.

A second input option is to buy scans from service bureaus that have more expensive scanners with more precise optical-mechanical systems. Keep in mind that the quality of a service bureau scan depends not only on the quality of the scanning equipment, but also on the operator's willingness to calibrate and maintain it, and on his or her understanding of color, and skill in operating the machine.

A third option is to have a color specialist scan the image on a high-end scanning system (even more expensive, with even better optics) of the type used by professional color separators for the last few decades. These systems provide excellent optical-mechanical quality for producing sharp scans, and the operators are typically very skilled.

Besides inputting images by scanning, you can also purchase libraries of photos and other artwork already scanned and provided on **CD ROM** (compact disc read-only memory). Many stock images, patterns, and textures are now available on CD ROM, with a variety of arrangements for use and payment (see Appendix A).

Kodak Photo CD technology is making it easy and inexpensive to have images from film (35 mm negatives or slides) stored on a compact disc. The easiest and least expensive way to get your images on Photo CD is to take your film to a photofinisher that offers the Photo CD service and get the Photo CD back along with the finished prints or slides. The images on the disc are relatively high-quality scans, made at high enough resolution so they can be enlarged to about 8 x 10 inches. They are very efficiently compressed and stored in Kodak's Image Pac format, which provides each image in five different resolutions, for use as thumbnails (Base/16 resolution), position-only prints for design purposes (Base/4), display

A known bug in the first released Windows version of Photoshop 2.5 makes opening Photo CD files that are higher resolution than the Base size excruciatingly slow. (If the disk you designate as the primary Scratch disk through the Preferences dialog is fragmented, the process may be even slower.) As this book went to press, Adobe planned to have a "fix" ready by late fall of 1993; you can get on a list to receive the update as soon as it's ready by contacting Adobe's technical support. Eastman Kodak Company, the maker of Photo CD, was also working on a solution.

When an image is scanned for Photo CD, the workstation operator can choose either a *scene space* option or a *universal film terms* option for color. Scene space adjusts the color of the image in an attempt to provide realistic-looking color, correcting for the photographer's incorrect control of the exposure if necessary. Universal film terms saves the image as it was recorded on the film. You may have chosen a particular film for its color characteristics and used a nonstandard shutter speed, so you don't want a standard scene space correction. If that's the case, request that the film be scanned using universal film terms when you take it in for Photo CD processing.

on a computer monitor or TV or for printing at relatively small sizes (Base), display on high-definition television or printing at intermediate sizes (4Base), and printing at large sizes (16Base). Photo CD images are scanned in RGB color and then translated to Kodak's Photo YCC color system because it's compatible with television and it allows efficient compression of data so the images can be stored in less space without losing image quality. To use Photo CD, you need a CD ROM-XA (eXtended Architecture) drive and software that can retrieve the Photo CD images and convert them to a form that Photoshop can use. For this purpose Photoshop includes a plug-in module that lets you open Photo CD files with the File, Open or Open As command.

Digital cameras, which bypass film altogether and record images as digital files on disk, are another potential source of images for manipulation in Photoshop. Although the quality of images taken with relatively inexpensive digital cameras is not as good as film, if the image is to be extensively manipulated for a photo-illustration, the convenience of having the image instantaneously available may outweigh the quality difference.

For imitating traditional art media such as the paintbrush, pencil, airbrush, or charcoal, a **pressure-sensitive tablet** with stylus provides a more familiar feel than a mouse. Photoshop is "wired" to take advantage of pressure-sensitivity to control a number of variables for its painting tools (see Chapter 6).

STORAGE AND TRANSPORT OF FILES

Even if you have enough RAM so you rarely need virtual memory, a large-capacity hard disk will be important for storing the files you work with. (With Photoshop, of course, you can never have enough RAM; as soon as you get more, you need *even more*.) For archiving (long-term storage of files you don't expect to need to work on often), tape backup provides a solution that's relatively compact and inexpensive. But tape cannot be used as a working storage medium; files must be copied from tape to be loaded into Photoshop.

Both Bernoulli systems and SyQuest removable-cartridge disks have become standards for transporting files that are too large — as many Photoshop files are — to fit on a floppy disk. As magneto-optical (MO) read-write drives and desktop CD-ROM writers become less expensive, they may become even more popular than tape or Bernoulli and SyQuest disks for transport and storage.

OUTPUT: PROOFING AND PRINTING

Like other desktop color files, Photoshop images can be printed

Use a defragmenting program such as Norton Utilities' Speed Disk or DOS 6's DeFrag to defragment your hard disks — that is, to collect all the small pieces of storage space that result when a disk is used and reused over time — and combine them into one large space. The goal is to make the Largest Free Contiguous disk space equal to the Free space. That way, when you store a file, it can stay together instead of being broken into parts that have to be sought out separately when Photoshop performs an operation on the file.

on inkjet printers, thermal transfer printers, dye sublimation printers, color photocopiers that can accept digital input, film recorders (as negatives or positive transparencies), or as color-separated film (for making plates for offset printing) from an imagesetter or a high-end color-separation system such as those of Linotype-Hell or Scitex. Typically, inkjet, thermal transfer, or even dye sublimation printers are used to achieve a particular kind of art print quality or to serve as a kind of comprehensive sketch to show generally what the image and the color will look like. Film recorders offer all the options traditionally available for color transparencies.

When color separations are made for offset printing, the contract proof, which a printer and client agree is the color standard that the printer will match on the printing press, is usually a laminate proof generated from the separated film that will be used to make the printing plates. However, a printer with in-house imagesetting capabilities may have enough confidence in a proofing printer such as a Canon Color Laser Copier with Fiery controller that it can be used for contract purposes for some print projects. As direct-to-press printing technology eliminates film altogether for some printing jobs, the film-based proof will be eliminated also, and the "soft" proof (one that is not made from color-separated film) will become more important.

If you've done color artwork on the computer and then printed it out, you know that the color can look quite different on screen than it does on paper. This difference is due to some fundamental differences in the way color is represented on screen and on the printed page. (See "Converting RGB to CMYK" on page 18 for references on getting predictable color.)

RESOLUTION

Resolution is the term used for the number of "spots" (or image units) per inch (or centimeter or some other measure) used in scanning, screen display, imagesetting, or printing. For monitors, scanners, and image files, these units are usually called *pixels;* for halftone printing screens, which are the patterns of tiny spots of ink used for printing, the units are *lines* of dots.

When you're trying to decide on a resolution for scanning or creating an image, the goal is to gather (or create) enough image information to output the image successfully and still minimize the file size — the more information, the bigger and more cumbersome the file. So to determine the appropriate resolution, you need to know how much information the output device will need.

For the many printing processes that use halftone screens, the printer or imagesetter needs at least one pixel of color in-

In scans and screen displays, images are made up of pixels. The pixels are all the same size but vary in color, with over 16 million color possibilities.

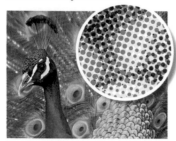

Many printed images are composed of overlaid screen patterns of halftone dots. Dots vary in size, but the number of lines of halftone dots per inch remains constant and the number of ink colors is limited. The spectrum of printed colors results from the visual "mix" of the tiny dots of color.

SIZING FOR COLUMNS

If you're sizing images for a publication whose column width you know, choose File, Preferences, Units and enter the column and gutter widths. Then when you size an image in the Image Size dialog box, you can choose "columns" as the unit of Width and set the number of columns wide that you want the image to be. If you specify more than one column, the calculation takes the gutter measure into account.

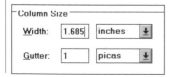

formation to figure out what size to make each halftone dot. The output device can't leave a blank spot if it runs short of information. Instead, it invents the information it needs to fill the blanks. Even if the device is pretty sophisticated in the way it goes about making up the information — averaging it from surrounding dots, for example — this *interpolated* color won't be as sharp and smooth as if the color information had been collected in the scan or painted into the image.

To figure out the setting for scan resolution (the number of *samples per inch* the scanner records) or for Resolution in the New dialog box that opens when you start a new Photoshop file, you can begin by answering the question, "Do you want to be able to see pixels?" That is, in the final printed image, do you want the individual square picture elements to be obvious, providing a kind of computer-age electronic grain? If so, you need only decide how big you want the pixels to be — 72 to the inch or 50 to the inch, for instance — and set your scan or file resolution at that number.

For most applications, though, you probably won't want the pixels to show. Instead you'll want the details and color transitions to be smooth, with the image as sharp as possible. For an image printed with a halftone screen, you'll get better results if the image file can give the output device more dots of information than the halftone *screen frequency*, which is the number of lines of dots per inch used by the printer or the press to put the image onto a page. (Some typical screen frequencies for printing color images on paper are 85 lines per inch for newspapers, 133 and 150 lines per inch for magazines and books. This book was printed at 150 lpi.) A good ratio of scan resolution to screen frequency typically falls within the range of 1.5:1 to 2:1. Under 1.5, image quality may go down noticeably. Over 2, the extra data is essentially wasted — it takes up space in the file but doesn't add significantly to the quality. So, for instance, if your halftone screen frequency for printing will be 150 lpi, you'll need about 225 to 300 dots per inch in your image. (The higher end of this range is needed for images with straight lines or abrupt color transitions.)

Photoshop provides a quick way to calculate the resolution you need for scanning an image on a desktop scanner or creating an image from scratch in Photoshop. Open a new file and choose Image, Image Size to open the Image Size dialog box. Click the Auto button and set the Screen (halftone screen frequency) you and your printer agree on. Choose Medium (1.5 times the halftone screen, for natural, organic images) or High (2 times the screen frequency, for images of man-made elements). Photoshop will tell you the resolution you need for printing.

In subtractive color (represented by the top illustration), cyan, magenta, and yellow inks combine to make a dark, nearly black color. In additive color (bottom), red, green, and blue light combine on screen to make white light.

If you're creating an image from scratch, you can click OK to accept these settings. But is this also the resolution you'll need for scanning an image? That depends on the relationship between the size of the original and the size of the final printed piece. Click OK in the Auto dialog box to return to the Image Size box. Make sure at this point that the Proportion and File Size boxes are not checked. Enter the final printed dimensions for Height and Width. Now measure the dimensions of the original; if you plan to crop the image, use the approximate cropped dimensions here. Next make sure that both the File Size and the Proportion boxes are checked in the Image Size dialog box. Then enter the critical dimension — Height or Width. The other dimension and the resolution will adjust automatically to show you the appropriate scan resolution.

The Image Size dialog box also shows the file size (New Size) of the image. This number can serve as a check when you scan. If you think you've set the dimensions and resolution correctly but the file size is very different from the one you saw in the Image Size dialog box, you'll know you need to investigate to see what's wrong. Likewise, if you order a scan from a service bureau, providing the height, width, resolution, and file size will help ensure that you get the kind of scan you expect.

COLOR IN PHOTOSHOP

Photoshop employs several different systems of color representation. These systems — Bitmap, Grayscale, Duotone, Indexed Color, RGB Color, CMYK Color, and Lab Color — can be selected through the Modes menu.

CMYK Color. Primary colors are the basics from which all other colors can be mixed. In four-color process printing, which is the type of printing most often used for reproducing the photos, photo illustrations, and other works produced in Photoshop, the primaries (called *subtractive primaries*) are cyan, magenta, and yellow, with the potential for adding black to make the dark colors. Black makes dark colors look crisper, and darkening with black requires less ink. This can be important because a press has an upper limit to the amount of ink it can apply to the printed page without problems with the ink adhering to the paper.

To print light colors, the bare paper is allowed to show through between the dots produced by the halftone screens. In halftone screens, the *density* (number of dots per inch) is the same for dark, medium, and light colors. The main characteristic that changes is the *dot size*. A pale yellow, for example, is printed with small dots of yellow and perhaps no dots of the other colors. An intense red might be printed with magenta and yellow dots that are as large as the screen density allows.

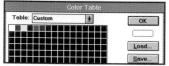

In Indexed Color mode, you can change colors quickly by clicking on the cells of the Color Table. Peter Kaye uses this method to try different colorways in fabric design, as shown here.

Photoshop's Duotone mode provides a way to store curves that can be used for printing a grayscale image in one to four ink colors. The program includes several sets of duotone, tritone, and quadtone curves. Or you can shape the curves yourself. By drastically reshaping the curves as in this tritone, you can make individual colors predominate in highlights, midtones, and shadows.

RGB Color. On the computer monitor, primary colors of light (called *additive primaries*) are generated by bombarding the phosphor coating of the screen with electrons. The mix of red, green, and blue light that results is perceived by the eye as color. When all three colors are ON at full intensity, the result is white light; when all are OFF, black results. Different intensities of energy excite the phosphors to different degrees, so that the three colors mix to form all the colors of the RGB spectrum. Because of the architecture of computer hardware and software, there are theoretically 256 different levels of energy that can be applied to each of the three colors; this means that there are 256 x 256 x 256 (or more than 16 million) colors that can be mixed. This is enough colors to very realistically represent the world we see. It takes 8 bits of computer data (a bit is a 1 or a 0, an ON or an OFF signal) to represent 256 different energy settings; therefore, to represent three sets of energy settings takes 24 bits. So full color as displayed on the computer screen is called 24-bit color.

Indexed Color. Many computers aren't equipped to display 24-bit color. Instead, they can display only 256 colors at once, or 8-bit color. In such a system, 256 colors are stored in a *color look-up table* whose storage addresses are identified by numbers between 0 and 255. The process of assigning 256 colors to represent the millions of colors potentially in a full-color image is called *indexing*. In Photoshop, colors can be indexed to an Exact palette (if the image includes 256 or fewer colors), the Uniform palette (this is the Windows system palette, a set of 256 colors chosen to provide a good color representation of a wide variety of images), an Adaptive palette (the set of the 256 colors most common in a particular image), a Custom palette (a set of colors selected for some particular purpose; several are supplied with the program, or you can make your own), or the Previous palette (the set of colors that was used the last time, within the current Photoshop session, that a file was indexed with a Custom or Adaptive palette.

Lab Color. Instead of being separated into three colors (plus black in the case of CMYK color), color can be expressed in terms of a brightness component and two hue/saturation components. Photoshop's Lab Color mode uses such a system. So does Kodak Photo CD (its Photo YCC color system) and so does color television. The range of colors that a particular color reproduction system can handle is called its *gamut*. Photoshop's Lab Color mode, because its gamut is large enough to include the CMYK, RGB, and Photo YCC gamuts, serves as an intermediate step in converting from RGB to CMYK and from Photo YCC to RGB.

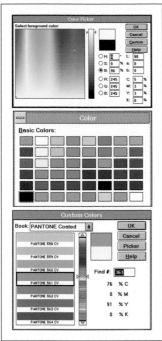

Color picker models shown here are the Photoshop mode (with Brightness selected), the Apple System color wheel, and the Pantone set of custom ink colors.

Grayscale. A Grayscale mode image, like a black-and-white photo, includes only brightness values. Only 8 bits of data are required for storing the 256 shades of gray (including black and white) that this Photoshop mode provides.

Duotone. Even though a Grayscale image can include 256 levels of gray, most printing processes actually produce fewer tones with a single ink color. But with two inks (or even one color of ink applied in two passes through the press), it's possible to extend the tonal range. By adding a second color in the highlights, for example, you increase the number of tones available for representing the lightest grays in an image. Besides extending tonal range, the second color can "warm" or "cool" an image, tinting it slightly toward red or blue. Or the second color may be used for dramatic effect or to visually tie a photo to graphic elements in a publication.

In Photoshop's Duotone mode, a set of *gamma curves* determines how the grayscale information will be represented in each of the ink colors. Will the second color be emphasized in the

Double-clicking Photoshop's gradient tool opens a dialog box that lets you accomplish some amazing color effects.

Choosing Counterclockwise or Clockwise in the Gradient Tool dialog box and then dragging with the tool creates a color blend from the foreground to the background color around the color wheel.

A Radial gradient from white to black in Normal mode made the large "atom." The smaller ones were made in Lighten mode. Then the color of the midtones was changed with Variations.

An amorphous multicolor background can be created by using the gradient tool in individual color channels. Select File, Preferences, General to choose to view color channels in color.

You can offset the "center" of a Radial fill by using the gradient tool inside an elliptical selection.

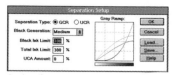

Setting the parameters for converting RGB to CMYK color

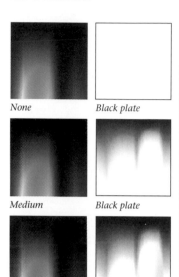

None   *Black plate*

Medium   *Black plate*

Maximum   *Black plate*

shadows but omitted from the highlights? Will it be used to color the midtones? The Duotone image is stored as a grayscale file and a set of curves that will act on that grayscale information to produce two or more separate files for printing (Duotone mode also includes tritone and quadtone options).

Bitmap. The least "bulky" mode in Photoshop is Bitmap, which uses only 1 bit of "color" data to represent each pixel. A pixel is either OFF (black) or ON (white). Photoshop's several methods for converting Grayscale images to Bitmap provide useful options for printing photos with low-resolution, one-color printing methods, as well as some interesting graphic treatments (see Chapter 3, "Enhancing Photos").

Color tools. Photoshop's interface for selecting colors includes color pickers (for selecting the foreground and background colors), the color palette (for mixing and selecting colors), and color tables (for assigning a limited range of colors to be used in an image file). The *Adobe Photoshop User Guide* and *Tutorial* explain how to use these powerful color tools.

CONVERTING RGB TO CMYK

Converting a color image from RGB (for display) to CMYK (to output film for printing) is a complicated process. First of all, not all the colors that can be displayed on screen can be printed, so it's possible to mix colors in RGB files that can't be reproduced on the page. Second, because you're moving from a three-color to a four-color system with black available to substitute for mixes of the other three colors, there are many different ways to represent a particular RGB color in the CMYK system, and because of the way ink pigments interact, all these ways potentially look slightly different.

Photoshop has some built-in features for helping with the RGB-to-CMYK transformation. For example, the Separation Setup function (under File, Preferences) lets you control how the translation from RGB to CMYK will be achieved.

In order for your computer monitor to be as accurate as possible in showing how an image will look when it's printed, all parts of the display and print production systems must be *calibrated,* adjusted to produce color consistently over time. The Gamma utility that comes with Photoshop helps with calibration. The viewing environment must be maintained constant also, so that changes in lighting conditions don't change your perception of colors on the screen. And the parts of the system must be coordinated with one another. To calibrate your system for using Photoshop, start by reading and following the directions in Chapter 15 of the Photoshop user guide. Additional references on prepress color and calibration can be found in "Publications" in Appendix C of this book.

■ **Jack Davis** created *Analog Flame* by applying paint with the paintbrush tool and then smearing it with the smudge (finger) tool. He used a Wacom tablet and stylus for a natural painterly feel, but found that he had to work with a fairly small brush tip in order to get the smudge tool to respond quickly enough to follow his strokes. So he created the painting at half the final size he wanted, with a half-size brush, and then scaled it up later with the Image Size function and with the default Bicubic Interpolation setting in the General Preferences dialog box. With a continuous-tone image like this without any hard edges, the interpolation that Photoshop does during the scaling-up process is very effective at maintaining smooth color transitions. Another technique Davis found helpful for this image with its upward strokes was to paint the image upside down, since it's easier to control the direction of the strokes if you "pull" the brush toward you rather than "push" it away, just as in painting or drawing with natural media.

■ To make *Glasses* **Katrin Eismann** started by placing two glasses at one end of the bed of a desktop scanner and then moved them as the scan was in progress. The original scan is shown at the right. Then she used Image, Adjust, Levels, moving the Input black point slider inward to intensify the colors. Then she used the magic wand (set at a tolerance of 32) to select part of the white background and chose Select, Similar to extend the selection. With the Shift key held down, she clicked the wand and used Select, Similar again to select greenish areas at the bottom of the image. She feathered the selection (Select, Feather); the Feather Radius for this 1800-pixel-wide version of the image is about 5 pixels. Then she filled the selected area with black (Shift-Backspace, with black as the foreground color).

SELECTIONS, MASKS, AND CHANNEL OPERATIONS

PHOTOSHOP PERFORMS MUCH OF ITS MAGIC by working on *selections,* areas of the image that you isolate so you can copy or move them, or so any changes you make will be applied only there. Selections can be made with selection tools, with choices from the Select menu, or with the pen tool from the Paths palette. When you make a selection, a flashing border, or marquee ("marching ants"), lets you see the extent of the selection.

Selections are ephemeral; clicking outside the selection border with a selection tool, choosing Select, Deselect, or pressing Ctrl-D makes the selection border disappear. Unless you first store it as a Quick Mask, an alpha channel, or a pen path, the selection is gone when you deselect it.

SELECTION BASICS

The tools typically used to make selections are the top four in the toolbox (the rectangular and elliptical marquees, the lasso, and the magic wand). The *Adobe Photoshop User Guide* and the *Tutorial* explain how to work the tools. Here are some pointers:

Constraining marquee selections. The rectangular and elliptical marquee tools offer a variety of options for selecting.

- The default mode for the marquee tools is to start the selection from the edge. To select from the center out, hold down the Alt key. You can press the Alt key at any time during the selection process.

- To select a square or circle, constrain the rectangular or elliptical marquee by holding down the Shift key as you drag.

- To make a selection of a particular height-to-width ratio, double-click on either of the marquee tools and set a particular height-to-width ratio in the marquee dialog box. This constrains the marquee to make selections of those proportions.

- To make a selection of a specific size, use the same dialog box that lets you set the height-to-width ratio. Specify the size in pixels. If you want to make a selection of a specific

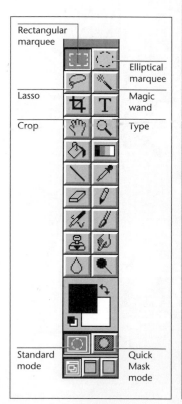

Rectangular marquee

Elliptical marquee

Lasso

Magic wand

Crop

Type

Standard mode

Quick Mask mode

continued on page 22

FINDING IMAGE RESOLUTION

To quickly find the resolution of an image, hold down the Alt key and press on the file size number in the lower left corner of the main image window.

LASSO ALTERNATIVES

With the Alt key held down, you can alternate between clicking straight-line segments with the lasso tool and dragging it freeform. Using the Alt key while dragging also safeguards against accidentally dropping or closing a selection if you inadvertently release the mouse button.

Antialiasing (right) smooths the appearance of edges.

measurement in inches or centimeters, multiply the dimension you want by the resolution of your image in pixels per inch or pixels per centimeter.

Operating the lasso tool. The lasso is probably the most versatile of the selection tools.

- In its default mode you drag it to define a selection border.
- To constrain the lasso to drawing straight-line segments, hold down the Option key and click from point to point. Clicking a series of short line segments to define a smooth curve is often easier and more accurate than trying to trace by dragging the lasso.

Setting magic wand tolerance. The magic wand selects the pixel you click and all other pixels for as far as that color continues. To specify how broad a range of color is included in the selection, double-click the magic wand tool to open its dialog box, and set the Tolerance to a number between 0 and 255. The lower the number, the smaller the range of colors.

Feathering a selection. Feathering is a way of softening the edges of a selection so it blends into the surrounding image. This kind of edge can be useful when part of an image is selected, modified, and then released back into unmodified surroundings. Feathering extends the selection outward but at less than full opacity so that some of the surrounding image is included. At the same time the opacity of the image is also reduced for a distance inside the selection border. The Feather Radius determines how far into and outside the selection border this transition extends. The lasso and both marquees provide feathering.

- To feather a selection as you make it, double-click the tool in the toolbox to open its dialog box so you can set the Feather Radius. Then make the selection.
- To feather a selection after you've made it (if you forgot to set the Feather Radius ahead of time, for example, or if the selection tool you used didn't have a Feather option), with the selection active choose Select, Feather and set the Radius.

Antialiasing a selection. Antialiasing smooths a selection's edge by adding partially transparent pixels to fill in any "stairsteps" of pixels at the selection border. When the antialiased selection is pasted into its new surroundings, these pixels pick up color from the pixels they're pasted on top of so they end up being a color intermediate between the colors on the two sides of the selection border. Of the four selection tools

TOLERANCE VALUES

The Tolerance value set for the magic wand also controls the range of the Select, Similar and Select, Grow commands.

TINY MOVES

Use the keyboard arrow keys to move selections a pixel at a time.

HYBRID SELECTIONS

To make a selection that's partly sharp-edged and partly feathered, set the tool's Feather Radius and make the feathered selection first; then set the Feather Radius to 0 and add the unfeathered selection by holding down the Shift key as you select. (If, instead, you make the sharp-edged selection first and then the feathered, the feather softens the junction of the two selections.)

Feathered selection made first; sharp-edged selection added

BORDER WARNINGS

The Border command doesn't work on a Select, All selection because there's no room in the window to add the border. Also, the Border function can leave some "stairstepping" artifacts on curved and slanted edges.

at the top of the toolbox, the lasso and magic wand can be antialiased; double-click on the tool icon to open a dialog box that lets you choose this feature. The elliptical marquee is antialiased automatically. The rectangular marquee, with its straight-sided selections, doesn't need antialiasing.

Moving a selection. When you move a selection tool icon to the inside of a selection, it turns into an arrow pointer. Drag to move the selection.

Moving the selection border but not the selection. To relocate the selection border without moving any pixels, hold down the Ctrl and Alt keys, place the selection pointer inside the border, and drag.

Extending a selection. You can enlarge a selection in any of these ways:

- To add to an existing selection, hold down the Shift key and use any selection tool. The area you add doesn't have to be in contact with the first selection area.
- To add pixels that are similar in color and adjacent to the current selection, choose Select, Grow (Ctrl-G). The selection will continue to grow as you repeat the command.
- To add all pixels in the image that are similar in color to the pixels in the current selection, choose Select, Similar.

Subtracting from a selection. Hold down the Ctrl key and use any selection tool to surround the area you want to remove from the current selection.

Selecting an intersection. To select the intersection of an existing selection and a new selection, hold down the Ctrl and Shift keys together as you drag to make the new selection. Only the intersection will remain selected.

Selecting a border area. To select an even border area around some part of an image, select that part and then choose Select, Border and specify the width you want that border to be.

Selecting the entire image. Choose Select, All (or use the keyboard shortcut, Ctrl-A) to select the entire image, including any part that extends beyond the current window.

Cropping an image around a selection. If you have an active, unfeathered rectangular selection and you choose Edit, Crop, the image will be cropped to that size, and its window will automatically shrink to fit the new dimensions.

To add or subtract a straight-line lasso selection that starts inside an existing selection, press the Shift or Ctrl key and drag the pointer a very short distance; then, still holding that key down, press the Alt key and begin clicking to make the straight-line segments.

To select something from a solid-color background, make a marquee or lasso selection, then hold down the Ctrl key and click on the solid-color area inside the selection.

If a selection is floating, pressing Ctrl-J or choosing Select, Defloat turns it into a fixed selection that's part of the overall image but is still selected.

Setting crop tool parameters

A one-step crop and rotation of a selection.

COPYING OR FLOATING A SELECTION

Photoshop selections can be either "fixed" or "floating." Moving, cutting, or deleting a fixed selection creates a hole in the image that lets the background color show through. A floating selection, on the other hand, hovers "above" the plane of the image and can be dragged to another position, or deleted, without disturbing the image underneath. Any changes you make to the selection (such as changing its color balance or darkening or lightening it with Levels) won't take effect in the main image until you deselect the selection. And when a selection is floating, you can use any of the controls in the Composite Controls (from the Edit menu) to determine how the selection combines with the image underneath.

You can also convert a fixed into a floating a selection by any of the following methods:

- Choose Select, Float (or press Ctrl-J) to make a copy and float it exactly above the original.

- Hold down the Option key and drag a copy of the selected area to another location in the image.

- Copy the selection to the clipboard (Ctrl-C) and paste it (Ctrl-V) wherever you want it in the image or in another image file.

THE CROP TOOL

The crop tool is a selection tool of sorts — it lets you select a particular area of an image to preserve while you eliminate the area outside. For some situations it provides an advantage over using the rectangular marquee selection tool and the Edit, Crop command because you can move the cropping borders in, out, up, or down by dragging on the corner handles, and you can rotate the cropping frame by Alt-dragging a corner. Click inside the crop with the gavel icon to accept the crop, or click outside with the "Not!" icon to release it so you can start over.

By double-clicking the crop tool icon in the toolbox, you can open a dialog box that lets you set the dimensions you want to crop to and the resolution you want in the cropped image. Note that setting Width and Height values doesn't set a fixed size the way a similar setting does for the rectangular selection marquee. Instead, it makes a cropping box of those *proportions*; the cropped image will then be resized to the dimensions you specified. If you have specified a Resolution value, this will be incorporated in the resizing as well. (Be careful that you don't accidentally increase resolution without realizing it, causing interpolation that can degrade the image.) If you don't specify a resolution, the current resolution will be used.

You can use the special selection properties of the type tool, designed to allow kerning of type, to manage other floating selections. With other selection tools, if you hold down the Ctrl and Shift keys to select only a part of a floating selection, the unselected part disappears. But if you use the type tool with Ctrl and Shift, instead of disappearing, the unselected part is dropped into the image.

Saving a selection as a path takes a lot less file space (only a few K) than saving it as an alpha channel.

Using the pen tool provides one advantage over using the lasso: You can move the anchor points and manipulate their handles to adjust the shape of a selection border, which can be quite a bit easier in some cases than making lots of little additions to and subtractions from a lasso selection.

THE TYPE TOOL

First and foremost, Photoshop's type tool provides access to fonts, allowing you to incorporate type into images. But it also acts as a selection tool, and it's beneficial to look at it that way.

When you choose the type tool and click in an image, the Type Tool dialog box opens so you can specify your typeface and style and enter the text you want to set. Clicking OK returns you to the image, where the type appears as a floating selection filled with the color that appears in the Foreground color square in the toolbox (so besides being a font tool and a selection tool, the type tool also has paint properties!). Because it's a floating selection, you can move the type around without disturbing the image underneath. Here are some tips:

Using ATM. Make sure you have Adobe Type Manager (ATM) installed in your System or that you're using TrueType fonts so Photoshop has access to smooth type outlines.

Turning on antialiasing. Unless you want stairstepped, jaggy type for some reason, always select the Anti-aliased Style option in the Type Tool dialog box to smooth the edges.

Clearing type with the Composite Controls. When you set type, it's filled with the current foreground color. Because the type is a floating selection, you can use the Composite Controls dialog box to clear it of color: Move the black or white point of the Floating Selection slider all the way to the other end of the slider; choose Darken or Lighten mode, whichever is opposite the tonality of the type.

Setting type in alpha channels. Whenever you need to set type, consider the advantages of setting it in an alpha channel rather than in the main image. First, you'll have a permanent selection available so you can reload it (Select, Load Selection) if you want to change the type in any way after you've initially loaded and filled it with color. You can also kern the type fairly easily in an alpha channel even after you've dropped the original floating selection: If your channel has white type on a black background, change the Background color icon to black. Then double-click the magic wand icon in the toolbox and set its Tolerance at 254. Click on a white letter you want to move; Shift-click to add letters to the selection. Drag the letters, or move them in small steps by pressing the arrow keys.

By using the Channels palette, you can set up the kerning operation so you can see the lettering in relation to the image as you kern. First click on the name of the alpha channel in the Channels palette to select it for both viewing and "writing." Then click in the "eye" column of the main channel. You'll be

The Paths palette

Clicking to make corner points

Dragging to make smooth points

Closing a path

Adding a point

Deleting a point

Changing the type of point

SETTING PATH TOLERANCE

With a selection active, choosing Make Path from the pop-out menu in the Paths palette brings up a dialog box that lets you set a Tolerance to specify how closely the Bezier curve will follow the selection boundary when a selection is converted to a path. A tolerance of 0 means the path must trace every little nook and cranny in the selection; this can make for a very complex and calculation-intensive path. The higher the Tolerance value, the more loosely the path follows the selection border, but the less likely it is that the path will create a limitcheck error on output if it's exported to another program.

viewing the image and the alpha channel (which appears in its mask color) but changing only the alpha channel.

THE PEN TOOL

Unlike Photoshop's other selection tools, the pen tool has a palette of its own, opened by choosing Show Paths from the Window menu. The Paths palette includes everything necessary to draw and edit a smoothly curving path (called a Bezier curve), to name it and save it so it can be recalled later, to turn it into a selection, and to combine it with an existing selection. The saving, loading, and selecting functions of the pen tool are found in the menu that pops out if you press the arrowhead at the top right side of the palette. The pop-out menu also allows you to stroke or fill a path or make a clipping path for silhouetting an image to be exported for use in a page layout, for example.

The shape of the Bezier curve drawn by the pen tool is controlled by the positions of anchor points and direction lines, or "handles," which direct the curve as it comes out of the points. The *Adobe Photoshop User Guide* explains how to work the pen tool, but here are some quick tips for using it:

Drawing a path. To draw a path with the pen tool:

- Click to place a corner point (without handles). Placing two corner points one after another draws a straight line.

- Drag with the pen tool to create a smooth point and to position its control handles.

- Constrain the position of the next corner or smooth point to any 45- or 90-degree angle by holding down the Shift key as you place the point.

- When you see a little circle to the right of the pen icon, clicking will close the path.

Editing a path. You can change a path after it's drawn:

- Drag a point with the arrow pointer to move that point.

- Click with the arrow pointer to select a control point or a curve segment. Shift-click to select more of the path.

- Click on the curve with the pen+ tool to add a point.

- Click on a point with the pen– tool to remove that point.

- Click on a corner or smooth point with the corner point tool (the open arrowhead) to turn it into the other kind of point.

- Drag on a handle with the corner point tool to reshape the curve by moving the handle independently of its mate.

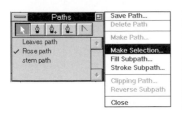

Converting a path to a selection

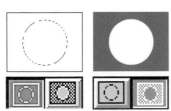

Making a selection in Standard mode (left) and converting to Quick Mask mode

• A path can be copied (Ctrl-C) or cut (Ctrl-X) to the clipboard and then pasted (Ctrl-V).

Duplicating a path. Hold down the Alt key and drag the path with the arrow tool.

Moving a path. Hold down the Alt key and just click — don't drag — with the arrow tool to select a path. Then release the Alt key and drag the path to move it without duplicating it or changing its shape.

Saving a path. Select the path and choose Save Path from the pop-out menu.

Converting a selection to a path. Convert a selection to a path by choosing Make Path from the pop-out menu.

Loading a path. To load a path, in the Paths palette, click the name of a path in the list under the row of tools.

Converting a path to a selection. Select a path and choose Make Selection from the pop-out menu. In version 2.5.1, press Enter (with any tool but a painting tool active) to turn a path into a selection.

QUICK MASK

Quick Mask is a feature that lets you store a selection temporarily. By making a selection and then clicking the Quick Mask icon (on the right side near the bottom of the toolbox), you can turn the selection into a clear area in a semitransparent mask. Unlike the ephemeral marching ants, the Quick Mask remains stable as you use the painting tools to edit it. Switching back to Standard mode by clicking the Standard mode icon (to the left of the Quick Mask icon) turns the mask into an active selection border again.

Double-clicking the Quick Mask icon opens a dialog box that lets you change mask color and opacity and choose whether the mask color should indicate the selected or nonselected area. Examples of using Quick Mask appear on pages 34 through 36 and elsewhere in the book

In Quick Mask mode, "Mask" is listed in the Channels palette. It also appears in the list of channels under the Select, Load Selection command.

ALPHA CHANNELS

Photoshop's alpha channels provide a kind of subfile for storing selection boundaries so you can load them back into the image and use them later. A selection stored in an alpha channel becomes a mask, with white areas that can be loaded as an

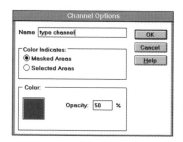

Giving channels meaningful names can help you identify their contents for loading.

ALPHA CHANNEL EFFICIENCY

To keep file size down by reducing the number of alpha channels, or to be able to use more selection masks than you have alpha channels available, you can use a single alpha channel to combine two or more selections that don't overlap. Then when you load the channel as a selection, you can use the lasso with the Shift and Command keys to select just the parts you want.

RGB channel   Channel 4

Selecting a complex subject by using the magic wand and Select, Similar on the background; using Select, Inverse; and Select, Save Selection

active selection, black areas that protect parts of the image where changes shouldn't apply, and gray areas that expose the image to changes proportionally to their lightness of the gray.

You can store any type of selection boundary in an alpha channel. When used with the program's Image, Calculate functions, alpha channels also provide some very sophisticated ways to combine selections — adding them together, subtracting one from another, and making them interact in a variety of ways far beyond what you can do with the selection tools and the Ctrl and Shift keys.

A Photoshop file can have as many as 16 channels in total. So an RGB file, for example, since it has four channels tied up in the main channel and the three individual colors, can have up to 12 alphas, each providing a way to recall a particular selection independently of any other selection. A grayscale file can have up to 15 alphas, and a CMYK file can have as many as 11. Here are some tips for using alpha channels:

Making a new alpha channel. To make an alpha channel:

- Make a selection and choose Select, Save Selection.

- Or choose Window, Show Channels and then choose New Channel from the Channels palette's pop-out menu. When you make an alpha in this way, you have the opportunity to give it a name that will help you remember its content.

Loading an alpha channel as a selection. To turn an alpha channel into a selection:

- Choose Select, Load Selection and, if more than one alpha channel exists, choose the channel's number.

- Or choose Image, Calculate, Duplicate; make the alpha channel the Source; and choose *Selection* as the Destination.

SMART SELECTING

With all the ways you can make and store selections, the most important selection tool of all is your brain. Knowing how the selection tools and operations work, as well as Photoshop's other functions, and then thinking about what part of your image you want to change and exactly what it is you want to accomplish can save lots of time and effort. Here are some tips for making complicated selections.

Inverting a selection. To select an object with a complex boundary (such as a person's hair) or with many parts (such as the leaves of a tree), it's often easier to select the background and then invert the selection by choosing Select, Inverse.

RGB | **Blue**

Working in a single color channel can make it easier to separate foreground from background for selection purposes.

CLEANING UP MASKS

A pixelated selection outline (A) can be cleaned up by blurring (B) and then using Image, Adjust, Levels to sharpen up the edge. Move the Input Levels black and white point sliders close together to reduce the blur to an antialiasing effect (C). The closer the two sliders are, the sharper the edge. By moving the group of three sliders right or left, you can shrink (D) or enlarge (E) the selection.

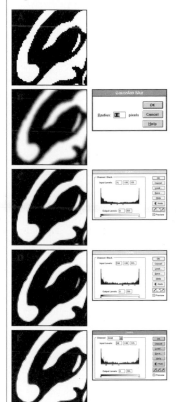

Selecting in a single channel. For some RGB and CMYK images, a subject may be more distinct from its background in one color channel than in the others. You can use this to your advantage: View each color channel by itself (by clicking on its name in the Channels palette) and pick the one with the most difference between subject and background. Then activate that channel by clicking its name in the Channels palette, make your selection with the selection tools, and save the selection in an alpha channel (Select, Save Selection; or Make Selection in the Paths palette if your selection is a pen path). Then load the selection into the main image (Select, Load Selection).

Using a luminance mask. If you paste a grayscale image such as a photo into an alpha channel, it becomes a selection mask that you can load back into the main channel to select the light parts of the image. Use this selection, or a part of it, to change the color, tone, or texture of the image. In the alpha channel, choosing Image, Map, Invert makes a negative mask that will let you reproduce the photo on a new background by filling the selection with color or darkening it by adjusting Levels.

Getting rid of a color "edging." Sometimes, despite the most careful selecting, a pasted selection retains some background color around the edge.

- To eliminate an "edging" picked up by images selected from a black or white background, use the Black Matte or White Matte modes in the Composite Controls dialog box.

- To remove edging in a color other than black or white, try the Select, Defringe command on the floating selection. This will "push" color from the selection into the edge pixels.

- Another way to remove color edging is to "choke" the selection, to shrink the selection border just slightly so the edging is eliminated. To do that, save the selection border in an alpha channel (Select, Save Selection). Then use Filter, Other, Minimum to shrink the white area in the alpha channel. Or load the alpha channel into itself as a selection and choose Edit, Stroke, Center, Black to shrink the white area. You can select the smaller, stroked mask to reselect and repaste the image into the new background.

Selecting with painting modes. Sometimes the easiest way to make a complex selection is not to select at all. By thinking in terms of Lighten and Darken modes, you may be able to avoid making complex selections. For example, suppose you wanted to repair light spots from water damage to the blue sky in a photo where it's difficult to separate sky from

Quick Mask with left-to-right gradient mask over image

Quick Mask turned to selection in Standard mode; delete to background color

Combining two images through a vertical gradient selection

Turning a photo into a drawing with Gallery Effects Chalk & Charcoal filter applied to a gradient selection

A radial mask protects the face from a Gaussian blur effect

PHOTOS: CRAIG McCLAIN

trees in making a selection. You could use the lasso with the Option key to make a roughly rectangular selection of the entire sky area, including the trees. Then click the eyedropper tool to pick up a Foreground color from the sky, a blue that's darker than the water spots but lighter than the green leaves. Then choose Edit, Fill and set the Mode to Darken, which will only apply the color to pixels lighter than that color. The sky blue will fill in the light spots without coloring the leaves.

USING GRADIENT SELECTIONS

You can use the gradient tool to make a graduated mask that lets you apply any change in a gradual way. To make the mask, either turn on Quick Mask and use the gradient tool to paint the mask, or open an alpha channel, create a gradient there, and then load the channel as a selection. Here are some things you can do with a gradient mask:

Making a one-color gradient. Make a top-to-bottom (or left-to-right) white-to-black mask and load it as a selection. To make an image "disappear into the mist," set the background color to white by clicking the default colors icon, and then press the Backspace key. The same technique can be used to delete to a color or to black.

Making a gradual pattern fill. Make a gradient selecton, define a pattern, and choose Edit, Fill, Pattern.

Turning a photo into a painting. Make a gradient selection and apply a filter through it.

Turning a color image into black-and-white. Desaturate the image by applying Image, Adjust, Hue/Saturation through a gradient mask. Or duplicate the color image and change the mode of the duplicate to Grayscale or Bitmap; then copy and paste the black-and-white version onto the colorful one, through a gradient.

Combining two images. Make a gradient mask and Paste Into it or Paste Behind it to blend the images.

Protecting part of an image. Use a radial gradient mask to protect a part of an image from a change that you apply to the rest of the file. 🌀

Using the Calculate Functions

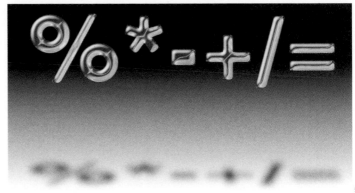

Overview Use the Image, Calculate functions to perform various combinations on files that have exactly the same pixel dimensions or to combine several channels of one file.

RULES FOR USING CALCULATE

To use the Calculate functions, the documents you combine have to follow certain rules.
1. All the documents whose channels you'll be working with have to be open.
2. They all have to have exactly the same dimensions — to the pixel! This is no problem if the channels are all from the same document, because they will automatically be the same size. But if you mix documents from different origins or from files that have been split into separate documents and then worked on, their sizes may be different, and you'll have to crop or resize to exact pixel dimensions before using the Calculate functions.
3. The Destination document and channel must be able to accept the kind of information you're trying to store. You can't, for example, store the result of a calculation that involves an RGB channel in a grayscale channel.

SOME OF THE MOST POWERFUL FUNCTIONS in Photoshop are hidden away in a submenu whose very name can strike terror into the hearts and right-brained minds of many of the program's potentially most devoted users. Many of the Calculate functions do their magic by performing mathematical operations using the values of corresponding pixels in two Source channels and storing the result in a third (Destination) channel.

Filters are mathematical operations, too, but they tend to have friendlier names, like Twirl and Blur. When you use filters and Calculate together, you can get some amazing results. The *Adobe Photoshop User Guide* explains the arithmetic of the Calculate functions. The two pages that follow show some of the magic of Calculate.

CLEANING UP THE EDGES

Running Calculate functions on channels (especially Lighter, Darker, Add, and Subtract, it seems) can sometimes result in a ragged edge, which can become a problem when you load a channel's contents and use it as a selection. The selection can pick up unwanted bits of the background, for example. To correct the problem, some people fix these artifacts by hand with the smudge or blur tool (this is tricky, painstaking work). Or if all the edges are supposed to be the same color or shade of gray, you can load the channel contents as a selection (Select, Load Selection, choose the same channel number as the channel you're working on) and add a stroke of the edge color (Edit, Stroke). Or you can leave the mask uncorrected, and instead, when you paste the selection, defringe that selection (Select, Defringe) or use the Black Matte or White Matte mode from Composite Controls when you paste.

Original pasted

Defringed and pasted

Channel Operations

Overview *The numbered images are provided on disk as a 16-channel Multichannel file you can experiment with. Chapter 8 includes step-by-step instructions for the Embossed Paper, License Plate, and Beveled Glass effects that appear in the last column.*

THESE IMAGES DEMONSTRATE HOW the Image, Calculate functions (or channel operations) work. A similar demo originated by Steve Lomas, as well as tips from Kai Krause, served as a starting point for our own exploration. The 16 numbered images were all developed by running channel operations on a single character typed into one channel of a Multichannel file and inverted. A caption under each image gives the menu and dialog box settings used to create it. To save space, commands have been shortened. For example, the caption for channel 15 means: "Choose Image, Calculate, Difference and specify channel 4 for Source 1, channel 6 for Source 2, and a New channel (it will be channel 15) for Destination; choose Image, Map, Invert; then choose Image, Adjust, Levels and click Auto; choose Select, Load Selection, #2; fill with white."

1 Original image (505 pixels wide)

2 Image, Calculate, Duplicate (1, New, Invert); Filter, Other, Minimum (5)

3 Image, Calculate, Difference (1, 2, New)

4 Image, Calc., Dupl. (1, New); Filter, Other, Offset (8, 5, wrap); Gauss. Blur (5); Image, Adjust, Contrast (–50)

5 Image, Calculate, Duplicate (4, New); Filter, Other, Offset (–16, –10, wrap)

6 Image, Calculate, Difference (4, 5, New); Image, Map, Invert; Image, Adjust, Levels, Auto

7 Image, Calculate, Add (1, 4, New, Scale 1, Offset 0)

8 Image, Calculate, Multiply (1, 4, New)

9 Image, Calculate, Subtract (1, 4, New, Scale 1, Offset 128)

10 Image, Calculate, Duplicate (1, New); Filter, Blur, Gaussian Blur (5); Filter, Stylize, Emboss (–60, 3, 100); Image, Adjust, Levels, Auto

Soft-edged metal *Load 15 in an RGB file; Image, Adjust, Color Balance; KPT Texture Explorer, Procedural Blends (metals, liquid gold puddles)*

11 Image, Calculate, Duplicate 10, New); Select, Load Selection, #3; Fill with a 50% gray

12 Image, Calc., Multiply (6, 10, New); Image, Calc., Dupl. (1, Selection); Select, Inverse; Fill with white

Embossed paper *Start with 10; extract shadow/highlight masks; Select, Load Selection, #2; Image, Adjust, Levels*

13 Image, Calculate, Difference (6, 11, New); Image, Map, Invert

14 Image, Calculate, Duplicate (5, New); Image, Adjust, Levels, Auto; Image, Calc., Dupl. (1, Selection); Fill with black

License plate *Load 2 in an RGB file; Blur; Emboss; Calc., Dupl. (Black, Selection); Image, Adjust, Levels; Image, Adjust, Hue/Saturation*

15 Calculate, Difference (4, 6, New); Image, Map, Invert; Levels, Auto; Select, Load Selection, #2; Fill with white

16 Image, Calculate, Composite (12, 6, 11, New)

Beveled glass *Start with 16; Select, Load Selection, #2; KPT Texture Explorer (Normal); Select, Inverse; KPT Texture Explorer (Procedural); Image, Map, Invert*

Using Quick Mask Mode

Overview *Make a selection; activate Quick Mask; add to the mask with the painting tools and eraser; return to Standard mode; save the selection in an alpha channel.*

CRAIG McCLAIN

Original images

Starting the selection

Setting up Quick Mask mode

THE QUICK MASK FUNCTION, the Channels palette, and the ability to vary the color and opacity of masks make it easy to construct complex masks in Photoshop. All these features make it possible to view an image while you tailor the mask. In making this montage, called *HQ,* from two of his own photos, photographer Craig McClain started with the magic wand and then used Quick Mask to generate the channels he needed for making the montage shown above.

1 Planning your strategy. Look at the two images you want to montage and decide how to go about it. McClain knew that he would have to resize one image or the other to put the two together to make the montage he wanted. He would either have to enlarge the sky image or reduce the building, which he planned to stretch even taller before combining it with the sky. Typically, it's preferable to reduce an image rather than scale it up. But in this case McClain probably could have done either: The sky was a "soft," natural subject and could have withstood the interpolation of scaling up; the building, because of its straight lines, might suffer a little from the interpolation involved in scaling down. In the end, he decided to scale the building down. This meant that the sky would be the "receiver" image, the file where the montage would be assembled, so he started in that file to make the mask for combining the two images. The plan would be to make a mask in the receiver image, scale the "donor" image, and then silhouette the subject from this image and paste it into the receiver file.

4

Editing the mask

5a

Converting the mask to a selection

5b

Saving an alpha channel

6a

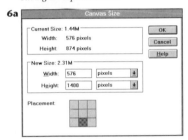

Canvas Size

Current Size: 1.44M
Width: 576 pixels
Height: 874 pixels

New Size: 2.31M
Width: 576 pixels
Height: 1400 pixels

Placement:

OK Cancel Help

6b   **6c**

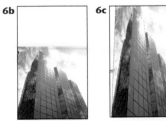

Adding canvas   *Using Perspective*

6d

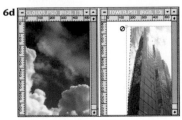

Scaling down the building

2 Making an initial selection. Working in the receiver image, use one or more selection tools to select as large a part of the foreground or background as you can. McClain knew that he could make an alpha channel to select either the clouds, in which case he would paste the building behind them, or the sky, in which case he would paste the building into it. He chose the sky and began by clicking the magic wand tool in the blue area.

3 Activating Quick Mask mode. With an initial selection active, turn on the Quick Mask by clicking on the Quick Mask mode icon near the bottom of the toolbox — it's the icon on the right; the Standard mode icon is on the left. Double-click either icon to open the Mask Options dialog box that lets you change the color and opacity of the mask. You can click the color square to open the color picker to change the mask color. McClain chose the default 50% red; the color would contrast nicely with the blues in the image, and the reduced opacity would let him see image details through the mask.

4 Cleaning up the mask. Choose the paintbrush or any of the other painting tools to clean up the mask. You can add to the masked area by painting in the foreground color, or subtract from it by clicking the switch colors icon (the double arrow next to the foreground and background squares in the toolbox) to switch the Foreground and Background colors before painting. McClain clicked the switch colors icon and used the paintbrush with a large, soft brush tip to remove some of the clouds from the mask, adding that area to the selection. For this image McClain felt that his selection didn't need to be precise because he could feather the edges of the clouds later.

5 Saving the selection. When the mask is complete, turn off the Quick Mask mode by clicking on the Standard mode icon. This will make the nonmask area into an active selection. Then choose Select, Save Selection to save the selection as alpha channel #4.

6 Preparing the donor image. Silhouette the subject in the donor image. Since McClain wanted to accentuate the height of the building, he made more space at the top of the image (by choosing Image, Canvas Size and clicking in the grid to position the existing image at the bottom of the canvas so the extra Height he specified would be added at the top). Then he selected the part of the building he wanted to distort and chose Image, Effects, Perspective; he dragged on one of the top corner handles to reshape the building, moved the cursor inside the selected area (where it became a mallet icon) and

Masking the building

Paste Into the selection

Defringing the building

Final editing

clicked to finalize the distortion. To resize the building, he opened both the building file and the sky and chose Window, Show Rulers in both files. By dragging with the rectangular marquee selection tool, he selected the part of the building he wanted to use and chose Image, Effects, Scale, dragging on a corner handle until the rulers showed it was the size he wanted.

7 Silhouetting the donor image. Use the selection tools and Quick Mask mode again as in steps 3 and 4. McClain used the magic wand to select the sky around the building and used the eraser to clean up the selection, erasing the red patches of mask. Then he clicked on the Standard mode icon to turn the Quick Mask into a selection.

When the selection is complete, copy the silhouetted subject (Ctrl-C). McClain chose Select, Inverse to switch the selection from sky to building before copying the selection to the clipboard.

8 Combining the images. Open the receiver image again and load the selection from channel 4 (Select, Load Selection). Then use Edit, Paste Into or Edit, Paste Behind to add the silhouetted subject from the clipboard. Drag the pasted image into position in the receiver image. Choose Select, Defringe if necessary to clean up the edge of the silhouette once it's in place, and then deselect it (Ctrl-D) to finish the pasting operation. McClain used Paste Into to put the building into the selected sky area and defringed it before dropping the selection. Then he used the rubber stamp tool set to Clone (Non-aligned), by double-clicking the tool to open its dialog box, to pick up cloud texture from various parts of the image (by Alt-clicking with the tool); using a soft, medium-sized brush tip on the rubber stamp, he clicked along the cloud edges. 🖌

HOW "DEFRINGE" WORKS

The Select, Defringe command doesn't clean up the edges of a floating selection by peeling off the pixels of the background that have adhered there. It doesn't shrink the selection at all. Instead it "pushes" color from the inside outward, into the pixels at the edge. The Width setting in the Defringe dialog box tells the program how far inside the selection it should look to find the colors that it will push outward. A setting of 2, for example, makes the program look 2 pixels in from the outermost shell of pixels. It then extends the colors of this third "shell" of pixels outward to the selection border, replacing the colors in the first two shells. Any setting higher than 1, or at most 2, pixels is likely to be perceived as an unnatural border.

Using a Photo as a Mask

Overview *Copy and paste a photo into an alpha channel of an RGB image; invert the channel to a negative; load the channel in the main RGB channel; colorize the selection.*

STEPHEN KING

Photo pasted into channel 4

Channel 4, image map inverted

Map scan

Graphics mask (channel 5)

Channel 4 loaded in RGB channel

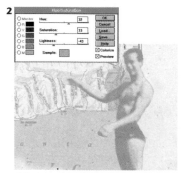

Colorizing the selection

THE GRAYSCALE INFORMATION in a photo can be a very effective tool for "pulling" an image out of a background texture. For this T-shirt design, Stephen King started with an RGB scan of kraft paper and then used a scan of a map, a photo, and graphics created in Adobe Illustrator to colorize and darken parts of this background. Additional photos were pasted in.

1 Making the luminance mask. Open an RGB file that will serve as the background for the image. Copy and paste the photo you want to use (Ctrl-C, Ctrl-V) into an alpha channel (New Channel from the Channels palette). Invert the image colors (Ctrl-I) so the channel contains a negative of the photo, which can now be loaded as a selection to reproduce the image on the RGB background. After working with his photo to make channel 4, King imported a graphics file from Adobe Illustrator into another new alpha channel (#5) (the process of importing an encapsulated PostScript [EPS] file is described in Chapter 7) and pasted in a map scan; he used Ctrl-I to produce a negative and then loaded the mask from channel 4 (Select, Load Selection, #4) and pressed Shift-Backspace to fill the selection with the black foreground color. Keeping photo and graphics in separate masks gave him the opportunity to colorize them separately.

2 Colorizing. Load each mask (Select, Load Selection, #4 or #5) and choose Image, Adjust, Hue/Saturation. Select the Colorize box and adjust the three sliders. After loading the two masks and colorizing with each, King also pasted in and framed three color photos and a grayscale image, which he also colorized with the Hue/Saturation controls.

Putting Text over an Image

Overview *Select the area you want to lighten; adjust Levels or use a Fill to lighten the selection.*

Original image

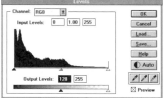

Contrast reduced with Output Levels

THERE ARE DOZENS OF WAYS to lighten a selected area of an image in Photoshop, with different amounts of detail and contrast preserved in the lightened area. The best method for a particular job will vary, depending on what kind of lightening you want to achieve. For example, if you want to put text over an image as in this mock magazine layout, you may want to eliminate the detail so it won't "fight" with the type.

1 Selecting the type area. Use the rectangular marquee to select the area you want the type to overprint.

2 Lightening the selected area. Use the Image, Adjust, Levels dialog box or the Fill command (or its Shift-Backspace shortcut) to lighten the area. Here are some ways to do it.

- **Using the Output Levels.** Move the black point slider to the right. This lightens the blackest black in the image to a gray and lightens all the other tones proportionally. Because it takes all the tonal levels from 0 to 255 and compresses them into a shorter range (from 120 to 255 in this example), the contrast is reduced. We used this method for the image above.

- **Screening with white.** Click the "swap" arrow in the Foreground/Background icon in the tool palette. Then choose the Edit, Fill command, select Screen or Normal, type in an Opacity value, and click OK.

USING A TINT

Instead of filling with white, try picking up a foreground color from the image with the eyedropper tool, and filling in either Screen or Normal mode, varying the opacity until you get the right tint.

2b

Filled with white at 50% opacity in Normal mode

2c

Filled with white at 50% opacity in Screen mode

3

Lightened display type

3 Lightening the display type. Display type can be lightened with the same method you applied to the text area (as in this example) or as described in "Making Type Stand Out" on the next page.

Adding the text type. To make the type as crisp and readable as possible, you can import the image into an object-oriented program such as Corel Draw, Adobe Illustrator, Aldus FreeHand, Aldus PageMaker, or QuarkXPress, and set the type there. For the "Cool Wool" image, the Photoshop file was converted from RGB to CMYK and saved in CMYK TIFF format, and then it was placed in the PageMaker page, where the type was added. 🖋

INTERACTIVE FILLING WITH THE BRUSHES PALETTE

Lightening an image by moving the black point slider for Output Levels in the Levels dialog box produces the same "bleaching" effect as applying the Fill command in Screen mode with white as the foreground color. Using the Levels box has an advantage: It's interactive. That is, the Preview option lets you see results and make adjustments without closing the box. But you can make the Fill command interactive by floating the selected area (Select, Float, or Ctrl-J) and pressing Shift-Backspace with white as the foreground color to fill the area. Then use the mode setting and the Opacity slider in the Brushes window to vary the effect.

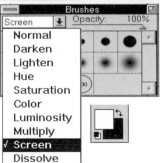

Varying the transparency of a floating white box using the Brushes palette mode and Opacity controls

Making Type Stand Out

Overview *Set display type in an alpha channel; load it as a selection; adjust brightness and contrast with the gamma slider.*

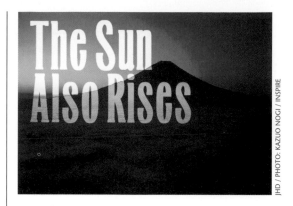

JHD / PHOTO: KAZUO NOGI / INSPIRE

1

2a

Moving the gamma slider left

INSTEAD OF MAKING A LIGHTENED BACKGROUND for text, your goal may be to emphasize display type as part of a photo. If that's the case, you can afford to preserve image detail as you lighten, since it won't interfere with readability. To make the words stand out, you can either brighten the type, as shown here, or leave the type area unadjusted and lighten the background instead.

1 Making the selection. Open the image and create an alpha channel (Window, Show Channels, New Channel) for setting the type. For an RGB document, the new channel will be channel #4. Choose the type tool, click with its cursor, and select Anti-aliased in the Type Tool dialog box. Click in the text area of the dialog box and type the words and style the type. Then click OK. The type appears as a floating selection in the alpha channel. Deselect the type (Ctrl-D) and choose Image, Map, Invert. This produces a mask with white type on a black background.

2 Lightening the type. Now, working in the main channel of the image, choose Select, Load Selection to bring in the type selection. Press Ctrl-H to hide the selection edges so they won't interfere with your view. The type can be brightened by moving the middle Input Levels slider (gamma) to the left in the Image, Adjust, Levels dialog box. Input Levels is set up so that all tones to the right of this gamma slider will be lighter than 50% brightness and all tones to the left of it will be darker than 50%. Here are two ways to use the gamma slider for lightening:

- **Moving the gamma slider alone.** Leave the black and white points in place, and move the gamma slider to the left. The selection will lighten without losing the detail in the image.

- **Moving the white point slider.** Move the white point

2b

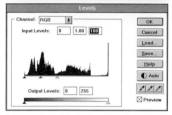

Moving the white point

3

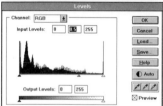

Darkening the background

slider to the left. The gamma point will move also, staying halfway between the white and black points. The selection is lightened, and at the same time, since the white point controls the detail in the light tones, the color is intensified.

3 Increasing the contrast by adjusting the background. Once the letters have been brightened, choose Select, Inverse to select the background image and deselect the type. Now you can use Image, Adjust, Levels on the background. For example, you can move the gamma slider to the right to darken the image without losing detail. This process worked well for this particular image to produce the effect shown in the opening illustration.

Lightening the background. Another approach to making display type stand out as part of an image is to leave the photo at full strength within the type and lighten the background in contrast, as shown below.

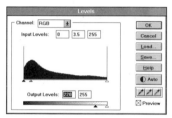

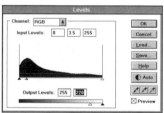

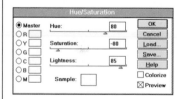

SETTING SMOOTH TYPE

To set type with smooth edges, not jagged and bitmapped-looking:
1. Install Adobe Type Manager (ATM) or use TrueType fonts.
2. Choose the Anti-aliased option in the Type Tool dialog box.
3. If the type still looks jagged and you're using ATM, increase the ATM font cache. (Double-click the Windows Program Manager's Main icon and then the ATM Control Panel icon to access the Font Cache setting).

ENHANCING
PHOTOS

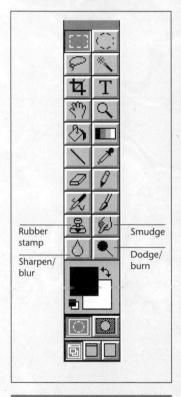

Rubber
stamp

Sharpen/
blur

Smudge

Dodge/
burn

CALIBRATING

For your printed image to match
your screen display, your display
and output systems need to be
calibrated and color-matched.
For information about color man-
agement and calibration check
Chapter 15 of the *Adobe Photoshop
User Guide,* the "Output" chapter
of *Designer Photoshop*, and "Adobe
Technical Notes" (see Appendix).

THIS CHAPTER DESCRIBES SEVERAL TECHNIQUES for enhancing
photos — from emulating traditional camera and darkroom
techniques such as motion blur, haze, and solarization, to
hand-tinting, to retouching. But much of the day-to-day production work done with Photoshop involves trying to get the
best possible print reproduction of a photo — correcting black-
and-white or color images so they print crisply and clearly
with a full range of contrast or color.

The Photoshop functions most often used for improving a
photo are chosen mainly from the Image, Adjust and the Filter, Sharpen submenus. The dialog boxes for two of the choices
from Image, Adjust — **Levels** and **Curves** — look very
"techy," and one — **Variations** — looks quite friendly. It's
precisely these characteristics that make them so useful. Levels
and Curves provide a lot of useful information about the image and a great deal of control (their various uses are described
throughout the book). What Variations offers is the opportunity to see in advance what will happen to the image with
each of your choices (for a step-by-step guide to the Variations
interface, see the *Tutorial* volume that comes with Photoshop).

One of the other choices in the Image, Adjust submenu —
Brightness/Contrast — is tempting, perhaps because, unlike
Levels and Curves, its name includes terms we can easily understand and relate to. But the Brightness/Contrast control has
a restricted set of functions that can cause distortion in the
color or tonal range of an image if applied alone. If we think of
using Levels and Curves on an image as analogous to tuning
up all the sections of an orchestra so it can play harmoniously,
then using Brightness/Contrast is more like the brass playing
loud to cover up problems in the woodwinds section.

The **sharpen/blur, dodge/burn, smudge,** and **rubber
stamp** tools can play an important role in correcting local
flaws in an image. Sharpen/blur applies the same functions as
some of the Sharpen and Blur filters (described in Chapter 5),
but with hand-held precision. Dodge/burn can be thought of
as Image, Adjust, Levels in a wand, varying contrast, brightness, and detail, with independent control in the highlights,
midtones, and shadows through the Brushes palette.

continued on page 44

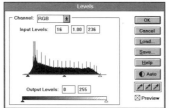

Moving black and white points to adjust tonal range; before (left) and after (right)

Adjusting Curves to bring out shadow detail; before (left) and after (right)

IMAGE CORRECTION

Is there a standard approach to evaluating a photo and preparing it for reproduction in print? Color correction is a skill that's refined through long and broad experience. If you ask a color expert where to start in correcting a black-and-white or color photo, you're almost certain to hear, "It depends on the photo." But here are some steps that may be generally helpful.

Extending dynamic range. In a typical image — not a close-up portrait of a black angus bull or a photo of lace appliquéd on white satin — you'll want to get the broadest range of tones (and thus the largest amount of detail possible) by making sure the lightest area in the image is pure white and the darkest is pure black. (Not everyone agrees that a grayscale image should include pure black and pure white. Some feel that for optimal printing the lightest tones should be at least 3% black and the darkest shades should be 95% black. For thorough coverage of grayscale images, refer to *Adobe Photoshop Version 2.5 in Black and White.*)

To see whether an image uses the full brightness range, choose Image, Adjust, Levels and inspect the *histogram*, the graph that shows what proportion of the pixels (the vertical measure) are each of 256 tones (spread along the horizontal axis, from black on the left to white on the right). If the histogram doesn't extend all the way across the horizontal axis, it means the full range of shades of gray is not being used in the image. You can expand the tonal range by clicking the Auto button or moving the white and black sliders of the Input Levels inward to the first bars of the histogram.

Correcting "exposure." One of the most common problems with photos is incorrect exposure — the image is too dark overall (underexposed) or too light (overexposed) or the shadows are too dark. Many of what at first appear to be color problems can be corrected by fixing the exposure. To increase or decrease the amount of detail you can see in the highlights, midtones, or shadows, choose Image, Adjust, Curves. Click on the curve to create a point; drag it to change its position. The rest of the curve will change shape to make a smooth transition from the black point to the white point through the new position of the point you've moved. You can make general corrections by reshaping the curve so it bulges left (toward the black end) and upward to correct for underexposure, or to the right (toward the white end) and down to correct for overexposure. (This kind of correction can also be made with the gamma [gray] slider in the Levels dialog box.) If you move the cursor out of the Curves dialog box, it turns into an eyedropper. Click on a particular tone in the image to identify its posi-

Adjusting Levels and Curves overall and using the dodge/burn tool on selected local areas can restore information that seems to be lost, as shown in this image restored by Jim Belderes of Digital Design, Inc. Where damage is severe, Belderes uses the rubber stamp in a Clone mode to paint missing features.

Posterizing an image

Silhouetting a subject with a clipping path so it can be exported without its background

tion on the curve. Then you can move that point to lighten or darken that part of the tonal range.

Removing a color cast. If the image still seems to have color problems after you've expanded the dynamic range and corrected for exposure, try removing a color cast by selecting the gray eyedropper in Levels or Curves and clicking it on some part of the image that should be neutral, without a color. Unlike the black and white eyedroppers, the gray one has nothing to do with brightness or contrast. Instead, it adjusts the color balance of the entire image based on the fact that you tell it what neutral should be.

Retouching. Once general corrections have been made, individual problems can be addressed. Here are some examples:

- **To correct the color of a particular area,** make a feathered selection (see Chapter 2) and use Image, Adjust, Variations or Color Balance to adjust it.

- **To remove blemishes,** use the rubber stamp, especially in Clone (Non-aligned) mode with a soft brush tip, Alt-clicking to pick up color and texture and clicking to deposit it.

- **To smooth the texture of a spotted area,** make a feathered selection, float it, blur it or fill it with a single color (or a shade of gray for a grayscale image), and then use the Brushes palette or Composite Controls to set the mode (try Lighten or Darken, depending on the kinds of splotches you're trying to eliminate) and opacity before dropping the floating selection to blend it with the original.

Sharpening. Sharpening often improves a scanned photo. Sometimes it's the last thing that should be done to an image before it's prepared for the press, because the synthetic effects of sharpening can be magnified in other image-editing processes, such as increasing saturation of the colors. Sharpening is discussed more extensively in Chapter 5, "Using Filters."

SAVE THAT PHOTO!

When you want to reproduce a photo in print, it's nice to have a good image to begin with — it may need a little tweaking of the exposure, or a color cast may have to be removed, but it's basically sound. It isn't too badly focused, it's well-framed or at least croppable, the subjects have their eyes open and aren't grimacing inappropriately, and the background doesn't include anything distracting. But there are times when a particular photo *must* be used in a publication — for example, it's the only picture of an important event, or it's free and the client's budget is limited, or the portrait is damaged but the subject is no longer alive — and the photo just can't be redeemed by the

Blurring the background (right) can eliminate the need for rubber-stamping to get rid of detail.

These are three of five scanned photos that were combined using the rubber stamp in a Clone mode to eliminate the seams, with care not to repeat textures. The sky was selected and filled with a deep blue; the selection was also saved as an alpha channel. The alpha was duplicated as a grayscale file; Image, Canvas Size was used to make room for the radial fill that would keep the sky from looking flat. The half-circle fill was made by starting the gradient at the lower edge of a rectangular selection. Then the entire new sky area was selected and reshaped into a squashed oval (Image, Effects, Scale). This selection was dragged over the silhouette of the mountains, and Darken was selected in the Brushes palette. The bottom portion of this window was then copied back into the alpha channel of the panorama document and loaded as a selection so that Image, Adjust, Levels could then be used to lighten the bottom of the sky.

normal correction processes. Here are some ideas for handling those kinds of photos:

- **To simplify and stylize an image,** choose Image, Map, Posterize and select a number of colors or shades of gray.

- **To show activity or setting but get rid of unwanted detail in the subject,** select the subject and fill it with black to create a silhouette against a backlit background.

- **To get rid of unwanted detail in the background,** select the background and blur it, or use the rubber stamp in a Clone mode to paint over some background objects with other background texture.

- **To get rid of a background altogether,** select it and fill it with a color. Or make a clipping path that will silhouette the subject and mask out the background when you export the photo to another program: Choose Window, Show Paths to open the Paths palette, where the pen tool resides. Outline the subject with the pen tool or make a selection by other means (refer to Chapter 2 for the specifics of operating the pen and selection tools). Save the path. In the process of saving you'll give the path a name. Then choose Clipping Path from the pop-out Paths palette menu, and select your named path from the pop-out menu in the Clipping Path dialog box. Enter a higher Flatness value if the path is very long and complex. Choose a Fill Rule: Use Non-Zero Winding if the path is a simple outline, or Even-Odd Fill if the path intersects itself or if it's a compound path (made by drawing two or more paths, selecting them together, and choosing Save Path). Save the file in EPS format to be imported into another program and printed. But before you save it, convert it to CMYK mode (choose Mode, CMYK) in case the other program can't separate RGB EPS files.

- **To piece together a panorama,** remove and replace the original sky. Blending the part of the scene that continues from one photo to another — often this is the sky — is usually the hardest part of making a panorama sequence into a single image. One solution is to remove the sky, and then replace it with a sky from a different photo, a stretched version of the sky from one of the montaged images, or a synthetic sky.

Making a Mezzotint

Overview *Define a pattern; convert an image to Bitmap mode using the pattern and increasing the resolution.*

PHOTO: CRAIG McCLAIN

Define Pattern
Take Snapshot

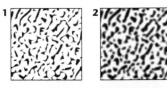

Original grayscale image

4b

Bitmap
Resolution
Input: 301 pixels/inch
Output: 301 pixels/inch
OK / Cancel / Help
Method
○ 50% Threshold
○ Pattern Dither
○ Diffusion Dither
○ Halftone Screen
● Custom Pattern

Converting to Bitmap mode

A TRADITIONAL MEZZOTINT is produced with a halftone screen made up of custom dot shapes. (Halftone screens convert continuous-tone images such as photos into the tiny dots needed for most printing processes.) In Photoshop you can create a mezzotint look by defining a pattern and then using it to convert a grayscale image to a black-and-white bitmap. The pattern you use can be one you produce yourself, one of those supplied with Photoshop, or one you import from a PostScript drawing program such as Adobe Illustrator or Aldus FreeHand.

1 Choosing a mezzotint pattern. Choose one of the patterns supplied in the Brushes & Patterns folder that comes with Photoshop and open the pattern file; or paint with black to create your own pattern (see "Making Paper for Painting" in Chapter 6 for instructions on making a non-uniform pattern tile that will wrap seamlessly). If you make your own pattern, be sure to keep the balance between black and white fairly even.

2 Blurring the pattern. To produce an effective mezzotint, so that parts of the pattern drop out gradually when it's used in light areas of the image and fill in gradually in the dark areas, blur the pattern to create a full range of grays: Choose Filter, Blur or Blur More.

3 Defining the pattern. When the pattern tile is complete, choose Select, All and then choose Define Pattern. The pattern will then be stored so that Photoshop can call on it when you want to convert an image.

4 Converting an image to a bitmap. Open your photo file. Convert it to Bitmap by choosing Mode, Bitmap (if the photo is in color, you'll have to convert it by choosing Mode, Grayscale first and then Mode, Bitmap). When the Mode of an image is converted from the 256 tones of grayscale to the black-and-white-only Bitmap, the intermediate gray shades are

Original grayscale image

Reduced and made into a pattern tile

Original converted to Bitmap using Custom Pattern

Original CMYK image

Color mezzotint effect

represented as dot patterns, which can be chosen in the Bitmap dialog box. Click the Custom Pattern button, enter an Output Resolution value that's two to three times the resolution of the Input photo file, and click OK. (Experiment with the Output Resolution to get the detail you want.)

Variations. Here are some other "mezzotinting" approaches you can try for a variety of effects:

- **Using low-resolution diffusion dither.** Low-res bitmaps can produce pleasing mezzotint effects; see "Dithering" on pages 50 and 51.

- **Using a nonwrapping pattern.** Working with a recognizable image rather than a random, seamlessly tiling pattern for a mezzotint effect can produce an interesting illustration. You can even use a smaller version of the image itself as the "halftone dot." The image you use should have a broad range of tones — black, white, and a full range of grays. Surround the small version with the rectangular selection marquee and choose Edit, Define Pattern. Then follow the directions for step 4.

- **"Mezzotinting" a color file.** If you have the patience, try producing a mezzotint effect in color. The process involves splitting the color image into its separate color channels, converting them to bitmaps and applying the mezzotint, and then recombining them into a single color file. Open a CMYK image; choose Window, Show Channels and select Split Channels from the pop-out menu of the Channels palette. You will now have four separate grayscale files. For each file define a pattern as described in steps 1 through 3 (we used the same pattern, rotated in 90-degree increments for the four files). Choose Mode, Bitmap, following the instructions in step 4. When all four files have been converted to bitmaps, you'll need to convert them back to a single CMYK file. For each bitmap file, choose Mode, Grayscale and accept the default Size Ratio of 1. Then choose Merge Channels from the Channels palette's pop-out menu; make sure CMYK Color is selected in the Merge Channels dialog box. The channels will be reassembled into a single CMYK document.

Mezzotinting with Noise

Overview *Float a copy of the image; apply a Noise filter; convert the floating selection to Luminosity mode; drop the selection to blend the two images.*

PHOTO: CRAIG McCLAIN

Original photo

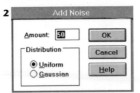

Noisy image composited with the original in Luminosity mode

A MEZZOTINT-LIKE EFFECT for a color image can be achieved quickly and simply with the Add Noise filter, applied so that it causes a random brightness pattern on the image without introducing random hue variation.

1 Floating a copy. Open a color image in RGB mode and Select All. Press Ctrl-J to float a copy exactly on top of the first.

2 Adding Noise. Choose Filter, Noise, Add Noise and choose Uniform. We used a setting of 50 for this 590-pixel-wide image.

3 Combining the two versions. With a selection tool chosen in the tool palette, the Brushes palette settings will apply to the floating selection as the two versions of the image are composited. Choose Luminosity from the pop-out menu, so that only the grayscale (brightness) information from the "noisy" image is transferred to the final composite. Click OK and then press Ctrl-D to drop the selection. (You could use Edit, Composite Controls to choose the Luminosity setting instead of controlling it through the Brushes palette.)

Variations. For a larger but softer "grain," apply the Despeckle filter (Filter, Noise, Despeckle) to the composited image.

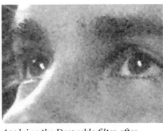

Applying the Despeckle filter after compositing

Dithering

Overview *Convert the image to Bitmap mode with a low-resolution Diffusion Dither; convert back to RGB color; replace black with one color gradient and white with another.*

TRANSPARENCY

In a black-and-white (Bitmap) image saved as a TIFF, the white parts are transparent when the file is imported into a page layout.

A MEZZOTINT-LIKE EFFECT can be achieved with Photoshop's Diffusion Dither. This kind of patterning can be useful for making the plates used for silkscreen printing or for adding a distinctive texture to a color illustration. Rob Day used a similar approach to color the leaf in the *Internet Companion* book cover shown on page 80.

1 Converting a photo. Start with a color or grayscale image. Convert it to Bitmap through the Mode menu: If the image is in Grayscale mode to start with, choose Mode, Bitmap. If it's in color, you'll have to choose Mode, Grayscale first and then Mode, Bitmap, because you can't convert directly from a color mode to Bitmap or vice versa. When you make the conversion, specify a low resolution in the Bitmap dialog box. We used 123 dpi, but you can use any resolution low enough to show a pleasing pattern. The resolution that looks best to you may vary, depending on the content of the particular image you want to apply it to.

2 Replacing the black pixels with a color gradient. To convert the dithered image to RGB mode so you can add color, choose Mode, Grayscale and then Mode, RGB. Double-click on the gradient tool to open its dialog box; set it for a Linear fill (or try a Radial fill if you like) and close the box. In the Brushes palette (Window, Show Brushes) set the mode to Lighten so the color will replace only the black pixels. Then click on the Foreground and Background color icons in turn and choose colors for the extremes of the color gradient; use any color except black or white. In the image, drag the gradient tool from where you want the gradient to begin to where you want it to end.

2c

3 Adding the second color gradient. Now select all the white pixels this way: Double-click the magic wand tool to open its dialog box; set the Tolerance at 0 and turn off antialiasing. Close the box and click the wand on a white area of the image. (Press Command-+ if you need to enlarge your view to place the magic wand tip.) Then choose Select, Similar to add all the rest of the white pixels to the selection. To apply a second gradient to the white pixels, set the Foreground and Background squares to new colors and use the gradient tool again, this time in Normal mode, to apply the color.

Filling with solid color. You can use a solid color rather than a gradient for either or both of the colors of the

3a

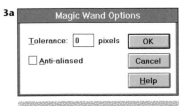

"mezzotint." Set one of the colors as the Foreground color and the second as the Background color. Instead of using the gradient tool in step 2, used the Edit, Fill command. Use Edit, Fill in Lighten mode so that only the black pixels are replaced with the foreground color. For the white pixels, make the selection as in step 3, and then press Backspace to fill with the background color.

3b

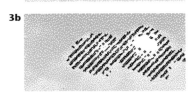

3c

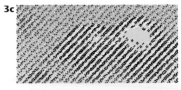

Changing the color scheme. If you want to experiment with different colors, you can convert the image you've filled with solid colors (described above) to Indexed mode and replace the colors in the Color Table: Choose Mode, Indexed. Then choose Mode, Color Table and click on the individual colors of the table to open the color palette and choose new colors. In the image the new colors are automatically substituted for the old.

3d

COMBINING RESOLUTIONS

If you want to use a low-resolution dither pattern with a higher-resolution element as we did for the final balloon image, choose a Bitmap resolution that's one-half or one-fourth of the higher resolution you plan to use. For information on combining the two resolutions, see page 80.

"Hand-Tinting" a Portrait

Overview *Convert the black-and-white image to RGB mode; select areas and adjust color, primarily in the midtones; desaturate light areas; add color details.*

JHD / PHOTO: INSPIRE

1a

Original grayscale image

1b

Image converted to RGB and Curves adjusted

THE COLORING OF BLACK-AND-WHITE PHOTOS with paints and pigments began very early in the history of photography, and its popularity persisted until color photography became widespread. Today the look is popular again — not a technicolor imitation of a color photo, but a subtle coloring reminiscent of early hand-tinting.

1 Correcting the tonality of the image. Whether you start with a color or a grayscale scan of the black-and-white image, you can use Photoshop's Levels (Ctrl-L) and Curves (Ctrl-M) adjustments to spread the tones in the image over the full range of possibilities and to bring out the shadow detail. For this image, which seemed a little dark to begin with, we used Image, Adjust, Curves to lighten the three-quarter tones, increasing the shadow detail. Clicking on the original curve at an Input value of about 15 and then dragging the point upward raised the entire curve. Clicking to form another point at an Input value of about 128 (halfway in the 0 to 255 range of the curve) and dragging downward closer to the center of the grid returned the midtones, quarter tones, and highlights to values close to their original settings. When making these kinds of Curve adjustments, it's important to maintain a smooth curve shape, without drastic changes in direction. Otherwise you can flatten the color or produce a sort of solarization effect with harsh tonal breaks.

2 Making selections. Now select various parts of the image so you can make color adjustments. Select one area, change it

2a

Magic wand selection

2b

Selection enlarged by Shift-clicking

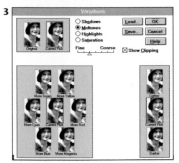

3

Adjusting color balance in the midtones

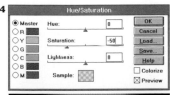

4

Desaturating white areas

by the method described in step 3, then select another, and so on. For this image the dress was selected by clicking on it with the magic wand tool with a Tolerance setting of 32 (double-click the magic wand in the toolbox to open the dialog box so you can change the setting). Additions to the selection were made by holding down the Shift key and clicking on other parts of the dress. The skin was selected with the lasso, feathered 5 pixels (double-click the lasso to open its dialog box). This selection was drawn loosely to imitate the old hand-tinting process, which often involved soft overlapping of colors.

3 Coloring the selections. Once selections have been made, open the Variations dialog box (Image, Adjust, Variations). The hue adjustment in the Variations box is especially good for skin tones — it's an electronic cosmetologist's dream that lets you see the tinting possibilities at a glance. Starting with fairly coarse adjustments (set with the slider at the top right of the dialog box), you can clearly see what color changes you're selecting. As you zero in on the changes you want, move the slider left to make finer adjustments. For the most part, change only the color of the midtones. Changing highlights and shadows, brightness, or saturation of selected areas tends to make selections look unnaturally distinct from their surroundings.

4 Desaturating white areas. Areas that have been colored too much can be desaturated or recolored by selecting them

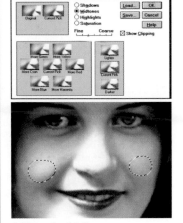

5

Adding color details

with an unfeathered lasso and choosing Image, Adjust, Hue/Saturation. For example, selecting the eyes and teeth and moving the Saturation slider to the left tends to take away most of the tint, while still maintaining the overall warm color cast that makes these features "at home" in this tinted image.

5 Adding color details. After hard-edged areas (such as the hat and lips in this image) have been selected with an unfeathered lasso and colored by using the Hue slider in the Hue/Saturation dialog box, subtle color variations can be added to the face. For instance, the cheeks in this image were selected with the lasso feathered to 5 pixels, and the Variations dialog box was used again to apply a little rouge. *Wow*

Popping Color

Overview *Select the subject; save the selection to an alpha channel and invert it; load the selection; adjust the hue and saturation of the background.*

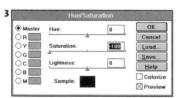

Selection converted to a path; adjusted

Alpha channel to select background

Background desaturated

A POPULAR EFFECT IN BOTH PRINT AND VIDEO is to isolate the subject of an image by "graying out" (or desaturating) the background. This effect is sometimes used to emphasize the subject, sometimes to simplify the background for overprinting text, and sometimes to tie an image to others in a publication.

1 Selecting the subject. Use the pen tool (choose Window, Show Paths and click on the pen) to outline the subject. In this case we started with the magic wand tool to make a rough selection, converted this to a path (Make Path, from the pop-out menu in the Paths palette), and then adjusted the path to fit the subject. Using a path lets you fine-tune the outline without worry of accidentally dropping and losing the selection.

2 Making a mask to select the background. The finished path was saved (Save Path from the pop-out Paths menu), converted back to a selection (Make Selection from the pop-out menu), and saved to an alpha channel (Select, Save Selection). The channel was then inverted (Image, Map, Invert) so it would select the background.

3 Desaturating the background. Load the background alpha channel as a selection (Select, Load Selection, #4) and choose Image, Adjust, Hue/Saturation (or press Ctrl-U). To turn the background gray, move the Saturation slider to –100, all the way to the left end of the scale.

4 Trying another variation. For the parrot image at the top of the page, we used a variation of the desaturation process.

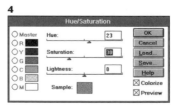

Settings for colorizing and desaturating

The Colorize box was selected, the Hue slider was adjusted to the desired color, and then the color was desaturated to 25. (When Colorize is off, the Saturation scale goes from –100 to +100; when it's on, the range is 0 to 100.)

Combining Positive & Negative

Overview *Copy the image; turn the copy into a negative; paste positive onto negative; adjust Composite Controls settings to blend the two versions of the image.*

Positive   *Negative*

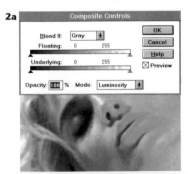

Composited in Luminosity mode

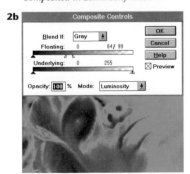

Input "trimmed" to 84 with some "fuzziness"

PHOTOSHOP'S COMPOSITE CONTROLS FUNCTION (from the Edit menu) lets you control how a floating selection combines with the image underneath. You can control the opacity of the floating selection, and you can choose, by brightness level, whether pixels in the combined image will come from the floating selections or the underlying image. For an illustration for *Entertainment Weekly* magazine, Jeff McCord found that the facial features in a negative version of an image from the "Director's Cut" of the movie *Basic Instinct* were too ghostly. So he used Composite Controls to combine positive brightness values and negative color.

1 Making a negative. Select All, copy (Ctrl-C), start a new file (Ctrl-N), and paste (Ctrl-V). Choose Image, Map, Invert (Ctrl-I) to make a negative.

2 Combining the two versions of the image. Now paste the positive image (still in the clipboard), and choose Edit, Composite Controls. Select Luminosity so only the brightness values of the positive image (not hue or saturation) will contribute to the composite. Use the Gray option and the Floating slider triangles to define exactly which part of the brightness range you want the positive to contribute. Hold down the Option key and drag a triangle to split its two halves in order to smooth the color transitions. After making the composite, McCord adjusted Levels and Color Balance of the finished image and pasted the patchwork of frame grabs on top.

"Sketching" a Portrait

Overview *Convert the grayscale image to RGB; apply a filter or special effect on the Red, Green, and Blue channels separately; experiment with removing the color from different channels.*

KATRIN EISMANN / PHOTO: DOUGLAS KIRKLAND

1

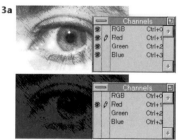

Grayscale converted to RGB and adjusted

2

Setting up to work on one channel

3a

Filter applied to the Red channel only; result viewed in RGB (top) and Red (bottom)

WORKING IN THE INDIVIDUAL RGB CHANNELS can produce some interesting treatments of color photos or of grayscale images converted to color. Katrin Eismann explored this technique in a portrait that began as a black-and-white photo. While there may be a number of different methods for accomplishing this effect in Photoshop, we reproduced it as shown in these steps. Looking at the steps that built the effect provides a good demonstration of how the positive and negative values in the individual channels can interact in the overall image. If you don't have the Aldus Gallery Effects filter set used here, you might want to experiment with the individual-channels technique by starting with one of the native Photoshop filters that produce random variations, such as Noise or Pointiilist, and then applying other effects, such as a Stylize filter or Distort, Displace, Mezzo, to the individual channels.

1 Converting the photo to RGB. Convert the image from Grayscale to RGB by selecting from the Mode menu. The conversion will put the same grayscale information in each of the color channels. For this photo, after the conversion to RGB, the gamma (gray) slider in the Image, Adjust, Levels dialog box was moved a little to the left to lighten the image overall.

2 Setting up to work on individual channels. Set black as the foreground color and white as the background color. (A quick way to do this is to click on the small default colors icon below the Foreground and Background color squares in the toolbox.) Select the first color channel you want to work on by clicking on that channel's name in the Chan-

COLOR CHANNELS IN COLOR

To view individual color channels in color rather than in grayscale, choose File, Preferences, General, Color Channels In Color.

3b

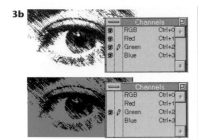

Filter also applied to the Green channel; result viewed in RGB (top) and Green channel (bottom)

3c

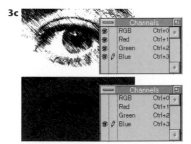

Filter also applied to the Blue channel; result viewed in RGB (top) and Blue channel only (bottom)

4a

Working in the Green channel only: Selecting All and filling with black; result viewed in RGB channel

4b

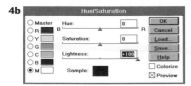

Working in the RGB channel: Removing the magenta by lightening it; the result is viewed here in the RGB channel

4c

Working in the RGB channel: Removing the magenta by lightening it; the result is viewed here in the RGB channel

nels palette. If you like, you can view the effect on the entire image by clicking in the eye icon column next to the RGB channel name.

3 Operating on the channels. Now make changes to the individual channels. For this image, the GE Graphic Pen filter was applied with the maximum Length setting (15), a Stroke Direction setting of Left Diag., and a Light/Dark Balance setting of around 30. The setting was the same for all channels, but because the filter operates with a degree of random variation, a slightly different effect was produced each time it was run. The filter was run first on the Red channel, then on the Green, and then on the Blue, although the order of operations would make no difference. Shown here are the progressive results as seen by viewing each color channel alone and by viewing all the channels together as each step was added.

4 Eliminating one color. Now you can eliminate the color effect contributed by one of the channels. To produce the red, blue, and black composition seen in the opening image, the Green channel was selected by clicking on its name, the entire content of the channel was selected (Ctrl-A for Select, All), and Shift-Backspace filled the channel with black. This effectively removed the green lines from the RGB image, but it also removed the green component of the white background, leaving a strong magenta component, since magenta is the complement (opposite, or negative) of green. To remove the magenta, leaving a white background, the main channel was activated by clicking on RGB in the Channels palette. Image, Adjust, Hue/Saturation was chosen, and the M (for magenta) color sample was selected; this would make the color adjustments apply only to that particular color. The Lightness slider was moved all the way to the right, to a value of +100. This turned the magenta white without affecting other colors. 🖋

Clicking one of the color buttons in the Image, Adjust, Hue/Saturation dialog box will let you adjust only one part of the color spectrum in an image. But be aware that this kind of adjustment in a photo can lead to artificial-looking color breaks — one color changes but the colors that blend it into the surroundings don't change with it.

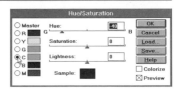

Painting a "Duotone"

Overview *Convert a Grayscale image to CMYK mode; set up two alpha channels with custom mask colors; copy and paste the image into both alpha channels; view both alpha channels while you work in one channel at a time to alter the masks; copy and paste the contents of the two alpha channels into two of the CMYK channels; output only those two channels.*

Original grayscale image

Experimenting unsuccessfully in Duotone mode

IN MOST OF THE COLOR PRINTING we see, the world is represented by the interaction of the four process printing ink colors: cyan, magenta, yellow, and black. We tend to think that this is the only way to get a wide variety of colors — a broad range of brights, neutrals, highlights, and shadows. But by using two complementary colors of ink, you can produce many more than two colors at less than half the price of printing a four-color piece. This rough comp for a wedding invitation in "retro" style is an example.

Printing a Photoshop image in two colors almost automatically suggests the Duotone mode. The program's Duotone function is ideal for taking advantage of custom color in a two-color printing job — either to add an obvious color accent to photos as part of the design of the piece, or as a subtle but effective way of extending the range of tones the printing press can produce. But Duotone mode has limitations. You can change the curves to modify the color treatment for a particular image, but no matter how you fiddle with the curves, it's virtually impossible to direct the colors to specific places in the image, independently of the highlight/midtone/shadow information present at those spots. The only way to put the color exactly where you want it is by "hand-painting." But how can you do that, see the results interactively on-screen, and still be able to separate the file into the two spot colors so you can make the plates for printing each of two custom color inks?

The way to approach it is to take advantage of Photoshop's ability to show more than one alpha channel of a file on-screen at the same time. You can specify a custom mask color for each channel and see a closer approximation of the colors

3a

Changing the color in the Channel Options dialog box

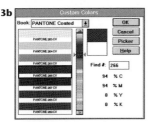

3b

Choosing a custom color

3c

Setting the opacity of the channel "ink"

4

Channels set to view both mask colors while working on the purple mask only

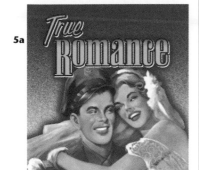

5a

Background removed from the gold channel; type outlines filled in the gold channel; channels viewed together

as they develop. After working with the two alpha channels until you have the color combination you want, you can assign the contents of the channels to two of the CMYK channels and output only those channels to make the printing plates for the two custom ink colors.

1 Setting up the file. Open the image in Grayscale mode. For this image, type outlines had been created in Adobe Illustrator and added (File, Place) to the image; the type outlines were also saved in separate alpha channels in the grayscale file.

2 Testing Duotone mode. Just in case a Duotone might produce the results you want, you can start out by experimenting with Mode, Duotone and loading and manipulating curves. You'll be "working blind," though, unable to see the result of your work until you click OK and close the color controls in the Duotone dialog box. Furthermore, although in most of Photoshop's default Duotone settings the two curves differ somewhat in shape, they both usually follow a basically lower-left-to-upper-right form. To get either of the two colors to appear alone anywhere in the image, you have to do some fairly drastic manipulation of at least one curve, as you can see in this Duotone Options dialog box.

3 Making a CMYK file and alpha channels. If Duotone mode doesn't do the trick, try making a hand-painted duotone. The first step is to convert the Grayscale image to CMYK mode. Choose CMYK Color from the Mode menu.

Create the first of the two alpha channels for the file by choosing Window, Show Channels and then choosing New Channel from the pop-out menu. When the Channel Options dialog box appears for this new channel (#5), click the color square to open the color picker, click the Custom button, and pick the lighter of the two colors you will use. We set the Opacity of the mask at around 85% to approximate the ink opacity.

Return to the main CMYK channel by clicking on CMYK in the Channels palette. To copy the image to the new channel, choose Select, All, and then press Ctrl-C; click on #5 in the Channels palette listing, and paste the image into this channel (Ctrl-V). Repeat the new-channel and copy-and-paste operations to create channel 6, to set your other custom color as its mask color, and to store another copy of the image in this new channel.

4 Setting up the two-color view. Now you can view both channels (by clicking in the "eye" column for both) as you

5b

Channels viewed separately: gold (left) and purple (right)

5c

Channels	
CMYK	Ctrl+0
Cyan	Ctrl+1
Magenta	Ctrl+2
Yellow	Ctrl+3
Black	Ctrl+4
PANTONE 266 ...	Ctrl+5
PANTONE 130 ...	Ctrl+6

Painting details in the gold channel, before (above) and after

6a

Viewing the C and Y channels after pasting

6b

The gold (left) and purple printing plates

work on only one of them (by clicking in the "pencil" column for just one). With only the two alpha channels set for viewing as you work, you can now see approximately how the two printed colors will interact.

5 Working in color. Use the painting and editing tools with the foreground and background colors set to black and white to alter each of the two channels. Since the CMYK file was a duplicate of the original grayscale file and therefore exactly the same dimensions, the type outlines that had been saved in an alpha channel in the grayscale file could be loaded as a selection in each of the two custom color channels (Image, Calculate, Duplicate as a Selection). The type was filled with black (the foreground color, representing the mask) in the gold channel, so that it showed up as bright gold lettering. The background of the original image was removed from the gold channel by painting with white (the background color). The airbrush was used to distribute color softly but precisely for the gold highlights on the hair and cheeks.

6 Making the printing plates. Now you'll paste the contents of the finished alpha channels into two of the four printer channels. (The C and Y channels were used in this case because they were the colors closest to the inks we were using.) Working in channel 5, choose Select, All and then copy. Click on Yellow in the Channels palette, and paste in the clipboard contents. Repeat the selecting, copying, and pasting process to put the contents of channel 6 into the Cyan channel. Save the file in CMYK mode. When the file is output, tell the image-setting service to output only the specified plates, at the screen angles that your printer recommends for your two ink colors. When you give the film to the printer, identify which of the two plates is to be printed in each of the custom colors. 🖉

Retouching a Photo

Overview *Scan the image; use Curves to adjust brightness and contrast in highlights, midtones, or shadows; select any large expanse of background; save the selection; clean up the mask; load the selection; replace the background; make repairs.*

1a

Original photo

PHOTO: ROY ROBINSON

1b

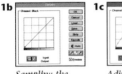

Sampling the shadows

1c

Adjusting the shadow tones

1d

Adjusted photo

2

Selecting the sky

3a

Making a Quick Mask

NOT ALL PHOTO-RETOUCHING JOBS are glamorous, but the technique can be practical and profitable. The San Diego Gas & Electric Company wanted to show the City Council of Oceanside, California how their streets would look if power lines were buried. The goal was to produce "before" and "after" photos the officials could hold in their hands for comparison.

1 Adjusting "exposure." Before you begin retouching, correct the brightness and contrast of the original image. Our original black-and-white photo had lost some shadow detail when we scanned it. So after the RGB scan (used to gain more information than a grayscale scan would have provided) was converted to grayscale (Mode, Grayscale), we applied Image, Adjust, Curves. The Curves function provides a way to isolate contrast and brightness changes to the highlights, midtones, or shadows. Move the cursor out of the Curves box and onto the image (it becomes an eyedropper) and click to sample the tone you want to change. A circle on the Curve shows the location of that tone. Drag to adjust the position of the point. Then move other parts of the curve back toward their original positions.

2 Selecting the background. It can be very hard to remove and seamlessly repair a background texture like the sky that extends over a large area with subtle color changes. Sometimes it's easier to select the background, make and edit a mask, and then replace the background. Instead of trying to remove the power lines by using the rubber stamp to paint sky over them, we decided to select the sky by Shift-clicking on various parts with the magic wand, add the power lines to the selection, and replace the selected area.

Repairing the mask

Saving the selection in an alpha channel

Replacing the sky

Cloning to cover the power pole

Copying elements from the image

Copying and flipping

Trimming away hard-to-replace details

3 Using Quick Mask. When the selection is complete, click on the Quick Mask icon in the toolbox. Then use the eraser and paintbrush to edit the mask. The goal was to create a mask to protect everything but the sky and power lines. We used the pen tool (choosing Window, Show Paths) to surround geometric areas accidentally included by the magic wand, such as parts of the "BOWL" sign. We converted each path to a selection (choosing Make Selection from the Paths submenu) and filled it with black (Shift-Backspace to fill with the foreground color), which made it part of the protective mask. We used the eraser to remove parts of the mask that covered the power lines.

4 Saving the selection. Convert the Quick Mask to a selection by clicking the Standard mode icon in the toolbox. Then choose Select, Save Selection to store the mask in an alpha channel for safekeeping.

5 Replacing the background. Now replace the background. We used a gradient fill between two shades of the sky color from the original photo. We started by clicking the eyedropper tool on the top of the original sky to set the foreground color; then we held down the Alt key and clicked on the skyline to set the background color. In the retouched image, we loaded the selection from the alpha channel (Select, Load Selection) and dragged with the gradient tool from the top of the sky selection to the bottom. To simulate the grain of the original photo, we added Noise (Filter, Noise, Add Noise).

6 Completing retouching tasks. Use the rubber stamp, lasso, and other tools and functions to retouch smaller areas of the image. We used the rubber stamp in Clone (Non-aligned) mode to grab (Alt-click) texture to paint over the power pole. We also lassoed and Alt-copied parts that could be reused, such as the "e" in the "Blue Palette" sign. For the "O" in "BOWL," we flipped a selection (Image, Effects, Flip) to mirror the intact half of the letter. Knowing what elements *not* to restore completely can save you a lot of time. For example, we shortened a palm frond by rubber-stamping the roof texture over it.

Printing the picture. So that city officials could compare "before" and "after," the original and retouched scans were output to negative film at a halftone screen of 200 lines per inch, and contact prints were made. *Wow*

Simulating Motion

Overview *Isolate and remove the subject, saving an alpha channel and storing a floating copy in a separate file; blur the background; add the subject back into the background; blur the edge of the subject.*

1a

Original image

1b

Red channel

1c

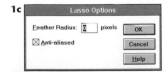

Alpha channel

2

New file with floating selection

ADDING A SENSE OF MOTION to a photo can draw the viewer into the excitement of the scene. Using blurring techniques in Photoshop, you can simulate the effect of a camera panning to follow the subject (as shown above) or of a stationary camera with the subject speeding by it (as shown on page 65).

1 Isolating the subject. Start by selecting the subject separately from the background. We looked at the three color channels of this RGB image of the skier and decided that the red channel showed the most difference between subject and background. So we copied the red channel (#1) (Ctrl-C), made an alpha channel (choose New Channel from the pop-out menu in the Channels palette), and pasted the selection into the channel (Ctrl-V); then we adjusted Levels (Image, Adjust, Levels) to emphasize the difference even more. The lasso, with Feather Radius set to 0 (so there would be no "halo" of background pixels associated with the selection) and Anti-aliased turned on, was then used to clean up the mask of the skier. Selected areas were lassoed, and Backspace and Shift-Backspace were used to fill the selections with white (the Background color) and black (the Foreground color) respectively. The Shift key was held down to add new areas to a selection, and the Alt key allowed the lasso tool to be operated either "freehand" (by dragging) or by clicking from point to point in straight-line segments.

2 Making a desktop "clipboard." When the subject is isolated, copy it (Ctrl-C), open a new file (File, New), click OK to accept the dimensions in the New dialog box, and paste the subject in — but don't drop the selection. Leaving the selection floating, you can use this file as a visible "clipboard" for storage. The advantage of leaving it floating is that you won't

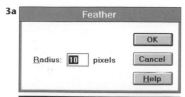

3a

Alt-dragging a patch of background

3b

Subject covered

4

Background blurred

5

Subject replaced

run the risk of picking up any of the white background when you come back to select and copy the subject to the clipboard again. Meanwhile, the alpha channel you made in the main file will hold the position of the subject so you can add it back later in precisely the same place.

3 Removing the subject from the background file. To blur the background, you have to eliminate the subject — otherwise it will become an obvious contributor to the blur. To do this, you can drag part of the background (in this case the sky) over the subject to cover it up. We used a lasso with a feather radius of 10 to select a soft-edged piece of the sky, held down the Alt key to make a copy, and dragged it over the skier. Feathering softens the transition between the patch and the original background, but a perfectly seamless transition isn't necessary. Because the background will be blurred and the subject will be pasted back in, the quality of the cover-up doesn't have to be precise. (Even a fairly busy background, such as a cityscape, is amenable to this cover-up and blur treatment.)

4 Blurring the background. With the subject eliminated from the background file, choose Filter, Blur, Motion Blur. We used a distance of 40 pixels in the apparent direction of the skier's motion for this image, whose width was 600 pixels.

5 Putting the subject back. Copy the subject that's still floating in the "visible clipboard" file that you made (Ctrl-C). In the background file, load the alpha channel you made (Select, Load Selection) and then paste the subject into place (Ctrl-V). The selection from the alpha channel will ensure that it settles in exactly the right spot. This makes the subject the center of focus.

6 Adding to the blur effect. If the image seems too perfect, you can add a little "blur detail" to the subject. For example, select the trailing edge of the moving subject and apply a motion blur. Or use a radial blur on a small part of the subject,

MEASURING AN ANGLE

To determine an angle of some object in an image, you can use the line tool with its width set to 0 to draw a line parallel to the object. Then check the angle in the Info box.

6a

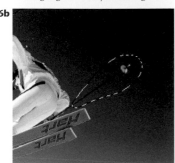

Trailing edge selected for blurring

6b

Detail selected for Radial Blur; blur center established

7a

Blur area selected

moving the blur center to correspond to a pivot point. In this case, for instance, the center for the spin blur was the part of the selection closest to the skier's hand holding the pole.

7 A different motion-blur effect: Blurring the foreground. Start with the original image and load the alpha channel from step 1 to select the subject. Then extend the selection with a feathered lasso with the Shift key held down. Select Filter, Blur, Motion Blur to create the effect of movement. Then paste the floating subject from step 2 on top of the blurred one. Again, to get rid of that "too perfect" look, make a rough selection with a feathered lasso (we used a feather of 10). Add a motion blur, using a two-step application; we used 20 pixels each time.

7b

Selection blurred

A TWO-STEP MOTION BLUR

Applying a motion blur in two steps eliminates the harsh edge that can appear with a one-step blur. Here the top image was blurred once at 40 pixels. The bottom image shows the effect of a two-step blur, with a 20-pixel motion blur applied twice.

40-pixel motion blur applied once

20-pixel motion blur applied twice

7c

Subject replaced and roughly selected; selection blurred

Solarizing a Portrait

Overview *Adjust the image map in the Curves dialog box to convert some of the tones to negative values.*

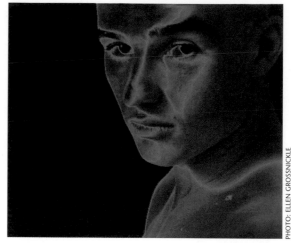

PHOTO: ELLEN GROSSNICKLE

Original portrait

Converted to grayscale

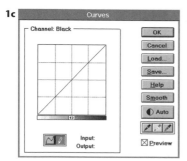

Standard curve

SOLARIZATION, FIRST OBSERVED BY Sabbatier in 1860 and later discovered accidentally by Lee Miller and Man Ray in 1929, is the partial reversal of a negative to a positive, caused by a brief exposure to light during development, often with dramatic effect. Today's photographic materials are much faster than they were in the 1920s, which makes it difficult to solarize a photo successfully in the darkroom. But you can get various similar effects by manipulating Photoshop's Image, Adjust, Curves command.

1 Opening the image map. Open your color or grayscale scan on-screen. (Both color and black-and-white images can be solarized. The portrait shown here started out in color and was converted by choosing Mode, Grayscale. The contrast and tonal range were improved by using the Image, Adjust, Levels dialog box, opened with the Ctrl-L shortcut.) Then open the image map by choosing Image, Adjust, Curves (Ctrl-M). Click the arrows below the curve to set the light-to-dark indicators so that white is on the left, and select the pencil icon below the curve. Also select the Preview icon.

2 Experimenting with solarization. A lower-left-to-upper-right diagonal line is the normal image map, with every input value represented by the same value on output. Redrawing the line to make an upper-left-to-lower-right diagonal produces a negative, with each input value represented by its opposite. It follows, then, that a V- or inverted-V-shaped line will produce a partial positive, partial negative. With the pencil icon selected, experiment by redrawing the line until you get a result you like. To get straight line segments, hold down the Shift key and click at the endpoints of the segments you want to draw.

2a

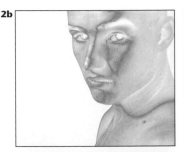

2b

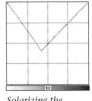

This setting produces the same effect as the Solarize filter.

2c

3

Solarizing the portrait

4a

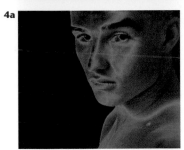

4b

Colorizing

5

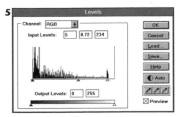

Making final adjustments

3 Solarizing the portrait. To make the solarized image shown in the opening illustration, we scanned a color photo and converted it to grayscale as described in step 1. Then we adjusted the Curves as described in step 2, settling on an image map that looked like the one shown here, and clicked OK to apply it.

4 Adding color. To get the colorized effect we were after, we had to convert the file back to RGB by choosing Mode, RGB Color. Before we opened the Hue/Saturation dialog box, we used the eyedropper tool to pick up a medium gray tone. Then we chose Image, Adjust, Hue/Saturation (Ctrl-U); the tone we had chosen appeared in the Sample box. We clicked to turn on the Preview and Colorize boxes, and adjusted the hue, saturation, and lightness.

5 Making final corrections. We again adjusted the tonal range with Image, Adjust, Levels. Besides changing the contrast, this changed the color somewhat. We also painted with the rubber stamp tool to repair a scratch and used the lasso and the Fill command set to Lighten and with Opacity set to 40 percent to lighten the dark spots that had started as a too-intense highlight on the nose.

Experimenting. Solarizing can produce some dramatic effects both in grayscale and in color, and it can be particularly effective for living subjects — plant or animal. The feeling created by a solarized portrait can be quite different than that of the original photo, and can vary a great deal depending on what parts of the image remain positive and which appear negative. Here are some examples of color images that were solarized with image maps similar to those used in step 2. Image maps can be saved by clicking the Save button in the Curves dialog box and opened again by clicking the Load button (see step 1c).

Solarizing a color image turns some tones into their complements.

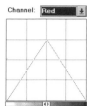

Solarizing one color channel produces a different result.

PHOTO: SUSAN HELLER

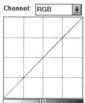
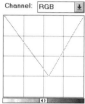
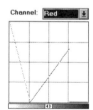

A black-and-white photo was scanned in RGB mode (above left). Altering the curves for two of the three channels colorized the photo.

REMAPPING COLORS

Adjusting the image map by working in the Curves dialog box can produce some wild color changes. Choose Image, Adjust, Curves and select the curve tool (rather than the pencil). Then click to establish a series of curve points. Shown below are the original image map and its straight diagonal Curve, along with three color variations and the Curves that produced them.

Original image

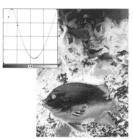

Curve adjusted in main RGB channel

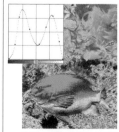

Curve adjusted in main RGB channel

Curve adjusted in Blue channel only

Coloring a Black & White Photo

Overview *Convert the grayscale image to RGB color; adjust color balance for highlights, midtones, and shadows.*

JHD / PHOTO: CRAIG McCLAIN

1

2a

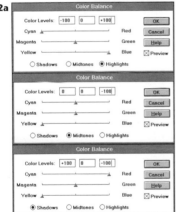

2b

ADDING COLOR TO A GRAYSCALE IMAGE can produce quite spectacular results. There are many ways to do it, and you'll see examples throughout the book. But here's a quick and easy approach, based on using Image, Adjust, Color Balance.

1 Preparing the grayscale image. Convert the grayscale image to color by choosing Mode, RGB Color.

2 Coloring. Choose Image, Adjust, Color Balance. In turn, click and adjust Highlights, Shadows, and Midtones. For a dramatic effect, use opposite settings for highlights and shadows. The image above was completed by placing clip art from an Art Parts disk in an alpha channel, loading it as a selection in the main image, copying the selected part of the background to the clipboard, feathering the selection and darkening with Levels, then loading the selection again, and finally pasting the original image from the clipboard and lightening slightly with Levels. (A similar technique is described in "Aglow at the Edges" in Chapter 8.) The right half of the image was selected with the rectangular marquee and Image, Map, Invert was chosen.

Experimenting. Try other Color Balance settings, or choose Mode, Indexed and then Mode, Color Table. Choose a particular color table from the pop-out menu or load one that you've previously created and saved.

Indexed Color, Black Body color table

Softening the Focus

Overview *Make a floating selection; blur it; recombine it with the original.*

JHD / PHOTO: VINTAGE

1a

1b

Gaussian Blur

Radius: 10.0 pixels

OK
Cancel
Help

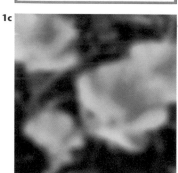

1c

SINCE THE END OF THE 19TH CENTURY, photographers have used haze and fog effects to impart a soft quality to an image, hiding the detail in the highlights, or in both the highlights and the midtones, or in the image overall. With a camera, the effect is sometimes achieved by smearing petroleum jelly very thinly on a filter placed in front of the lens, or by breathing on the filter, or even by placing fine nylon mesh over the enlarging lens in the darkroom. This technique is often used to hide small skin blemishes in portraits, to make hair look softer, or to add a romantic air. In Photoshop you can achieve a similar effect with Gaussian Blur and Composite Controls.

1 Blurring a copy of the image. Select all or part of an image. If you select a part, feather the selection a few pixels. Press Ctrl-J to float the selection — that is, to make a copy of it that sits exactly over the original. Choose Filter, Blur, Gaussian Blur. We selected the entire image and used a setting of 10 for this 505-pixel-wide image.

2 Compositing to make haze. Select Edit, Composite Controls and make one of the following changes to the Composite Controls dialog box:

- To refine the haze effect to soften the highlights only, choose Lighten and click OK. Adjust the Opacity.

- To refine the haze effect but apply it to all the tonal values in the selected area, choose Normal, enter an Opacity value to control the strength of the haze effect, and click OK.

- To soften the image within a particular tonal range, hold down the Alt key and drag the Underlying black and white sliders. Holding down the Alt key as you drag will split each slider triangle, so you can smooth the transition by defining a range of colors that are to be only partially composited. Move the two parts of each triangle apart slightly to avoid harsh color breaks. Experiment with the slider positions. The settings that work best will depend on the colors in the

2a

2b

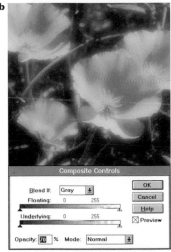

2c

image and the effect you're trying to achieve. When you have an effect you like, click OK in the Composite Controls dialog box and then click outside the floating selection (or press Ctrl-D) to deselect it. *彩*

"FLOATING" AND "UNDERLYING" SLIDERS

The sliders in the Composite Controls dialog box determine how the pixels of the floating and underlying images will contribute to the final composite:

• The sliders of the Underlying bar define the range of colors in the underlying image that are made available so they can be affected by the floating selection. So if you want to protect light or dark pixels, move the sliders inward to eliminate these tones from the available range.

• The sliders of the Floating bar determine what range of colors in the floating selection will be allowed to contribute pixels to the composite image by replacing the corresponding underlying pixels.

Together, the two sliders set up a sort of "if . . . then" proposition for each pixel in the underlying image: "If the pixel falls within the range established in the Underlying slider bar and the corresponding floating pixel falls within the range established in the Floating slider bar, replace the underlying pixel with the floating one; otherwise, leave the underlying pixel as it is." Of course, this can be further complicated by the Opacity setting (which determines what percentage of the final pixel colors the floating image will contribute) and the mode setting.

PRODUCTIVITY SINKHOLES

Some of Photoshop's image editing and compositing functions are so powerful and offer so many options that it's hard to stop experimenting once you get started. Like the Filter menu, the Composite Controls dia-

log box is one of these interfaces. A Photoshop devotee could get lost for days in the Filter menu or the Composite Controls. In fact, if the artist didn't have a clear goal in mind for a particular image before choosing Edit, Composite Controls, the dialog box could tend to take over the aesthetic development (not to mention the schedule) of the work. We've found that experimenting is a great way to learn about Photoshop's capabilities, but not necessarily when we have a specific design goal and a job to finish.

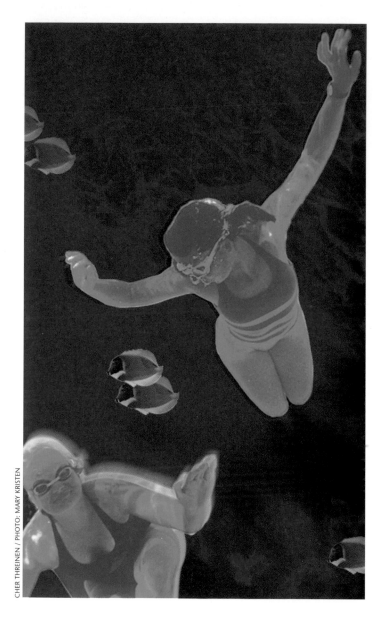

■ To create *Swimmers,* **Cher Threinen** started with a grayscale scan of a black-and-white photo of swimmers in a pool. She used the rubber stamp tool in Clone, Aligned mode to erase some lines that were painted on the side of the pool. She used the lasso to select the two figures, adding to and subtracting from the selection by holding down the Shift and Ctrl keys respectively as she lassoed parts of the figures. When the selection was complete, she feathered it slightly (Select, Feather, 2 pixels) and saved it in an alpha channel (Select, Save Selection). Then she duplicated the selection as a third channel and inverted it, to provide a mask that would select the water. Next, she converted this multichannel document to RGB. To color the image, she loaded a selection from an alpha channel, chose a color from the color picker, and used Edit, Fill in the Color mode to add a tint to the selection. For the figures, she also used Lighten mode, filling the swimmers with "layers" of aqua and blue. For the water, she used the lasso, the magic wand, and the Select, Feather command on areas that were still heavy with black to fill patches with magenta and red in Lighten and Color modes. The "halos" were created by loading the alpha channel for the figures to select them, copying the figures to the clipboard, and using Paste Behind to put the copy behind the original. With the pasted figures still selected, Threinen moved them to the left, and then feathered the edges of the selections and filled them with color in Normal mode at full Opacity. Fish were selected from another photo, colored, and pasted into the image.

Channel 1, Red

Channel 2, Green

Channel 3, Blue

■ To assemble his portrait of *Katrin Eismann*, **Russell Sparkman** started with two photographs he had taken with a digital camera. He combined negative and positive versions of these two images, using a different combination in each of the three (red, green, and blue) channels of the image, in which separate gradations of light and dark had already been created. The bevel was created with pen paths that were converted to selections so that the sides could be individually lightened or darkened with Image, Adjust, Levels to increase the feeling of depth. Noise was added to the frame, and feathered selections were darkened to create shadows at the top and at the left.

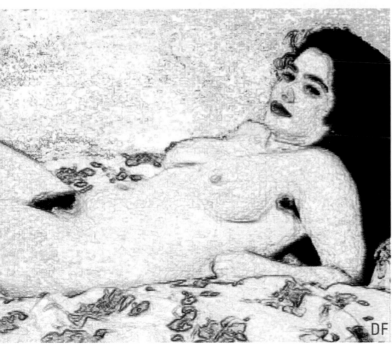

■ **Diane Fenster** started with a still video image to create *Rena Sketch*. She selected all and copied the image to the clipboard, and then chose from the Filter menu to run the Gallery Effects Find Edges filter on the image in the window. Next she pasted the color version from the clipboard back onto the "charcoaled" image, selecting the Color mode from Composite Controls to blend the two versions of the image.

MONTAGE AND COLLAGE

IN TRADITIONAL PHOTOGRAPHY and photo-illustration the distinction between montage and collage is significant. *Montage* is a method of making a single photographic print by superimposing several negatives. *Collage* is the assembly of separate photographic images mounted together, sometimes with other nonphotographic elements, to form another picture. With Photoshop, since photos and nonphoto elements can be combined, and since the "print" is likely to be output as part of a complete page layout, the distinction between montage and collage breaks down. But whatever you call it, the process becomes much easier, with no need for darkroom or glue.

Some of Photoshop's most useful compositing techniques involve feathered selections; gradient selections; alpha channels; the rubber stamp tool; Paste Into and Paste Behind from the Edit menu; Image, Calculate, Composite; and the Composite Controls, also from the Edit menu. In addition to reading about the montage/collage projects described in this chapter, check the index for more information on these topics.

Making a successful "seamless" photo montage, when that's your goal, involves more than choosing the right kind of selection and compositing techniques — like using a feathered lasso or marquee to create a soft, blending edge for the selection, or getting rid of background pixels at the edge of a selection to get a clean silhouette, or using Gaussian Blur on the background image to create a realistic depth of field.

To blend two or more images seamlessly, they should match in several respects. For example, the light should be coming from the same direction, and the detail and color cast of the shadows and highlights should be the same. Highlight and shadow detail can be manipulated by using Image, Adjust, Curves and Image, Adjust, Levels. And color cast can be identified with the eyedropper and the CMYK readings in the Info window (choose Window, Show Info to open it); then the color cast can be adjusted with Image, Adjust, Color Balance or Image, Adjust, Variations.

Changing the light source is much more difficult than managing shadow detail or color cast. In fact, it's so difficult that it's generally better to continue your search for photos that match in this respect than to try to make adjustments.

Fading One Image into Another

Overview *With the first image at the correct width and resolution for the final illustration, enlarge its canvas to the size you want the final illustration to be; adjust the second image to a size and resolution to fit within the expanded first image; use Quick Mask to make an alpha channel mask that will "fade" one image into the other; load the mask as a selection, and paste the second image into the first.*

JHD / PHOTOS: NASA, GRANT HEILMAN

FADING ONE PHOTO "seamlessly" into another requires that the two have certain qualities in common to begin with — for example, lighting, contrast, color saturation, and shadow detail. Beyond matching the way the two images look, you have to make adjustments so that you'll end up with the two parts

1a

Scan A: 2.377 inches wide at 300 samples per inch

1b

Scan B: 4 inches wide at 600 samples per inch

2a

Duplicating parts of the image

2b

Lasso Options	
Feather Radius: [3] pixels	OK
☒ Anti-aliased	Cancel
	Help

sized properly. If you know at the time you make scans what size and resolution you want the final illustration to be, you can scan one or both images to the proper size. But if you start with existing scans, or need to experiment before combining the images, you may be starting with images at two different resolutions and sizes, in which case you'll have to make the kinds of adjustments used for the image on page 76, made to illustrate the concept of decibel levels and the effect of sound for an introductory psychology textbook.

A NASA photo of a space shuttle launch was combined with a stock photo of a forest. The shuttle was chosen as the primary image, so it wouldn't have to be disproportionately resized to fit the other image; to do so would make it look obviously distorted. The forest image, on the other hand, provided more leeway — the trees could be stretched or compressed a little and still look like natural trees. The same could be done with a sky image, for example.

The shuttle was scanned from an 8 x 10-inch print on a desktop LaCie SilverScanner. The scan was set up to deliver the image, cropped appropriately, at a width of 2.377 inches (the column width into which the final image had to fit) and at 300 samples per inch (twice the 150 lpi screen resolution at which the book would be printed). (For information on how to figure scan resolution, see Chapter 1.)

The forest image had previously been scanned by a service bureau from a 4 x 5-inch transparency at a resolution of 600 samples per inch. So at the start of the Photoshop work, the images were two different sizes and resolutions.

1 Preparing the images. Open the RGB TIFF scans in Photoshop. In this case the first image (shuttle) had been scanned to the right size and resolution. If this were not the case, though, you could choose Image, Image Size, make sure Proportion was selected and File Size was deselected, enter the resolution you wanted, and then enter the critical dimension (in the case of this illustration, it would be width).

2 Retouching the images. After adjusting the tonal range, saturation, and overall color cast of the images, paying special attention to shadow and highlight density, edit the images as necessary to make the two photos work together. In this case the smoke from the launch had to be extended downward to get rid of the sharp edge of the launch pad. This was done by selecting some smoke with the lasso after setting a feathered edge, holding down the Alt key to copy the selected area, and dragging the selection to its new location; this operation was repeated until the smoke hid the structure.

3

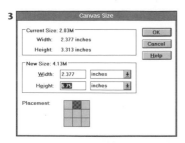

3 Making room for the second image. With the first image at the correct width and resolution, choose Image, Canvas Size and increase the size to the dimensions of the final image; this makes a space for the second image. For the shuttle image, width was left as it was and height was increased. Choose File, Save As to save the image in its new form.

4 Figuring size for the second image. Use the selection rectangle to select an area the entire width of the canvas and tall enough to overlap the first image where you want the two photos to fade into each other. Check the Info window (Window, Info Palette) to read the dimensions of the image in pixels.

5 Sizing the second image. Click on the second image to make its window active. There are several ways you can make the second image the same size as the expanded first image. (A) If the size and resolution of the second image allow it, you can crop the second image: Double-click on the cropping tool and enter Height, Width, and Resolution values to set a fixed size and shape for cropping; then after you reset the resolution of the image (as described next), you can drag the cropping tool to select a section that's exactly the right size and

4

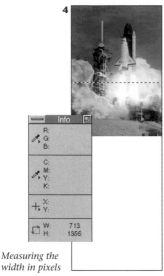

Measuring the width in pixels

5

Reshaping the photo

You can let Photoshop automatically choose the right resolution for reproducing an image. Choose Image, Image Size to open the Image Size dialog box; click the Auto button. Set the halftone screen resolution and choose Medium or High. The Medium setting, which multiplies the screen resolution by 1.5 to arrive at image resolution, works well for "soft," organic images. But if your image has sharp color breaks or straight lines, choose High; the High setting multiplies halftone resolution by 2. (Multipliers higher than 2 increase file size without further improving image quality.) The Draft setting, good for experimenting with an image before you begin work but not for print reproduction, produces a resolution of 72 dpi or the initial scan resolution itself, whichever is lower.

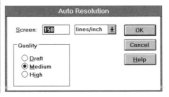

MEASURING DISTANCE

You can use Photoshop's line tool with Width set to 0 pixels to measure distances in an image: Double-click the line tool, set the Width to 0 in the Line Tool Options dialog box, and click OK. Then draw a line across the span you want to measure, and read the "D" value in the Info window.

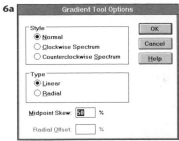

6a

6b

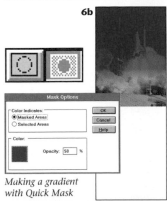

*Making a gradient
with Quick Mask*

7a

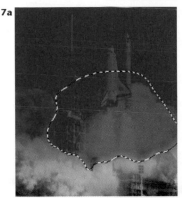

Adding to the mask

7b

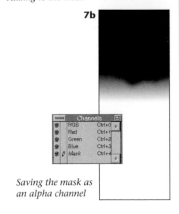

*Saving the mask as
an alpha channel*

shape. (B) If the nature of the image will allow you to resize it disproportionately, you can do what was done for the forest image here: Choose Image, Image Size; make sure that both Proportion and File Size are turned off; then enter the resolution and pixel dimensions you noted in the Info window of the first image and click OK. (Compare this image to step 1b to see that the image has been narrowed.) (C) You could use some combination of cropping and resizing.

6 Making the mask. As the basis for the mask for fading the two images together, click the Quick Mask icon near the bottom right corner of the toolbox. Double-click the icon to open the Mask Options dialog box to make sure the Masked Areas setting is chosen. You can change the color or opacity of the mask, if necessary, to make both image and mask clearly visible. Now select the gradient tool (if necessary, double-click the tool and set up a Linear blend). Drag the gradient tool on the Quick Mask to make a transition band where you want the two images to merge; put the white end of the blend where you want the second image to show.

7 Refining and saving the mask. Modify the mask, if necessary, to preserve additional areas of the first image at full strength when the second image is pasted in. For example, for this image, the lasso was used (with a feathered edge — Select, Feather, 10) to select part of the smoke, and Shift-Backspace was used to add this selection to the mask that would protect the first image when the second was pasted in. Click on the standard (nonmask) icon, choose Select, and Save Selection to save the finished mask in an alpha channel.

8 Combining the images. With the first image (from step 4) active, choose Select, Load Selection to load the mask from channel 4 into the RGB channel. Then click on the second image to make it active. Choose Select, All (Ctrl-A) and then Edit, Copy (Ctrl-C) to copy the second image to the clipboard. Then

> **IMAGE SIZE SETTINGS**
>
> If you find that you can't keep both File Size and Proportions selected in the Image Size dialog box as you change the Height or Width of an image, check to see if Width or Height is set to pixels. Changing to another unit of measure will allow you to keep both File Size and Proportions constant as you change the dimensions.

click on the first image and choose Edit, Paste Into to combine the two images through the mask. Reposition the pasted image, if necessary, to align the two images. (The finished image is shown in the opening illustration.)

Mixing Resolutions

Overview *Create a coarse-textured, low-resolution image; change the resolution of the low-res artwork to the higher resolution without losing the coarse texture; import a high-resolution element; create a glow.*

ROB DAY / PHOTO: NASA / COVER DESIGN: VIRGINIA EVANS

61 dpi mezzotint effect

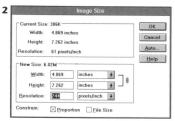

Setting the interpolation method to maintain the mezzotint

HOW CAN YOU COMBINE TWO RESOLUTIONS in a single Photoshop image? For instance, what if you want to import a photorealistic element with a high-resolution look into a purposely coarse, textured bitmap? In his illustration for a book cover, Rob Day used the following technique to get what appear to be two different resolutions into a single image.

1 Starting in low resolution. Create or scan a low-resolution image at the final size you will use to print it. Choose a resolution that's a quarter of the high resolution you'll need for the photorealistic element. Day scanned a leaf at 244 dpi in grayscale and used the scan to create a custom mezzotint-like effect in RGB mode at 61 dpi (see Chapter 3).

2 Changing the interpolation method for resizing. The next step is to increase the real resolution of the image so you can maintain the precision of the high-resolution image you will import, while preserving the low-res look — in this case, Day wanted to preserve the low-res mezzotint pattern. To do this, you can alter the way Photoshop will interpolate when it changes the resolution. Choose File, Preferences, General and select Nearest Neighbor for the Interpolation setting. Nor-

3

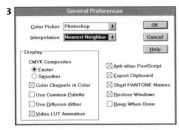

Increasing resolution

High-resolution image

5a

5b

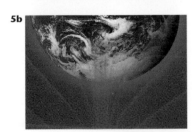

mally, you would use the default Bicubic interpolation method (or Bilinear, which is faster) for increasing the resolution of an image, so that when Photoshop assigns color to the pixels it adds, it will average the colors of the existing pixels and make a smooth color transition. But this time you want to preserve the pixellated look, so the right choice is Nearest Neighbor.

3 Increasing the resolution. Next choose Image, Image Size. In the Image Size dialog box, set the Width and Height units to Inches. (You can use any units that are a fixed measure; that is, any units but pixels.) Select the Proportion box, but deselect the File Size box. Leave the Width and Height the same, and quadruple the resolution. For Day's book cover, 244 dpi (four times the original 61 dpi) would provide plenty of data for a 150 lpi halftone printed image. (244 ÷ 150 = 1.62, which is within the range of 1.5 to 2 times the halftone screen resolution appropriate for an image that doesn't need the higher resolution required for diagonal lines or hard edges.)

4 Importing the high-resolution element. Open the high-resolution file. Select the element you want to add, and copy and paste it into the first image. Day imported a public-domain earth image from NASA, scanned to fit the cover design at a resolution of 244 dpi. (While the selection is floating, you can reduce its size by using Image, Effects, Scale.)

5 Adding finishing touches. Day also created a glow behind the earth. One way to do this is as follows: Before dropping the pasted-in selection, copy it to the clipboard (Ctrl-C). Then choose Select, Save Selection to make an alpha channel. With the selection still active in the image, choose Select, Feather and specify the size of the feather effect. Click on the Foreground color square and choose a color for the glow. Press Shift-Backspace to fill the selection with color. Load the selection into the image, so that you can now paste the clipboard contents (Ctrl-V) into exactly the right spot. The pink veins were added by making a mask from the original 244 dpi grayscale scan of the leaf, loading this selection, and filling it with pink. The file was saved in EPS/DCS format and opened in Illustrator, where Virginia Evans incorporated it into her cover design and added the type. 🐾

HIDING SELECTION BORDERS

You may want to keep a selection active so you can move, resize, or otherwise modify it. But you can't always get a good look at the image if the selection border pulsating is across the screen. To hide the selection border without releasing the selection into the image, press Ctrl-H (for Hide). Press it again to toggle the selection border back on.

Casting Shadows & Reflections

Overview *Draw a mask for the objects; make luminance masks for reflections and shadows; add objects, reflections, and shadows to the new background.*

1a

Original product shot

1b

Product selected and selection saved in alpha channel (#5)

2

Image copied and pasted into channel 6

3

Levels adjusted and Motion-blurred

SUCCESSFULLY INTEGRATING A FOREGROUND OBJECT from one photo into a new background image involves more than just cutting out the object and sticking it on top of the background. Adding a shadow cast by the object can help to make it part of the scene, but adding a reflection does an even better job. To put together this collage illustration for a packaging design for Pioneer, Japan, we borrowed the reflections present in the original studio shot of the products and used them as alpha channels to selectively lighten and darken the new background.

1 Making a mask for the objects. From a scanned image, select the object you want to transplant by tracing its outline with the lasso or the pen tool. We began with a scan made from a 4 x 5-inch transparency, a studio shot of the products. The CMYK scan was 2500 pixels wide; we used the crop tool to eliminate parts of the image above and below the products to make the file smaller and easier to work with. To use the pen tool, open the Paths palette by choosing Window, Show Paths. Click and drag with the pen tool (as described in Chapter 2) to outline the object you want to transplant. When you've completed the path and closed it by clicking on the original point, save it (Save Path from the pop-out menu in the Paths palette). To convert the path to a selection, choose Make Selection from the pop-out menu. Then save the selection as an alpha channel (Select, Save Selection). In this case, the alpha channel created by the Save Selection command was #5, since 0, 1, 2, 3, and 4 were occupied by the main CMYK image and the four color channels.

2 Starting a mask for the reflections. Back in the main channel of the image (the CMYK channel in the case of this example), choose Select, All (Ctrl-A), copy the selection (Ctrl-C), open a new channel by choosing New Channel from the Channels palette, and paste the copied image into the channel

Channel 5 loaded into channel 6 and filled with black

5a **5b**

Image copied into channel 7; color inverted

Channel 5 loaded into #7 and filled with black

6a

Darkening the shadows after lightening the highlights

6b

Reflections and shadows in place

(Ctrl-V). The reflections mask for this example was channel 6. Choose Image, Adjust, Levels and move the white point on the Input Levels slider to emphasize the highlight areas of the mask.

3 Creating a surface texture. If you want to "texturize" the background of your image — the surface on which the objects will rest — you can do it at this point by adding the texture to the reflection alpha channel. We used Filter, Blur, Motion Blur with a setting of 20 pixels to create the feeling of a "brushed" surface consistent with the high-tech nature of the products. The rubber stamp tool in Clone (Aligned) mode was used to touch up areas where the products had blurred into the background area.

4 Completing the highlight channel. Now load the original outline channel into the highlight channel as a selection: Working in the highlight channel (in this case, #6), we chose Select, Load Selection, #5 (the original mask). Fill the selection with black (by pressing Shift-Backspace with black as the foreground color). This isolates the reflections alone in this channel. Use the lasso and Shift-Backspace or a paintbrush and black paint to clean up the mask.

5 Making the shadow mask. Open another new channel (#7), and paste the copy of the scan stored in the clipboard into this new channel as you did for channel 6. Choose Image, Map, Invert to make a negative version of the image, turning the shadows into light areas that can act as selections. Again, as you did for the highlights mask, adjust the Levels, add texture, and then load the original outline channel and delete to black, leaving behind a mask that represents the object's cast shadow.

6 Making reflections and shadows. We used Image, Image Size on the product photo to find its exact dimensions in pixels. Then, in the background image file, we double-clicked the rectangular selection marquee and set its size at those dimensions. We used the marquee to select the part of the new background image where we wanted the products to end up, and copied the selection to the clipboard. In channel 0 of the product shot, we loaded the original mask channel (Select, Load Selection, #5) and then pasted the background from the clipboard behind this selection (Edit, Paste Behind). Then we loaded the reflection and shadow masks in turn (Select, Load Selection, #6 and Select, Load Selection, #7) and used Image, Adjust, Levels to lighten and darken the selected areas. Finally, we selected All, copied. and pasted the image back into the larger background file.

Wrapping One Image Around Another

Overview *Make a "sketchpad" file; copy parts of the first ("material" source) image into this file and alter them to fit the second image; select part of the second image; rubber-stamp from the sketchpad into the selection; copy the altered second image into the first; rubber-stamp to blend the two images.*

ABSOLUT COUNTRYSIDE.

JACK CLIGGETT

1

2

3a

THE MONTAGE PROCESS sometimes involves using textural "material" from one photo to modify a second image so it will blend realistically with the first. Jack Cliggett, head of the Graphic Design Program at Drexel University, did just that in creating this Absolut Vodka ad for Concept 3 Advertising to run in *Countryside* magazine. He couldn't simply composite the two images, regulating the opacity of the transparent water and glass. He had to make the water flow over the physical structure of the supersize bottle. A similar approach might also be used to drape hair around a face or cloth around an object.

1 Making a "material" file. Open a file that can supply the image material you need. Cliggett began with a scan of a stock waterfall photo from Comstock. When the image was scanned at a large enough size so that the part he wanted to use could be enlarged to the final 7 x 10-inch ad, the file was 54MB, far too large and slow to work with conveniently. So he copied the waterfall — the only part of the image he would manipulate — into the clipboard, opened a New file, and pasted in the clipboard contents.

2 Selecting the subject. Select the area in the second image that you want to fill with visual information from the first. Cliggett used the lasso with the Alt key held down and a feather setting of 2 pixels. (Set the Feather Radius by double-clicking the lasso in the toolbox to open its dialog box.)

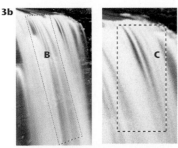

3b

B **C**

3c

D

3d

A   D

C

B

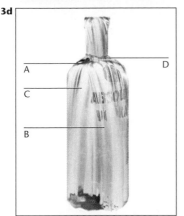

3 Painting with the image. Use the selection and rubber stamp tools to isolate textures from the first image and add them to the second. Cliggett created a new document to use as a sketchpad and worked first on the shoulders of the bottle. He copied and pasted an oval selection from the waterfall file (A) to his sketchpad file, flipped it horizontally, and then rubber-stamped it in Clone, Aligned mode from the sketchpad file onto the bottle file. (To "load" the rubber stamp with an image from any open file, hold down the Alt key and click to identify the area you want to clone.) Cliggett rotated an oblique rectangular selection on the sketchpad before the bottom part of it was applied to the bottle (B). Another vertical selection was flipped (C). A flat area of the falls was used to make the transition from the bottle's neck to its shoulder (D). He motion-blurred selected areas to make the water "flow." He rubber-stamped the Absolut logotype from the original bottle image, using a small brush tip, 40% Opacity, and vertical strokes to blend it with the water.

4 Montaging the images. Add the textured image to a copy of the other one, using the rubber stamp tool as necessary to blend the images together. With the bottle still selected, Cliggett copied it to the clipboard and then pasted it onto a duplicate (Image, Calculate, Duplicate) of the 7MB version of the waterfall. He inverted the selection (Select, Inverse) so his next edits would not affect the bottle. He cloned parts of the waterfall from the left to obscure the unacceptable parts of the waterfall that appeared alongside the bottle. He then held down the Shift key and used the lasso to add the bottom of the bottle to the selection and blended the bottom of the bottle into the mist at the bottom of the waterfall by rubber-stamping from other parts of the image. Details such as the branches in front of the waterfall bottle were rubber-stamped from the uncombined waterfall image.

Finishing the ad. When he had finished the montage of bottle and waterfall, he selected all, copied the composite picture, and pasted it into the original 54MB image. (To ensure that a selection is replaced in exactly the right position, save the selection to an alpha channel in the original image when you first select it; then load this selection before pasting the altered area back into the original file.) The finished image was cropped and saved. It was merged with a type file and output as film separations. ░

■ **Jack Davis** began the design for The *Journeyman Project poster*, a collage of overlapping disc shapes filled with images from this interactive game, in Adobe Illustrator. He drew borders to define the discs, saved the file in EPS format, and opened it in Photoshop as a Grayscale file. Then he used the magic wand tool with Tolerance set at 250 to select one of the disc shapes and copy it as a selection into an RGB background file of exactly the same dimensions by using Image, Calculate, Duplicate. With the selection active, he used Paste Into to add the image. After all the discs had been filled in this way, he made two other alphas. The first was a fatter version of the original alpha (Select, Load Selection and then Edit, Stroke), which he loaded as a selection in the RGB file so he could adjust Levels to lighten the rims of the discs. The second was a shadow mask, created by blurring and offsetting a copy of the mask used for lightening, and then loading the first mask and filling it with black; again he loaded the mask into the RGB channel and adjusted Levels to darken. The last step was to load the original alpha and fill the selection with black to clean up the edges left by the wand selections.

■ **Russell Sparkman** collected the raw material for *Dollar Signs* by photographing the dollar bill and the coins and using a 35mm slide that he had taken of painters on ladders. He determined the size of the image by how large he could scan the painters without their becoming too "soft." He used the Trace function in Fractal Design Painter to "sketch" the dollar to give it a partially painted feel. He made a feathered selection in Photoshop to merge the original dollar with the sketch by pasting it into the selection to complete that component. The faux sky was created with KPT Texture Explorer; the faux floor was created by generating a Noise texture, applying a vertical Motion Blur, adding vertical lines to define the boards, and making hue and saturation adjustments; then it was given perspective with Image, Effects, Perspective. The men on ladders were selected and the selections were saved in alpha channels and offset; these selections were then loaded and darkened to create the shadows. The buckets on the ladders came from another image of painters. Sparkman added a little green paint to the sides of the buckets to fit these elements into this image. The paintbrushes in the men's hands were drawn with the pencil and paintbrush tools with very small brush tips.

■ *Terra* by **Michael Gilmore** consists primarily of imported elements. The sun and planets were created in a 3D modeling and rendering program, and the gold color was added using Color Balance after the file was converted to RGB mode. The star map began as an Aldus FreeHand drawing and was successfully imported as an EPS. The lettering for "TERRA" and "The Human Perspective" was also done in FreeHand. The "TERRA" type was converted to paths, the construction lines were added, and an image was pasted into the letters. To import these elements into Photoshop, Gilmore used "an extremely low-tech" approach: A screen-capture program was used to take a "snapshot" of the on-screen FreeHand artwork, and that screen capture was pasted into the Photoshop file. The background of the image came from an earlier version of the *Terra* file: The Syquest disk on which Gilmore had been creating *Terra* developed a bad block. When he recovered the *Terra* file from the damaged disk, he opened it to find only "TV noise and garbage." As a "kind of tribute" to the original file, he made part of it into a pattern (by selecting it and choosing Edit, Define Pattern) and used this pattern to fill the background (Edit, Fill, Pattern).

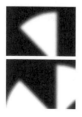

■ **Jack Davis** designed the type and graphics for this *Packaging Label* for a desktop drum scanner in Adobe Illustrator and placed them in a Photoshop background file. The background was an enlarged scan of printed halftone dots, though Photoshop 2.5's Stylize, Color Halftone filter could have approximated the effect. The halftone dot pattern was altered with Image, Adjust, Hue/Saturation. To create the metamorphosis of pixels to halftone dots, the Mosaic filter was applied through graduated masks in two stages with progressively larger cell sizes. The type was filled with clouds, using the Edit, Paste Inside command, and shaded as described in "Dropping a Shadow" in Chapter 8. The small type was given a glow as described in "Aglow at the Edges," also in Chapter 8. The photos and collage in the lower right-hand corner were pasted into soft-edged selections made by applying the Gaussian Blur filter to the pie shapes that were imported from Illustrator into alpha channels.

■ *Cupid* by **Michael Gilmore** started as a grayscale composition that was converted to RGB and colored with the Image, Adjust, Color Balance and Hue/Saturation commands. He also added Noise to the photo of the angel statue. The background behind the angel and the 3D elements is made up of a scanned photo of the wall of the office building where Gilmore works and a scan of a 16th-century map.

■ Characteristic of **Michael Gilmore**'s *False Prophet* is that although it's composed of distinctly different elements, the components are so well-integrated that they seem to have been photographed together in a single space. Gilmore achieves this effect by combining the elements in a grayscale file, then converting the grayscale file to RGB, and selecting and coloring the parts. Working in this way allows him to compose for tonality and then to achieve consistency of color by doing all his coloring in one file. In *False Prophet*, working at 150 dpi in a 20MB file, Gilmore selected the kewpie, chose Select, Border, 3 pixels and applied the Noise, Median filter to that border. The effect was a kind of after-the-fact antialiasing that smoothed and blended the edge. To make the postage-stamp-like elements, he scanned one edge of a stamp, copied parts of it, and rotated them into place to create the border; he used scanned 19th-century etchings for the stamp artwork. A photo of elements from a friend's "gizmo" collection, a scan of an old map of Ireland, and objects created in a 3D program completed the image.

■ To produce the magenta spots in the background of *Laura Stretching*, **Lance Hidy** used the magic wand tool and the Select, Similar command to select sun reflections from an ocean image; he loaded the selection into a white background and used the Fill command to turn it magenta. The silhouetted nude is simply a negative produced by choosing Image, Map, Invert. Hidy captured the spiky elements in the foreground by using the magic wand and Select, Similar to capture the highlights in a photo of dried grass. He pasted these highlights into the composite image and used Filter, Sharpen, Unsharp Mask with high settings, applied several times. He likens this "oversharpening" effect (the edges become black and the interior becomes brighter) to the sound distortion that can result from turning up the volume on an amplifier.

■ In *Neptune*, an image that stems from his long-standing interest in sea life, **Lance Hidy** explores light in ways that he never found possible in paint or traditional photographic processes. The effect, in some ways similar to solarization, is created with negative values and positive colors. Starting with a snapshot of his son David, Hidy used Image, Map, Invert to make a negative. Then he applied Image, Adjust, Hue/Saturation to turn the *color* positive again: To restore the color, he moved the Hue setting to the right end of the slider and and also adjusted Saturation to the right. He used the rubber stamp tool to clone out water drops on the boy's skin; the drops, highlights in the original photo, had turned to dark spots in the inversion process. He also used the rubber stamp tool in the From Saved mode to restore the original values to the mouth and eyes.

■ *Cactus Montage* by **Lance Hidy** was composed from four images: The trees in the background were a magic wand–Select, Similar selection turned negative with the Image, Map, Invert command and colored blue with Image, Adjust, Hue/Saturation; the cactus was selected with the lasso tool; the sea foam was prepared by selecting the blue water with the magic wand and deleting it; the lobelia flowers were another magic wand selection, with the hue changed from blue-violet to red. The four images were layered together by cutting and pasting on top of a three-color blend, made with the blend tool by blending from black to purple and then from purple to gold.

■ In *Q.P. Doll,* to illustrate the concept of "quality printing" on a promotional postcard for a printer, **Louis Fishauf** montaged the face of his son Jackson with the kewpie doll. He made a feathered selection on the face of the doll and then used the Paste Inside command to paste Jackson's face in place. Then, with the selection moved into place and still floating, he hid the selection outline and chose Image, Adjust, Hue/Saturation to modify the color of the face to match the color of the doll. The images in the corners are from still video and film-based photos. The type and other shapes were imported from Adobe Illustrator. The image was "layered" by placing (in the case of PostScript elements) and pasting the elements into the image in order. To make the hand appear to be holding the swash of the letter "P," Fishauf selected the thumb and used Paste Behind.

USING
FILTERS

PHOTOSHOP'S FILTERS ARE SMALL PROGRAMS that you can select from the Filter menu to run on an entire image or a selection. Within this menu, filters are grouped in submenus by type or software developer. Along with filters for special and painterly effects (described later in this chapter), Photoshop supplies three kinds of filters that can do a lot to improve the quality of scanned photographs, and can even improve painted images. You'll find these "workhorse" filters in the Sharpen, Blur, and Noise submenus.

SHARPEN

Photoshop provides four sharpening filters. Sharpen and Sharpen More accentuate the color differences between adjacent pixels of different colors. Sharpen Edges and Unsharp Mask find "edges," areas where a continuous run of pixels of one color comes up against other colors, and then they increase the contrast between that run of pixels and the pixels nearby; areas that aren't edges are left pretty much unchanged, so they still look smooth, or "soft." The use of sharpening filters comes up again and again throughout the book, but here's a quick list of sharpening tips:

Use only Unsharp Mask. In general, forget the other sharpening filters and use Unsharp Mask. Unlike Sharpen and Sharpen More, which sharpen images by accentuating the difference between adjacent pixels of different colors, Unsharp Mask accentuates the differences only at "edges."

Use it last. Because it can create artifacts that can be magnified by other image-editing operations, Unsharp Mask should generally be applied after you've finished editing the image.

Use it after scanning. As a rule, run the Unsharp Mask filter on a scanned photo to see if it improves the image by getting rid of any blurriness that may have been introduced by the scanning process.

Use it when changing size or orientation. Whenever you use Image, Image Size or Image, Effects, Scale to make a

continued on page 94

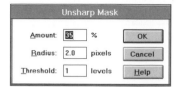
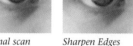

Original scan   *Sharpen Edges*

Sharpen   *Sharpen More*

Unsharp Mask default: 50, 1, 0   *Unsharp Mask: 100, 1, 0*

Unsharp Mask: 100, 3, 2   *Unsharp Mask, 4 times: 25, 3, 2*

PHOTO: NASA

Original scan

Enlarged   *Unsharp Mask 100, 1, 0*

PHOTO: KIDS / GAZELLE TECHNOLOGIES

Original scan   *Unsharp mask, 4 times: 25, 3, 2*

change that affects the file size, use Unsharp Mask afterwards. Any such change in file size involves interpolation (see astronaut). If you're enlarging the image or increasing the resolution, interpolation adds pixels of intermediate colors between the original pixels; if you're decreasing the dimensions or resolution of an image, it averages the color of adjacent pixels. Interpolation also takes place when you apply any of the functions in the Image, Effects submenu, such as Shear or Rotate. In each case, interpolation tends to "soften" the image.

Try different settings. With Unsharp Mask, you can set:

- The Amount (the strength of the application, or how much the difference at an edge is enhanced by the filter).

- The Radius (how many pixels in from the color edge will have their contrast increased). Increase the Radius with increasing resolution, because at higher resolutions the individual pixels are smaller relative to the image components.

- The Threshold (how different the colors on the two sides of an edge have to be before the filter will sharpen it). Use higher settings for images that are "grainy" or have subtle color shifts, such as skin tones, so the filter won't sharpen the "noise."

Use Unsharp Mask more than once. Running Unsharp Mask more than once at a lower Amount will sharpen more smoothly than if you run it once at a setting twice as high. (Note that this is not true for Sharpen More and Sharpen, which multiply the artifacts they create if you apply them more than once.)

BLUR

Photoshop's blurring filters can be used to soften all or part of an image. Blur and Blur More (which is three or four times as strong as Blur) smooth an image by reducing the contrast between adjacent pixels. With the Gaussian Blur filter, the transi-

Sharpening or blurring can help add depth and form to a painting or photo. Sharpen the areas that extend toward the viewer and leave unsharpened (or even blur) the areas that are farther away. For pinpoint, handheld control of the Sharpen filter, use the sharpen tool. (If the tool isn't visible in the tool palette, select it by Alt-clicking the water drop [blur] tool.) You can change the settings in the Brushes palette to control the area (brush size) and intensity of sharpening. (Restroking with the sharpen tool can produce an "overdone," unrealistic effect, like that produced by applying Sharpen more than once.)

After François Guérin painted a still life of fruit in Fractal Design Painter (left), he used Photoshop's Sharpen tool to add dimension (right).

Blur the background to reduce the apparent depth of field and focus attention of the foreground.

tion between the contrasting colors occurs at a particular mathematical rate, so that most of the pixels in a black-to-white blur, for example, are in the middle gray range, with fairly few pixels in the very dark or light shades. And you can increase the amount of blurring that occurs by raising the Radius value. The other three Blur filters fall into the special effects category: Motion Blur, which lets you set a direction and an amount for the blur, produces an effect like taking a picture of a moving object. Radial Blur provides two options: With Spin you can simulate the effect of photographing an object spinning around a center that you specify in a Blur Center box; Zoom simulates the effect of zooming the camera toward or away from the center.

Here are a few ways the workhorse Blur filters can come in handy.

Use Blur to make the background recede. One of the most common errors in Photoshop montage is combining a sharply focused subject with an equally sharply focused image used as background. You can fix the problem by blurring the background slightly to simulate the depth of field a real camera lens would capture. You can also apply this background-blurring technique to a single photo to reduce the perceived depth of field and focus attention on the foreground subject.

Use Gaussian Blur to smooth out flaws in a photo. Part of the repair of damage to a photo (such as water spotting) can be accomplished with the Gaussian Blur.

Use Gaussian Blur to control the edge characteristics in an alpha channel. Once a selection has been stored in an alpha channel, the Gaussian Blur filter can be run on the chan-

In color photo film, the grain is larger in the blue than in the red or green parts of the emulsion. Since the blue emulsion controls the yellow in the final image, and yellow is lighter than cyan or magenta, the blue channel is least likely to show this larger grain artifact. But if you run a sharpening filter on all three channels in an RGB image, this noise is made more obvious. To avoid "enhancing" the noise, try clicking off the blue channel's pencil icon in the Channels palette before you sharpen. You'll sharpen the red and green channels only, so you'll get the sharpening effect without magnifying the noise in the blue channel.

Channels before sharpening, (left to right: red, green, and blue)

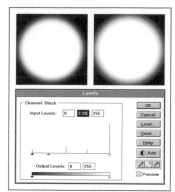

Gaussian Blur: Moving the Input Levels gray point slider to enlarge (here) or shrink the mask

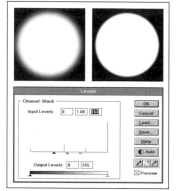

Gaussian Blur: Moving the Input Levels black and white point sliders to control the softness of the edge

nel to soften or smooth out the transition between black and white. Then the Image, Adjust, Levels function can be run on the channel to fatten, shrink, or harden the edge of the selection area.

Use the blur tool to apply the Blur filter by hand. This tool (the counterpart of the sharpen tool) gives you pinpoint control of the blur.

NOISE

Under Noise in the Filter menu are two filters that smooth the color in an image (Despeckle and Median) and one that roughens it (Add Noise). Add Noise creates random or Gaussian variation in pixel tone or color, Despeckle detects edges and then leaves these alone while smoothing out less abrupt changes in color, and Median averages the brightness of pixels within an image or selection. To make use of these filters:

Add Noise to improve a color gradient. Color gradients created in a PostScript-based graphics program can be too "slick"-looking or can show unwanted color banding. Adding Noise can make the gradient look more natural. For an especially subtle effect, you can run the filter on one or two of the channels, or run it on the individual CMYK channels.

Add Noise as the basis for generating a texture. Adding Noise and then applying other filters can generate some interesting textures. Some examples appear on the next few pages and in Chapter 6, "Painting."

Despeckle to reduce scan artifacts. The "ridges" that can appear in desktop-scanned images can be reduced or eliminated by the Despeckle filter. Despeckle can also help eliminate *moiré*, an interference pattern caused by the interaction of the scan pattern and the halftone screen pattern in a printed image being scanned.

HUE-PROTECTED NOISE

In a color image, Photoshop's Noise filter draws from the entire spectrum to change pixel colors; this can produce an artificial "electronic rainbow" look. But you can introduce noise without color change by floating a copy of the image (Ctrl-J), applying Add Noise, and then using the mode control in Edit, Composite Controls (or the Brushes palette) to set the mode to Luminosity before releasing the selection (you can use 100 percent opacity or reduce it for a subtler effect). A more limited hue-protected noise effect can be achieved with three filters of that name from the Kai's Power Tools set of third-party filters.

Noise, Add Noise, Uniform, 50

Float; Add Noise as at left; Composite Controls: Luminosity mode

Combining Filter Effects

Overview *Start with at least two copies of the file; apply separate filter or color effects to each; combine the effects with the Blend command.*

MICHAEL GILMORE

FILTERS OFFER ENDLESS POSSIBILITIES for combining their potentially spectacular effects. For an illustration for the Japanese edition of *Step-By-Step Electronic Design,* Michael Gilmore was inspired by *Jurassic Park* to use this dinosaur as the centerpiece.

1 Choosing an image. An out-of-the ordinary original image works well as the subject for the unusual effects that filters can apply. Gilmore started with a photo he took of a toy dinosaur from a local hobby shop. He scanned the photo and began experimenting to make it look a bit more fearsome.

2 Duplicating the file. In the rush of inspiration, it's sometimes hard to remember to save a copy of your original so you can start fresh if you want to. Fortunately, you can Revert to the original as long as you don't save an intermediate version. But it's a good idea to start by duplicating, and then save often during development of an image. Choose Image, Calculate, Duplicate to quickly make a copy to work on.

3 Applying the first filter. Choose an effect from the Filter menu and, if necessary, set its parameters. Gilmore had installed the Aldus Gallery Effects Vol. 1 filters (see page 108 for more about these filters). He chose Filter, Gallery Effects, GE Chrome and tested various settings on a part of the image in the interactive dialog box. When he was happy with the result, he clicked the Apply button.

4 Applying a second filter. Return to the original image you saved. You can duplicate it again, still maintaining an original, before you apply another filter. Gilmore applied Photoshop's Find Edges and then used Image, Map, Invert to get bright lines on a dark background.

4

5

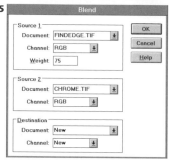

5 Blending the two effects. If, as in the case of this image, your two "filtered" images started out as copies of the same file and have not been altered in size or shape, you can apply the Image, Calculate functions to combine them. Gilmore used Image, Calculate, Blend, specifying 75% for Source 1 so the Find Edges filter would have a stronger effect than the Chrome. The result is shown at the top of the preceding page.

Experimenting with filters. Try out other filter combinations. Shown here are some of Gilmore's experiments combining filters with adjustments to color (through Image, Adjust, Hue/Saturation) and to the color map (Image, Map).

To produce the image above, the original was solarized (Filter, Stylize, Solarize) and Image, Map, Equalize was applied to brighten the result.

For the effect above, Photoshop's Ripple filter was applied (at its default settings) to the original; color was adjusted through Image, Adjust, Hue/Saturation; and the GE Dry Brush filter was applied.

For the version at the left, the color in a copy of the original was inverted (Image, Map, Invert); then the Mosaic filter was applied (above left). Hue and saturation were adjusted (Image, Adjust, Hue/ Saturation) (above right). Then this version was combined with the original (Image, Calculate, Difference).

USING DISTORTION FILTERS

When you apply a distortion filter, you can often get better, smoother results by running the filter at a lower setting several times than by running it at a higher setting once. The difference is especially apparent if the image includes straight lines. For this example we started with a screen dump of one of the color palettes supplied with the Photoshop program.

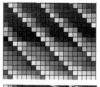

Original Pantone palette

Twirl applied 10 times at an Angle setting of 50

Twirl applied once at an Angle setting of 500

Distressed Type

Overview *Use Photoshop effects — particularly the Noise, Blur, and Diffuse filters — to "distress" type for use in bitmapped or PostScript illustrations.*

JHD / PHOTO: TAIZO TASHIRO / INSPIRE

Setting type in an alpha channel, #4

Mask after inverting

Loading the selection into a second alpha channel, #5

Gaussian Noise, 500   Stroke, 2 Pixels, Inside

Diffuse, deselect, Diffuse   Blur (4 times)

THE SMOOTH TYPE OUTLINES produced by PostScript illustration programs like CorelDraw, Adobe Illustrator and Aldus FreeHand, or even by Photoshop with Adobe Type Manager, are just too polished for some situations. Designer/consultant Peter Kallish of The Kallish Group in New York found that he could simulate the "distressed" appearance produced by a photocopy, or a weathered stencil, or a poorly inked rubber stamp, with Photoshop effects. The techniques shown here are variations on his process. Many are centered around the use of the Blur filter, which softens transitions between contrasting colors or grays, and the Diffuse filter, which shuffles pixels to "deteriorate" an image inward from the boundaries between colors.

1 Setting type in an alpha channel. Open the image to which you want to add the distressed type. Then create an alpha channel (Window, Show Channels, New Channel). If you're working in RGB, the new channel will be channel 4.

With black as the foreground color, use the type tool (with Anti-aliased selected in the Type dialog box) to set type in the alpha channel. The resolution of your file and the size of the type will affect the way the filters act on the letters. For the example shown in these steps, we started with 40-point type set in Adobe's Stencil font in a 72 dpi file.

2 Adjusting and saving the type. With the type still active as a floating selection, adjust the spacing between letters by defloating the type (Ctrl-J) and then holding down the Ctrl key to select the letters individually or in groups (selection techniques are described in Chapter 2) and moving them, pressing the Shift key after dragging begins in order to keep the letters aligned on their original baseline. When the lettering is complete, press Ctrl-D to drop the selection. This alpha channel will preserve your original lettering, so you'll have it if you need to start over. Choose Image, Map, Invert so that you end up with white lettering on a black background.

Levels: 84, 0.56, 241

Threshold: 185

Completed mask in channel 5

10a

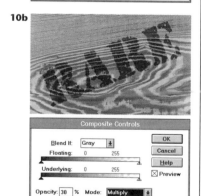

10b

10c

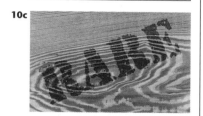

3 Making a second alpha channel for distressing the type. To make another channel (channel 5 if you're working in RGB) in which to "distress" the type, choose New Channel again to open a completely white channel. Then choose Select, Load Selection, #4 to make the type a selection in channel 5.

4 Generating a texture with the Noise filter. Now, to generate the texture from which to build the distressed lettering, choose Filter, Noise, Add Noise, Gaussian. (We used a setting of 500 pixels.) Don't deselect the lettering.

5 Building up the edges with a stroke. With black as the Foreground color, choose Edit, Stroke, 2 Pixels, Inside.

6 Modifying the texture with Diffuse and Blur. Choose Filter, Stylize, Diffuse, Normal and click OK. Then deselect the lettering (Ctrl-D) and press Ctrl-F to apply the Diffuse filter again with the same setting. Next choose Filter, Blur, Blur and apply it with the default settings; then press Ctrl-F three times to increase the blur effect.

7 Setting the darkness with Levels. Choose Image, Adjust, Levels and move the black point, midpoint, and white point triangles until you have the overall darkness you want for the lettering. For this example, we used settings of 84, 0.56, and 241. Click OK to apply your changes.

8 Setting the openness with Threshold. If you want a strictly black-and-white mask, choose Image, Map, Threshold to turn all pixels in the image either black or white. Move the slider farther right for more black areas or farther left for more white, open spaces. We used a setting of 185. Click OK to apply.

9 Completing the lettering. To save the distressed type as a mask that you can load into the RGB channel, choose Image, Map, Invert.

10 Coloring the type. Click on the RGB channel in the Channels palette to activate the background image you started with in step 1. Choose Select, Load Selection, #5 to load the distressed type selection. Now press Ctrl-J to float the selection so you can fill and rotate it and adjust its opacity. Click the Foreground color square and choose a color, and then press Shift-Backspace to fill the active selection. You can control the opacity of the floating selection, to make it look like opaque paint or transparent ink, by adjusting the sliders in the Composite Controls dialog box (under Edit).

A Helvetica Extra Compressed type, 72 points; Gaussian Noise, 500; Stroke, 2 Pixels, Inside, Black; Deselect; Diffuse, Lighten Only; Blur (5 times); Levels 151, 0.38, 220.

B Bauer Bodoni Bold type, 72 points; fill with black; Diffuse, Lighten Only (7 times); Image, Map, Invert (Ctrl-I); Blur (5 times); Levels 107, 0.58, 225.

C Futura Bold type, 72 points; fill with black; Deselect; Gallery Effects Spatter, Spray Radius 5, Smoothness 8; Blur (4 times); Levels, 79, 1.88, 191.

D ITC Century Bold type, 72 points; fill with black; Deselect; Gallery Effects Ripple, Ripple Size 15, Ripple Magnitude 2.

E Triplex Bold type, 72 points; Gaussian Noise, 400; Gallery Effects Spatter, Spray Radius 25, Smoothness 9 (2 times); Diffuse, Darken Only (2 times); Levels, 200, 1.00, 255; Diffuse, Normal (3 times); Diffuse, Lighten Only (2 times); Diffuse, Normal (3 times); Image, Map, Invert the selected character (Ctrl-I); Threshold, 221.

F Stone Serif Bold type, 72 points; fill with 40% black; Pointillize, Cell Size 5; Diffuse, Darken Only; Threshold, 185; Diffuse, Darken Only (2 times).

G Stencil type, 72 points; fill with black; Deselect; Wave; Threshold, 185.

H Times type, 72 points; fill with black; Gallery Effects Ripple, Ripple Size 10, Ripple Magnitude 6.

To get the effect shown in the opening illustration, we pasted the type several times. First we pasted at 60% opacity with the underlying selection controlled so that its lightest colors weren't affected by the pasted image. Then we pasted again in Multiply mode, to intensify the color on the dark areas and add some "worn" color to the light areas. To give the paint some thickness of its own, we loaded the selection again, and chose Filter, Stylize, Emboss. Because only the type itself was selected, the embossing effect was subtle. A beam of light was created by selecting a pear-shaped area with a highly feathered lasso, adjusting Levels to brighten the selection, and then choosing Select, Inverse and using Levels to darken the surrounding wood.

11 Trying other formulas. You can use other combinations of filters to create different distressed looks. All of these were created at 300 dpi, starting with the type loaded into channel 5 as at step 3. In some cases the Threshold adjustment (step 8) was omitted to get a mottled effect with several levels of opacity. (Settings for the various filters are shown in the caption. If no settings are given, the defaults were used.)

12 Exporting distressed type. Once the modifications to the letters are complete, the Photoshop-distressed type can be saved as PostScript outlines: In channel 5, choose Select, Load Selection, #5. Choose Make Path from the Paths palette. (The Tolerance setting in the Make Path dialog box will determine how closely the path follows the details of the selection border. in the process of making the path.) Then choose Save Path (also from the Paths palette); finally, choose File, Export, Paths To Illustrator to save the lettering as an Adobe Illustrator file. (The Paths To Illustrator filter must be in the Plug-ins folder.) The distressed type can then be scaled, skewed, and otherwise modified as a PostScript object.

PATHS FROM GRAYSCALE

When a selection that includes gray shades is converted to a path, the path is drawn at the 50% gray boundary.

Filter Demos

Overview *Drag the plug-in filter to the Plug-ins folder inside the Adobe Photoshop folder; start the Photoshop program; open an image; select the area you want to filter (make no selection if you want to filter the entire image); choose Filter and select a filter from the pop-out submenus.*

IN ADDITION TO PROVIDING PLUG-IN FILTERS with Photoshop, Adobe has made available to other software developers the program code they need to write more filters. Among the software developers now creating filters for Photoshop are Aldus, Andromeda, and HSC Software. The following pages provide a catalog of many of the available filters, showing the effects of applying them to two kinds of photos — a still life and a portrait, shown here at the left. The caption for each filtered image shows the settings used to produce it. Numerical settings are listed in the order they appear in a filter's dialog box, from upper left to lower right. If the default settings were used, no settings are shown.

Because filter effects require a good deal of calculation, applying a filter can be a time-consuming process. Besides showing you the results of applying the filters themselves, this gallery includes tips for using filters efficiently and effectively.

FILTER RERUNS

To reapply the last filter effect you used, press Ctrl-F. To select that filter but open its dialog box so you can change the settings before you apply it, press Ctrl-Alt-F.

Adobe

Filter effects are grouped alphabetically by submenu name, with individual filters shown alphabetically within submenu. Some filters (such as Blur: Radial Blur) can be set to produce two or more very different effects.

Blur: Blur

Blur: Blur More

Blur: Gaussian Blur (2)

Blur: Motion Blur

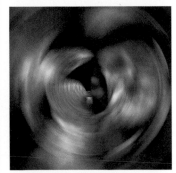

Blur: Radial Blur (25/spin)

Blur: Radial Blur (50/zoom)

Distort: Displace (12-sided)

Distort: Displace (crumbles)

DISPLACEMENT MAPS

Some of the Displacement maps Adobe supplies for the Distort, Displace filter are two-color files that produce fairly uninteresting effects when applied in the Tile mode. But using the Stretch mode develops a range of tones, which can produce effects that are more interesting.

Distort: Displace (fragmt lyrs/2/2/tile)

Distort: Displace (fragmt lyrs/5/5/stretch)

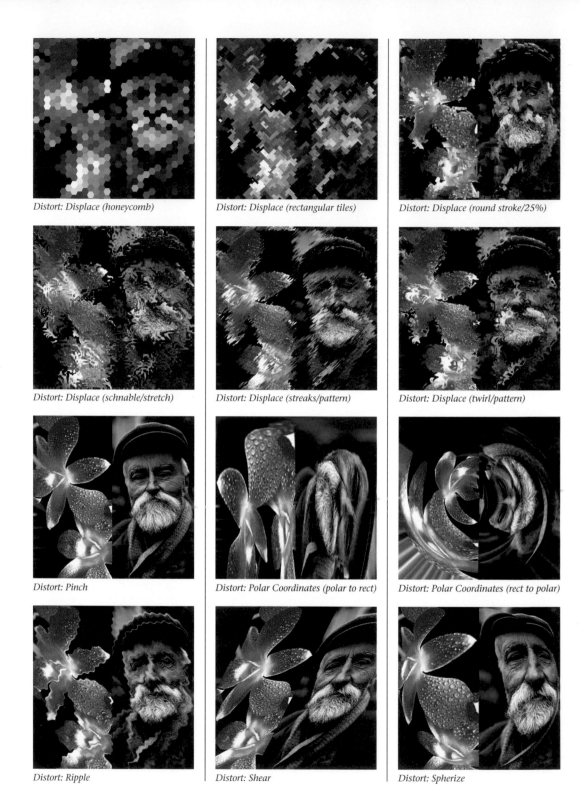

Distort: Displace (honeycomb)

Distort: Displace (rectangular tiles)

Distort: Displace (round stroke/25%)

Distort: Displace (schnable/stretch)

Distort: Displace (streaks/pattern)

Distort: Displace (twirl/pattern)

Distort: Pinch

Distort: Polar Coordinates (polar to rect)

Distort: Polar Coordinates (rect to polar)

Distort: Ripple

Distort: Shear

Distort: Spherize

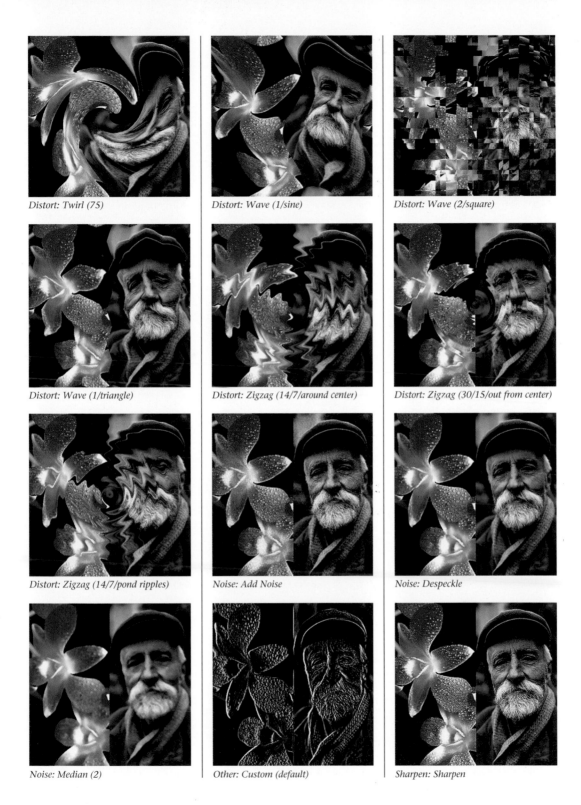

Distort: Twirl (75)

Distort: Wave (1/sine)

Distort: Wave (2/square)

Distort: Wave (1/triangle)

Distort: Zigzag (14/7/around center)

Distort: Zigzag (30/15/out from center)

Distort: Zigzag (14/7/pond ripples)

Noise: Add Noise

Noise: Despeckle

Noise: Median (2)

Other: Custom (default)

Sharpen: Sharpen

Sharpen: Sharpen Edges

Sharpen: Sharpen More

Sharpen: Unsharpen Mask (100)

Stylize: Color Halftone (6)

Stylize: Crystallize

Stylize: Diffuse

Stylize: Emboss

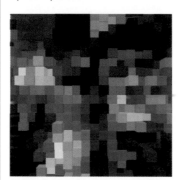

Stylize: Extrude (blocks/random/solid)

Stylize: Extrude (blocks/level)

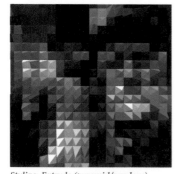

Stylize: Extrude (pyramid/random)

Stylize: Extrude (pyramid/random 20/80)

Stylize: Facet

Stylize: Find Edges

Stylize: Fragment

Stylize: Lens Flare

Stylize: Mosaic (6)

Stylize: Pointillize

Stylize: Solarize

Stylize: Tiles

Stylize: Trace Contour (32)

Stylize: Wind (blast)

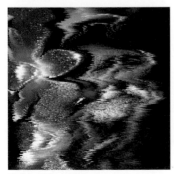

Stylzie: Wind (stagger)

Stylize: Wind (wind)

TESTING A RADIAL BLUR

The Radial Blur filter gives you three options for Quality: Draft, Good, and Best. Use Draft (which is quicker but rougher) to experiment with the Amount and the center of the blur. Then use Good (or on a very large image, Best) to generate the final effect.

Aldus Gallery Effects 1

The first set of Gallery Effects filters includes effects that can make a photo look like a painting or drawing.

Chalk & Charcoal

Charcoal

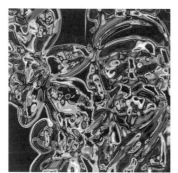

Chrome (7/3)

Craquelure

Dark Strokes

Dry Brush (texture 1)

Dry Brush (texture 3)

Emboss

Film Grain

Fresco

Graphic Pen (15/64)

Moszic

Poster Edges

Ripple

Smudge Stick

Spatter

Watercolor (texture 1)

Watercolor (texture 3)

"SOFTENING" A FILTER

If you run a painterly effects filter and the result seems too strong, one option is to Undo and run the filter again with a "milder" setting. But Gallery Effects and other special effects filters can take a long time to run. Here's a way to avoid the rerun time: Before you run the filter, float a duplicate of the image (Ctrl-J). Then run the filter on the floating copy. If the effect is too strong, use the Opacity slider in the Brushes palette to "soften" the effect.

PHOTO: PHOTOTONE / LETRASET

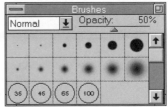

Original image

Duplicate, filtered

Composited image

Aldus Gallery Effects 2

Along with painterly filters, Gallery Effects 2 includes three — Rough Pastels, Texturizer, and Underpainting — that simulate a textured surface.

Accented Edges

Angled Strokes

Bas Relief

Colored Pencil

Diffuse Glow (2/7/13)

Glowing Edges

Grain (enlarged)

Grain (horizontal)

Grain (regular)

Grain (soft)

Grain (speckle)

Note Paper

Palette Knife (7/3/2)

Patchwork

Photocopy

Rough Pastels

Sprayed Strokes

Stamp (3/6)

Texturizer (brick)

Texturizer (burlap)

Texturizer (canvas)

Texturizer (custom pict file)

Underpainting

Aldus Gallery Effects 3

Gallery Effects 3 includes filters that simulate halftone screens and graphic and other special effects.

Conté Crayon

Crosshatch

Cutout

Glass (blocks)

Glass (blocks, frosted)

Glass (tiny lens)

Halftone Screen (circle)

Halftone Screen (line)

Halftone Screen (dot)

Ink (outlines)

Neon Glow

Paint Daub (dark, rough)

Paint Daub (sparkle)

Paint Daub (wide blur)

Plaster

Plastic Wrap

Reticulation

Sponge

Stained Glass

Sumi-e

Torn Edges

Water Paper

Kai's Power Tools

HSC Software's KPT filters include Gradient Designer and Texture Explorer — either of which is like a cross between your favorite toy and a bagful of electronic lollipops.

KPT Extensions: Gradient on Paths

KPT Ext.: Grad. Designer (spfx, glow jade)

KPT Extensions: Julia Set Explorer

KPT Ext.: Mandelbrot Set Explorer

KPT Ext.: Texture Explor. (proced.; not face)

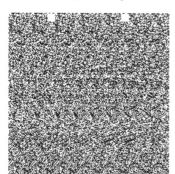

KPT Filters: 3-D Stereo Noise (see KPT Help)

KPT Filters: Diffuse More

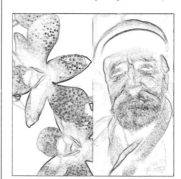

KPT Filters: Find Edges Charcoal

KPT Filters: Find Edges & Invert

KPT Filters: Find Edges Soft

KPT Filters: Glass Lens Bright

KPT Filters: KPT Grime Layer

KPT Filters: KPT Hue Protected Noise Max

KPT Filters: Hue Protected Noise Med

KPT Filters: Hue Protected Noise Min

KPT Filters: PixelBreeze

KPT Filters: PixelStorm

KPT Filters: PixelWind

KPT Filters: Scatter Horizontal

KPT Filters: Sharpen Intensity

KPT Filters: Smudge Darken

KPT Filters: Smudge Lighten

Andromeda Series 1

Andromeda Software's Photography Filters provide special effects similar to those you can achieve with 35mm camera lenses.

cMulti

Designs (mezzo/basic #3)

Designs (mezzo/pattern grains)

Diffract

Halo

Prism

Rainbow

Reflection

sMulti

Star

Velocity

Wow Filter "Widgets"

To get these effects, displacement maps from the Wow disk were used with Photoshop's Distort, Displace filter. See "Creating Crystal" and "Working with Widgets" for tips on making and using displacement maps.

Distort: Displace (dropsdisp.psd/5/5/tile)

Distort: Displace (dropdisp.psd/5/5/stretch)

Distort: Displace (puzldisp.psd/3/3/tile)

Distort: Displace (wovedisp.psd/3/3/tile)

Distort: Displace (icedisp.psd/5/5/tile)

Distort: Displace (tiledsps.psd/3/3/tile)

Distort: Displace (tiledspm.psd/3/3/tile)

Distort: Displace (tiledspm.psd/3/3/stretch)

■ **Louis Fishauf** created *Money Swirl* with the Twirl, Spherize, and Radial Blur filters. The image was composited from two files: one for the vortex in the middle and another for the bills on the outside. For the vortex, Fishauf started with a black "+" shape on white and applied the Twirl filter. In the other file, he arranged scans of four bills in the four quadrants of a square, applied the Spherize filter to achieve the distortion, and then applied a Radial Blur (Spin) to the ends of the bills, using the center of the illustration as the center of the spin. "It took about 20 tries to get the effect I wanted," says Fishauf. "I wish I had written down exactly how I finally did it."

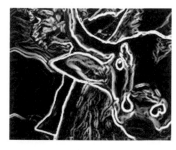

■ To create *Neon Cowboy,* **Ellie Dickson** started with a scanned photo of a bull and one of a cowboy. She cut and pasted the two images together and made changes to the color with painting tools and Image, Adjust functions. Then she selected the edge of bull and rider with a lasso with a 15-pixel feather (the image itself was about 1100 pixels wide altogether) and copied the selection to the clipboard. With the selection still active, she used Paste Behind and Composite Controls to paste the copy from the clipboard at 50 percent opacity. She offset the pasted-behind edge by dragging it to the left. Then she pasted behind again, this time at 40 percent opacity, again offsetting the pasted edge. She repeated this at 30 and 20 percent opacity. Then she used the Motion Blur filter, applying it to the image in the same direction as the fade she had been creating. She applied the Wave filter and then Trace Edges, and finally finished the piece by choosing Image, Map, Invert to create the neon effect.

■ To make *Neo Fragile*, **Kai Krause**, co-developer of HSC's KPT filters (see page 114) used the KPT Mandelbrot Set Explorer filter with the Copper Something setting and the Interior set to black to generate a fractal design. Then he applied the KPT Glass Lens Bright filter and adjusted the color through the Hue sliders in the Image, Adjust, Hue/Saturation dialog box. To clean up the edges, he Shift-selected the resulting highlighted sphere with the elliptical selection tool, copied this circular selection to the clipboard, and pasted it into a new black background. He made a mask from this file, adjusting Levels to increase the contrast of the mask, to which he added some black lines to match some of the spikes in his "plasma green sphere" file, which he generated with a star explosion displacement map. He used Image, Calculate, Composite, with the fractal image as Source 1, the altered mask as Mask, and the plasma green sphere as Source 2. Where the mask was white, Source 1 contributed to the *NeoFragile* image; where it was black, Source 2 contributed.

■ In *The Mother Zone,* a typographic design for a book cover, **Louis Fishauf** "distressed" the American Typewriter type using the Spatter filter from Aldus Gallery Effects Vol. 1 and the Photoshop Blur filter. He saved the type in an alpha channel so that he could make a mask to protect the white lettering from the scribbled color. He wanted to make a mask that would partially protect the area just outside the letter outlines so that it would not accept the color at full intensity and would thus remain darker to set off the type. To make this mask, he started by duplicating the white lettering in an alpha channel (Image, Calculate, Duplicate, New). Then, working in this new channel, he chose Select, Load Selection to activate the selection; copied the selection to the clipboard (Ctrl-C) to store it while he modified the channel; chose Select, Feather to soften the edges of the selection in the channel; pressed Backspace to fill the modified selection with the white background color; and pasted the type from the clipboard into the channel (Ctrl-V) on top of the feathered selection so that the feathering would no longer extend into the body of type, only outward. The finished mask was loaded from the alpha channel into the main RGB channel (Select, Load Selection, #4) and the inverse of the mask was selected as the active area (Select, Inverse). The color was then scribbled with a Wacom pressure-sensitive tablet, with pressure determining the thickness of the strokes.

■ **Sharon Varley** began work on *Atlantis* with a scan of a photo of a tile mosaic that she took at the House of Dolphins in Delos, Greece. She added blue with a transparency setting and used the Ripple filter to give the appearance of water. She placed a copy of the fairy, part of the original tile work, on top, selected its trailing edge, and applied the Motion Blur filter. The wave in the border was part of the original mosaic. Varley selected it, then chose Select, Border and filled the border with color to stylize the wave. She then recolored, enlarged, and duplicated the wave to make the final bottom border. The border at the top is a repeating design she drew in Illustrator using a scan of a Greek vase as a template. The sun is a clip art file in EPS format that was placed in Photoshop and colorized. The soft drop shadow behind it was made by pasting a copy of the sun behind the active sun selection, feathering it, and filling it with a partially transparent gray. To make the rectangular frame around the image, she drew a selection rectangle and chose Select, Border; She filled the border with color and then used the Crystallize filter to make this frame match the mosaic look of the tile.

■ To generate *Marble,* **Nino Cocchiarella** started with a single scan of a piece of marble. He selected areas of the image with the selection ellipse and the selection rectangle, saved the selections as masks, and loaded them to experiment with color. He used Image, Adjust, Hue/Saturation to color selected areas and Image, Adjust, Levels to make the drop shadows. He had made some of the masks with linear or radial gradient fills, so that the coloring, lightening, or darkening effect was applied differentially through the mask. The airbrush was used to add detail to the shading. The round but slightly flattened shapes were made by selecting areas and applying the Spherize filter twice, once with a setting of 100% and then again with a setting of 50%, and then adjusting Levels to light the objects.

■ **Jack Davis** used elements from three 3D files — rocket ship and trail, letterforms, and large planets — to assemlble this *Planet Studios Logo.* He set the type in Adobe Illustrator and then extruded it in a 3D program, but he couldn't get the exaggerated perspective he wanted, so he imported it into Photoshop and applied the Image, Effects, Distort command to complete the illusion. To emphasize the edges on the type and the rivets on the rocket, he used the Photocopy filter from Gallery Effects Vol. 2: He floated a copy, applied the filter, and used the Multiply mode and a slightly reduced opacity in the Brushes palette to composite the filtered image with the original. The large planets in the background were from a ray-traced image, which was rendered at low resolution and without antialiasing; this relatively crude rendering was possible because Davis planned to use Photoshop's Gaussian Blur filter on the planets to create depth of field between the lettering and rocket in the foreground and the planets in the background.

■ To create the spark for the *Megamorph Logo Comp,* **Kory Jones** used the KPT Julia Set 3 filter (see page 114). Working in an RGB Photoshop file, he specified black-and-white output for the filter and cut and pasted together parts of the fractal design to make the spark the shape he wanted. When the spark was complete, he cut it from the RGB channel and pasted it into an alpha channel he created for that purpose. He created a black background in the RGB channel, loaded the selection from the alpha channel, and filled it with blue. To emphasize the spark's main trunk, he drew a path with the pen tool and stroked the path with the airbrush tool, first with a medium-size brush tip with blue in Color mode and then with a smaller brush with white in Normal mode. He pasted the two spheres and the coils (created in a 3D program) into the RGB channel, using Composite Controls to make the spheres partially transparent so that the ends of the sparks would show through. A copy of the spark was pasted into the lettering, and its color was adjusted by using Image, Map, Invert to turn the white part dark and then adjusting the Hue to restore the blue color.

6

PAINTING

AS THE WORK IN THIS CHAPTER shows, Photoshop painters have extended their toolkits beyond the brushes and pencil, to use the editing tools, alpha channel "friskets," and many of the program's color and compositing controls. But if we define painting tools as those that can apply foreground color, background color, or pixels from an image, Photoshop's painting tools include the paint bucket, gradient, line, eraser, pencil, airbrush, paintbrush, rubber stamp, and smudge. All of these tools can be operated by selecting the tool and then clicking to make a single "footprint" on the canvas, or by holding down the mouse button and dragging to make a stroke. Most of these tools can also be constrained to a straight line by holding down the Shift key and clicking from point to point; the line tool, which always paints in a straight line, is constrained to 45- and 90-degree angles when the Shift key is used. Each of the tools has two sets of controls — one set in a Tool Options dialog box that appears when you double-click the icon in the toolbox, and another set that appears in that tool's Brushes palette (accessed by choosing Window, Show Brushes).

Here's a list of the painting characteristics that can be controlled through the Options dialog boxes:

Antialiasing: For the paint bucket only; the line, airbrush, paintbrush, rubber stamp, and smudge tools are always smooth-edged except in Bitmap or Indexed Color mode; the pencil tool is not; for the gradient tool, antialiasing depends on the selection into which the gradient is applied.

Arrowheads: For the line tool only, you can put custom arrowheads on the beginning or end of a stroke or both.

Fade-out: For the airbrush, paintbrush, and pencil, strokes fade from the foreground color to the background color or to nothing (transparent); the Distance setting affects the total distance from the beginning of the stroke (at full-strength foreground color) to the point where the background color is full-strength or the paint is completely transparent. The gradient tool always operates in Fade-out mode, applying a color gradient from foreground to background color.

Finger Painting: For the smudge only, which normally

continued on page 124

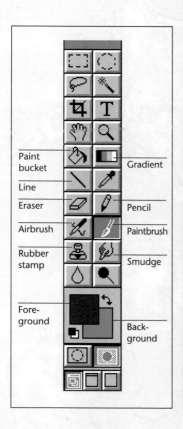

Paint bucket

Gradient

Line

Eraser

Pencil

Airbrush

Paintbrush

Rubber stamp

Smudge

Foreground

Background

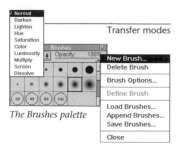

Transfer modes

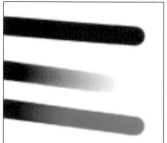

The Brushes palette

Painting with no Fade-out setting (top), with Fade-out To Transparent (center), and Fade-out To Background (bottom)

The pen tool can also act as a painting tool: Draw a path (as described in Chapter 2). Then choose a painting tool and choose Stroke Path from the pop-out menu in the Paths palette to paint the path.

If a document contains an active selection, the painting tools will work only inside that selection. If a painting tool doesn't seem to be working, it might be due to an active selection that you can't see — either because it's outside the window, or because you've pressed Ctrl-H to hide the selection border. You can deactivate, or drop, the selection by pressing Ctrl-D.

smears existing paint, but can instead apply the foreground color.

From Saved: For the rubber stamp, this Option restores the last saved version of the file in the areas you stroke. (The eraser, which normally applies the background color, restores the image From Saved mode when the Alt key is held down.)

From Snapshot: For the rubber stamp, as you apply strokes, this Option restores the version of the file or selection that was temporarily stored by choosing Edit, Take Snapshot.

Gradient Tool Options: These are covered briefly in Chapter 1.

Impressionist: For the rubber stamp, painting produces an Impressionist (somewhat smeared) rendition of the last saved version of the file; Impressionist is a kind of "filter in a brush."

Pattern: For the paint bucket, which can fill an area with the currently defined pattern; and the rubber stamp, which can paint with the currently defined pattern, either Aligned (painting as if the pattern filled the area behind the image and the rubber stamp was erasing to it) or Non-aligned (starting a new application of the pattern from the same pattern area each time the mouse button is pressed to start a new stroke). Defining a pattern is described on page 124.

Stylus Pressure: For the airbrush, smudge, paintbrush, pencil, and rubber stamp, lets you set the characteristic that will vary when pressure is applied to the stylus of a pressure-sensitive tablet; characteristics that can be varied, depending on the tool, are Size, Opacity, Color, and Pressure.

Width: For the line tool, set in terms of the number of pixels.

The parameters controlled in the Brushes palette include transfer modes (how the paint interacts with the underlying image) and a continuously variable characteristic such as opacity, controlled by a slider. To find out about the transfer modes, consult the *Adobe Photoshop User Guide* and experiment. To operate the slider, drag with the pointer. Or press the number keys on the keyboard to change the setting in 10% intervals; the "1" key produces a 10% setting, the "2" key 20%, and so on, with "0" producing 100%.

The pop-out menu in the Brushes palette allows you to add a brush up to 999 x 999 pixels in size to the palette (by choosing New Brush and specifying characteristics in the New Brush dialog box, or by selecting an area of an existing image and choosing Define Brush); edit an existing brush (by choosing Brush Options); name and save a particular palette of brushes (choose Save Brushes); load a palette you've previously saved (choose Load Brushes); or append a palette to the current one (choose Append Brushes).

Making Paper for Painting

Overview *Use filters to generate a paper texture; run the Offset filter and repair any edge artifacts so the texture will be able to wrap seamlessly; define the texture as a pattern; fill the RGB channel and an alpha channel with the pattern; load the selection from the alpha channel into the main channel; hide the selection border; paint.*

1

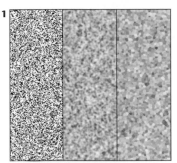

Noise   Gaussian Blur   Facet

2a

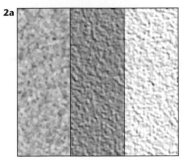

Blur More   Emboss   Adjust Levels

2b

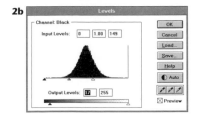

ELECTRONIC IMAGES "painted" on a clear, white background lack the texture that comes from the interaction between natural media and canvas. Several filters are available for applying texture after you've finished a painting (see "Filter Demos" in Chapter 5). But you can also set up a paper or canvas texture that interacts as you paint. Here's one to get you started.

1 Generating the basis for the texture. Start a new Grayscale file. Choose Filter, Noise, Add Noise. Here, for a 225 dpi file, we used a setting of 500, Gaussian. Then apply a blur (we used Blur, Gaussian Blur, with a setting of 1.0). Next apply the Facet filter (Filter, Stylize, Facet). Try different filter settings and different kinds of Noise and Blur to get different textures.

2 Finishing the texture. Experiment until you have a texture you like. (We used Filter, Blur, Blur More and then Filter, Stylize, Emboss.) Then use Image, Adjust, Levels to whiten the paper, moving the white Input slider to the left to increase detail in the highlights and moving the black Output Levels slider to the right to reduce contrast. The painting surface should be white, and shadows caused by the texture should be medium to very light grays. The greater the tonal difference between surface and shadows, the coarser the "paper."

3 Making the texture into a pattern. So your paper texture will fill any size canvas you want to paint on, turn the texture into a repeating pattern by making it seamless: Choose Filter, Other, Offset and set both the horizontal and vertical offset values at 50. Choose Wrap Around for the treatment of edge pixels; the pixels that are pushed out of the file at the right side and the bottom will reappear at the left and top to fill the empty space created there. Use the rubber stamp tool in one of the Clone modes to clean up any obvious discontinuities where the edges wrap. Save the texture.

3a

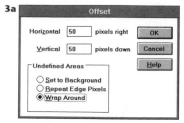

3b

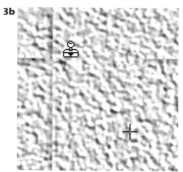

4a

4b

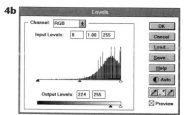

5a

Hard brush with-out alpha channel *Hard brush with alpha channel*

5b

Soft brush without alpha channel *Soft brush with alpha channel*

4 Getting ready to paint. When you want to paint on your paper texture, open an RGB file at 225 pixels per inch and at the size and shape you want for your painting. Now, to turn your pattern into an interactive paper texture, open the texture file you made and define it as a pattern: Select All and choose Edit, Define Pattern. Now you can put the texture into the main RGB channel or an alpha channel or both:

- To put an image of the paper in the main RGB channel so it will appear even in the unpainted parts of the picture, click on RGB in the Channels palette and fill the channel with the pattern by choosing Select, All and then Edit, Fill, Pattern. Use Levels to lighten the texture if you like, as we did.

- To put the texture into an alpha channel so you can load it to control how the paint interacts with the paper, repeat the pattern-filling process for a new channel (channel 4), created by choosing New from the Channels palette pop-out menu.

5 Painting. Choose a painting tool; select its mode and set its Opacity in the Brushes palette. If you load the selection from channel 4 (Select, Load Selection), the paint will be applied differentially, with more color going onto the white "surface" of the selection and less into the gray "recesses." (You can reverse this effect, letting paint accumulate in the troughs, by choosing Select, Inverse after loading the selection from channel 4 and before beginning to paint.) To paint naturally on a constantly shimmering selection would be impossible. So to keep the selection active but get rid of the shimmer, press Ctrl-H (for Select, Hide Selection). The selection will be invisible, but when you start to paint, the texture will become apparent. Results will vary, depending on which tool you use, whether you use a hard- or soft-edged brush tip, and whether you load the pattern from the alpha channel.

- Choose Multiply as the mode in the Brushes palette to intensify the color as you paint over your strokes.

- For a wet, transparent look like watercolor, reduce the opacity. Any color accepted by the gray areas will interact with the gray in the RGB channel and will darken. As you apply more of the semi-transparent paint, the color will build.

- For a dry look like charcoal, pencil, or dry brush, use Image, Adjust, Levels in the alpha channel to increase contrast before you load it into the RGB channel as a selection, and use a fairly opaque setting in the Brushes palette.

Experimenting. For the image at the top of page 125, we used a darker paper with a small, hard-edged brush in Multiply mode for most colors and in Normal mode for white. *WOW*

Painting with Light

Overview *Start with a sketch; rough in the color; build volume; add highlights and detail.*

FRANCOIS GUÉRIN

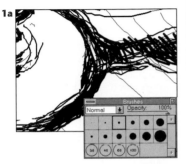

1a

1b

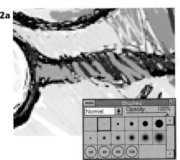

2a

2b

ACHIEVING A PAINTERLY EFFECT with the computer involves some mental translation from traditional tools to electronic ones. Artist/illustrator Francois Guérin, who also works with oils, pastels, gouache, and Fractal Design Painter, has found several ways to work effectively with Photoshop as a painting program. For *The Meal*, painted from memory, he used primarily the painting tools, the lasso, the Gaussian Blur, and functions from the Image, Adjust submenu. Guérin worked with a Quadra 700 and a Wacom cordless pressure-sensitive tablet. He likes the brushlike feel of the stylus but doesn't vary the pressure much.

1 Making a sketch. To start out, click the pencil tool and begin drawing. Choose pencil tips of different sizes from the Brushes palette. Guérin used a larger tip to darken the shadow areas.

2 Laying down color. Choose Window, Show Colors to open the color palette, and choose a color. You can apply the first strokes of paint with brushes from the top row of the Brushes palette, which provide smooth-edged strokes. Paint in Normal mode so the strokes cover the black-and-white sketch.

THE BEST SKETCHING TOOL

The pencil gives you hard-edged lines regardless of the size tip you use. Because Photoshop doesn't have to antialias the strokes, the pencil draws dramatically faster than a brush, providing a very responsive stroke.

COLORFUL SLIDERS

To make the color palette update its sliders as you mix colors in RGB, CMYK, and Lab modes (the HSB sliders are dynamic by default), use the File Manager to open the Windows folder and then open the Photoshop.ini file. Under the [Photoshop] line, type in the line DYNAMICSLIDERS=1 and restart Photoshop.

3a

3b

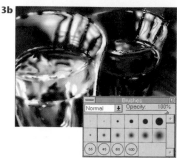

4a

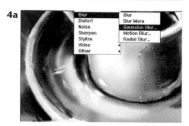

4b

5

6

3 Building volume. Use the palette square to mix the color variations you need to begin painting shapes. At this point, use the paintbrush and airbrush tools, which have softer edges, to achieve color blending in the painting.

4 Indicating textures. Guérin used the smallest pencil point to add "grain" to the wood of the table, which he later smoothed with the smudge (finger) tool. He also used the Blur filters to add a smooth sheen to some of the surfaces in the image. For instance, he used a feathered lasso to select some areas of the cup and saucer, and applied a Gaussian Blur. (Double-click the lasso icon in the toolbox to open the dialog box for setting the Feather amount; choose Filter, Blur, Gaussian Blur to open the dialog box for setting the amount of blur.)

5 Putting the colors in context. To modify the colors to be consistent with the light in the scene, you can use a feathered lasso and the Hue/Saturation, Levels, and Color Balance commands of the Image, Adjust submenu. Guérin used a more highly feathered lasso to surround parts of the image so he could change their tonality with the Image, Adjust functions.

6 Adding modeling and highlights. You can use traditional painting techniques, such as applying strokes to follow the form of an object, to mold elements in the painting. Guérin shaped the napkin beneath the fork in this way, for example. The blur tool (water drop) can be used to smooth areas such as the reflections on the glass. (If the water drop isn't showing in the tool palette, Alt-click the sharpen tool — the pointed icon at the lower left of the toolbox — to toggle it on.) The smudge (finger) tool does a good job of adding texture and making color transitions in some areas where light and shadows meet, in the wood of the table, for instance. It can also be used to pull specular highlights out of white paint, as on the tine of the fork.

Developing electronic painting technique. For a painting of his cactus collection, Guérin again started with an electronic pencil sketch. He poured color into the pencil-drawn shapes with the paint bucket tool and added some detail with

ADDING TO THE PALETTE

Normally, when you select a painting tool to paint on your image or to mix colors in the palette square, it turns to the eyedropper when you move it to one of the small color cells to pick up a color. But if you hold down the Alt key, the tool becomes the eyedropper on the canvas or in the large square (to pick up a color you've mixed) and turns into the paint bucket when you move it to the color cells (to fill a cell with the new color).

Sketching with the pencil and filling sketched areas with paint

Smoothing color with Gaussian Blur

Differential blurring to create depth

the paintbrush. Then he used a feathered lasso and the Gaussian Blur filter to blend the colors. He used the smudge tool to blend the edges where colors met, and added more color with paintbrushes. With the paintbrush and airbrush he built volume in the rounded plants, and added spines with the paintbrush and pencil. To capture the lighting on the scene, he selected areas of the image with the lasso and played with the color balance, brightness, contrast, hue, and saturation, as he had for *The Meal*. When he selected areas to adjust color, he used alpha channels to store complex selections such as the flower in the foreground so he could make additional color adjustments without having to draw the selection border again. To create the illusion of depth, he used the Blur filter, applying it three times for the round cactus on the right side of the painting, which was farthest in the background, twice for the closer, spiky one in the upper left corner, and once for a still closer one in the center. 🖌

CLEARING THE MIXING AREA

To clean up the mixing square in the Colors palette, use the rectangular marquee to select the contents of the square and then drag the selected area out of the palette.

EXTRACTING A PALETTE

To pull a color palette from a painted RGB or CMYK image so you can use it as a resource for a related painting, follow this procedure (be sure you don't miss the Revert step!):

1. Convert the painting to Indexed Color mode (temporarily — you'll be changing it back to full color) by choosing Mode, Indexed Color and then selecting 8 bits, Adaptive.

2. Choose Mode, Color Table, click the Save button, and give the table a name. Now choose File, Revert to convert the painting back to its original color mode. (Use Revert, not the Mode menu, to make this change so you won't lose any of the original color from the painting.)

3. In your new painting file, choose Window, Show Colors. Choose Load Colors and select the named color table. The small squares of the palette will fill with the colors you saved from the first painting.

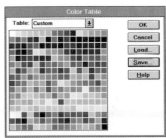

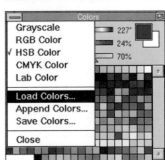

Beginning with Gray

Overview *Paint an image in grayscale; select areas of the image and fill with color, varying the opacity and mode; add finishing touches with painting and editing tools.*

CHER THREINEN-PENDARVIS

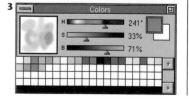

WHEN CAPTURING THE LIGHTING is all-important in a painting, you can sometimes get good results by starting out in grayscale and laying in the color later, taking advantage of Photoshop's Lighten, Darken, and Color modes. To paint *Tranquil Beach*, Cher Threinen-Pendarvis started out in grayscale, painting from memory and a pencil sketch.

1 Establishing lights and darks. Open a file in Grayscale mode and use the painting tools to rough in the light and dark areas. Threinen-Pendarvis used primarily the brush, airbrush, smudge, and blur tools to make her gray painting.

2 Smoothing transitions. To eliminate abrupt color changes and hard stroke edges, you can soften the image (or a selected part of it) by choosing Filter, Blur, Gaussian Blur. Threinen-Pendarvis applied a 2-pixel Gaussian blur to the entire image.

3 Making a palette. Choose Mode, RGB Color to convert the file from grayscale to color. Open the color palette: If the palette is collapsed on the desktop, clicking on the small squares at the right end of of its title bar will expand it. If the palette isn't visible at all, choose Window, Show Colors or press the F key assigned to the Show/Hide Colors command (F7). Use the palette to mix the colors you'll need for your painting.

4 Selecting areas to color. Use the lasso tool to select areas of the gray image where you want to apply color. As you make each selection, choose Select, Save Selection to save it in an alpha channel. Being able to load the selection again later will make it possible to add color in stages. Threinen-Pendarvis

4

Shore *Sky*

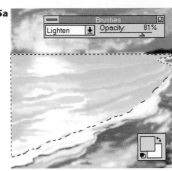

Ocean *Glow/water*

5a

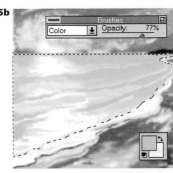

Brushes — Lighten | Opacity: 81%

5b

Brushes — Color | Opacity: 77%

5c

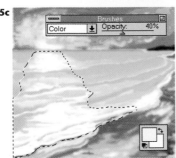

Brushes — Color | Opacity: 40%

used the lasso with various feather settings to make selections for the sky, the water, the beach, the glow in the sky and in the water, and other areas, and saved the selections in alpha channels.

5 Laying in color. When you have an area selected, press Ctrl-J to float the selection; this will make it possible to use the Brushes palette to control the mode and opacity of the paint you apply. Click with the eyedropper tool to select a foreground color from the palette. Then press Shift-Backspace to fill the selected area. Use the Opacity slider and the pop-up Mode list in the Brushes palette to experiment with adding color to the image. Use Lighten (which affects only those pixels that are darker than the foreground color), Darken (which affects only those that are lighter), or Color (which changes hue and saturation but not tonality).

CONTROLLING A FLOATING SELECTION

If the mode menu and Opacity slider in the Brushes palette won't work on your floating selection, you can activate them by clicking on any selection tool (or the type tool) in the toolbox.

Threinen-Pendarvis loaded and floated selections from the alpha channels she had made and colored the selected areas of her image. For the glow in the water, for example, she filled the floating selection with a greenish blue in Lighten mode and adjusted the opacity. Then she dropped the selection to set the color, loaded and floated the same selection again, and filled it with the same blue in Color mode, again with opacity adjusted. Next she loaded and floated the glow selection and filled it with a pale yellow in Color mode; setting the opacity at 40% blended the blue and yellow to make a light green, and the highlights took on a yellow tint. As she filled the remaining areas with color, the feathering at the edges of the selections blended colors to soften transitions between areas.

6 Adjusting the darks and lights. Use the painting tools and smudge and blur; vary the painting mode and the percentages of opacity to emphasize the dark and light areas of the painting. Among other final changes, Threinen darkened some of the shadow areas of the waves and altered the beach.

OPACITY KEYS

Even without a pressure-sensitive tablet, you can vary the opacity of paint without moving the pointer from the painting to the Brushes palette. Press a number key, either in the main keyboard or in the keypad, to vary the opacity in 10% steps — "1" produces 10%, "2" is 20%, and so on, with "0" being full opacity. This works with all the painting, drawing, and editing tools, including the gradient tool.

Colorizing Line Art

Overview *Make a background; combine it with scanned line art; use alpha channels, the lasso, and solid and gradient fills to colorize the artwork.*

TOMMY YUN

"THOUGH IT MAY NOT SAVE TIME," says Tommy Yun about the way he uses Photoshop to color hand-drawn line art, "you can get clean, slick visual effects a lot easier than with an airbrush."

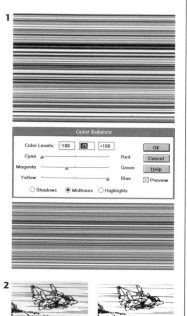

1 Creating a color background. Working at the same resolution as your scanned line art, paint a background for the image. Yun made this "speed blur" by dabbing with the paintbrush and gray paint onto a 1-pixel-wide RGB file. He used Image, Effects, Scale to stretch the strip of gray shades sideways to the width of his scanned drawing. Before he could colorize the resulting lines with Image, Adjust, Color Balance, he had to reduce the contrast (Image, Adjust, Brightness/Contrast), since the Color Balance function doesn't affect pure black or white. When he finished colorizing, he used Image, Image Size to scale the background to the right height, and copied it to the clipboard (Select, All; Edit, Copy).

2 Cleaning up the scan. To increase the contrast of the scanned line art to get black lines on a white background, Yun used Image, Adjust, Levels, dragging inward on the black and white points of the Input Levels slider.

3 Adding the background. Make a mask that will let you use Edit, Paste Into to add the color background. Yun traced the planes and text bubbles with the antialiased lasso to select them. He saved this selection in an alpha channel (Select, Save Selection) and inverted the new alpha channel (Image, Map, Invert). Then he activated the main RGB channel by clicking its name in the Channels palette. He loaded the mask as a selection (Select, Load Selection) and used Edit, Paste Into to add the background he had stored in the clipboard at step 1.

4 Softening harsh lines. To get rid of black lines from the background of the scanned drawing, Yun pasted a negative version of the original (made by applying Image, Map, Invert to a copy of the sketch) on top of the mask shown in step 3. He used Edit, Composite Controls in Darken mode to combine the two masks, and then did some additional painting with

4

5a

5b

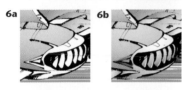

6a   **6b**

6c

7

8

black paint. He loaded the new mask as a selection in the RGB channel and used Levels to lighten the black lines.

5 Using radial fills. By making masks in alpha channels and loading them into the main RGB channel, you can isolate parts of the linework for coloring. Yun started by duplicating the mask in step 3 as a negative in another alpha channel (Image, Calculate, Duplicate, New, with the Invert box checked). Working in the new alpha channel, he used the selection rectangle to surround the left side of the mask and Shift-Backspace to fill it with black so that only the text ballons stayed white. Yun loaded his text balloons mask as a selection in the RGB channel and used the gradient tool to fill the balloons with a white-to-yellow gradient. (Double-click the gradient tool and set it to Radial; click on the Foreground and Background squares in turn to open the color picker and set the beginning and ending colors of the gradient. Draw a line with the gradient tool from the center to the edge of the area you want to fill; the selection will keep the fill from spreading across the whole image.)

6 Making gradient color fills. Next Yun worked with the lasso and the gradient tool. He filled large areas of the planes, then smaller ones, varying the feather on the lasso he used for selecting. (Double-click the lasso tool to be able to set the feather radius.) To add harsh-edged fills for a painted-cel look, he used straight-line selections (Alt-click with the lasso) and moved the Input slider's gray point in the Levels dialog box.

7 Adjusting background lighting. You can alter the background mask (from step 3) to select the background to adjust its color. Yun made two white-to-black vertical gradients, upward and downward from an imaginary horizon, using the gradient tool in Darken mode so it wouldn't lighten the black planes. After loading the mask as a selection in the RGB channel, he used Levels to lighten the sky through the gradient.

8 Finishing color details. Next Yun added color to the thrusters. Starting in a new channel filled with black, he used the gradient tool to make radial fills of white to black in Lighten mode. Then he used the lasso and Shift-Backspace to fill parts of the white areas with black. He loaded this new thrusters mask into the RGB channel, filled it with white, and colored the thrusters with Image, Adjust, Color Balance, pushing the highlights toward yellow and the midtones toward red and magenta. To finish the work, Yun loaded the mask from step 3 into the RGB channel and applied a 10-pixel motion blur (Filter, Blur, Motion Blur). The outline of the planes was slightly blurred also, enhancing the look of a painted cel.

■ **Ellie Dickson** had tried to paint *On Vine Street* with traditional artists' brushes but had failed to get the result she wanted. Then she tried Photoshop. She scanned the color snapshot, converted it from color to grayscale to retain the tones but remove the color, and then changed the mode back to RGB so she could add her own tints. She began by selecting areas with a feathered lasso and applying color with the Fill command at 10 to 15 percent opacity in Color mode. Once the tint areas were established, she deselected everything and used the airbrush to add paint in the same colors as the tints. She painted in Normal mode, varying the opacity. Finally, she added finishing touches with the paintbrush with a small brush tip setting.

■ To make *Still Life* **Nino Cocchiarella** used the pen tool to draw the shapes, which he saved as paths. He used the paths in two ways: He turned them into selections (Make Selection from the Paths palette's pop-out menu) and saved them as alpha channels. Then he clicked each path's name in turn to select it and chose Stroke Path to paint the paths. To round the shapes of the objects, Cocchiarella used the gradient tool in Lighten or Darken mode in the alpha channels to create masks; then he loaded the masks and adjusted Levels to highlight or shade the shapes. The lichen-like texture in some areas of the image was created by running the Pointillize filter and then the Noise filter in some of the channels and then loading these masks in the main image and adjusting Levels. Colors were adjusted by loading masks and applying Image, Adjust, Hue/Saturation.

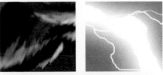

■ To make this cover illustration for his comic book, *Buster the Amazing Bear,* **Tommy Yun** began by scanning a faint pencil sketch. Working in Photoshop's Grayscale mode, he used the lasso tool to "block out" regions that he filled with different shades of gray. Then, with the tones of the illustration set, he used the smudge (finger) tool with a Wacom tablet and stylus to smear the grays to make the fur. He converted the image to RGB mode and added a storm image behind the bear. Then he created an alpha channel (choosing New in the pop-out menu of the Channels palette), turned it black by selecting it all (Ctrl-A) and filling it with black (Shift-Backspace), and painted a bolt of white lightning in it. He duplicated this channel (Image, Calculate, Duplicate) as a new alpha channel in the same file and ran a Gaussian blur on this new channel (Filter, Blur, Gaussian Blur) to make a mask for the glow around the lightning. After adding some finer streaks of lightning to the first alpha channel, he returned to the main RGB channel and used these two channels (Select, Load Selection) to select the lightning and the glow separately from each other and from the other elements of the illustration; he turned them white (Backspace). To select other areas, he set a large Feather on the lasso. Then, for each area that he selected, he used Image, Adjust, Color Balance to add color to the illustration.

■ To "paint" *Parker's,* **Bert Monroy** used a different technique than he had used for many earlier photorealistic paintings. As usual, he began with a photograph as visual reference but didn't scan it. This time, however, instead of starting out in Photoshop, he used Adobe Illustrator's drawing tools to construct the building as one file and the complex bridge elements as four separate Illustrator files, breaking the construction down into layers and drawing "fine detail that would have been impossible in Photoshop." In Illustrator he assigned flat color fills to the elements he had built. Then, after saving them in EPS format and placing them in Photoshop, he "texturized" them by selecting areas of the image and adding Noise, with settings between 8 and 24 for this image that was over 1500 pixels wide. To simulate street grime, he made selections with a feathered lasso before texturing and darkening them, so their edges would blend with the surroundings. The cars in the parking lot and the reflections in the windows were not begun in Illustrator, but painted entirely in Photoshop. For these "I started with blobs of paint," says Monroy, "and used the smudge tool to connect them; then I blurred the connections with the water drop. I worked the same way I do with paints." In Monroy's current digital painting, Photoshop stands in for paints and brushes, and Illustrator plays the role once performed by ruler and Rapidograph pen.

COMBINING PHOTOSHOP AND POSTSCRIPT

YOU CAN MOVE ARTWORK between Illustrator and Photoshop almost seamlessly, and you can import both kinds of files into page layout programs such as PageMaker and QuarkXPress. How do you decide when it makes sense to combine Illustrator (or other PostScript object-oriented) artwork with an image created in Photoshop? And when it does, how do you decide whether to import a Photoshop illustration into Illustrator, or an Illustrator drawing into Photoshop, or when to assemble the two in a third program? These pointers can help you decide.

- Although the pen tool in Photoshop can draw smooth Bezier curves, the program doesn't have the snap-to-grid features of object-oriented drawing programs such as Adobe Illustrator and Aldus FreeHand. So, if you need precise geometry, it's often easier to do the work outside Photoshop.

- Photoshop's text tool, working with Adobe Type Manager (ATM), can set smooth-looking antialiased type, and the program can produce some amazing type treatments. But for really designing with type or fitting type to a particular shape, PostScript drawing programs excel.

- When you want to maintain the PostScript nature of certain elements — for instance, for a brochure cover in which the Photoshop artwork is just one element of a page that includes logos and a lot of type — incorporate the Photoshop artwork into the PostScript file. That way, you can incorporate the painted or photorealistic Photoshop art and still take advantage of the highest resolution of the output device to produce crisp type and the clean edges of the PostScript elements.

- Bring both the Photoshop files and the PostScript artwork into a page layout program for a multipage document, or to assemble a number of things with precise alignment, and especially if large amounts of text will be typeset. A page layout program also provides a way to assemble Photoshop elements of different resolutions.

Although PostScript elements play a role in techniques described elsewhere in the book, this chapter presents some how-to examples of using PostScript programs extensively.

Rasterizing with Photoshop

Overview *Make the drawing in a PostScript program; export it to Photoshop; apply filter effects; print to a composite color printer from Photoshop.*

MAX SEABAUGH / ADAPTED FROM BALTHUS

1a

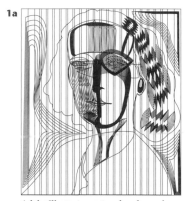

Adobe Illustrator, artwork only mode

1b

Adobe Illustrator, preview mode

IN ORDER FOR A COMPUTER-GENERATED IMAGE to be printed, it has to be *rasterized,* or converted into the dot pattern the printer (or high-resolution imagesetter) needs to put it on paper (or film). Typically, the printer does the rasterizing with a built-in or added-on *RIP (raster image processor)*. But a PostScript drawing, such as an Adobe Illustrator or Corel Draw file, can also be rasterized through Photoshop. And once the image is rasterized, even fairly simple Photoshop modifications can produce some dramatic changes in artwork.

Max Seabaugh of San Francisco's MAX studio drew this portrait in Adobe Illustrator. He wanted to soften its precise PostScript lines, create a pointillistic effect, and print it on his 300 dpi non-PostScript desktop inkjet printer, because he likes the color quality it produces.

1 Drawing and saving the file in Illustrator. You can use any of Illustrator's tools and functions to complete your artwork. You can save the file without a Preview.

2 Opening the file in Photoshop. In Photoshop choose File, Open and select the name of the Illustrator file. In the EPS Rasterizer dialog box, enter the size, mode, and resolution you

2

Image Size: 254K

Width: 3 inches
Height: 4.179 inches
Resolution: 72 pixels/inch
Mode: CMYK Color

[OK] [Cancel] [Help]

☒ Anti-aliased ☒ Constrain Proportions

3a

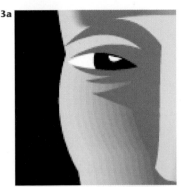

Rasterized by Photoshop at 72 dpi

3b

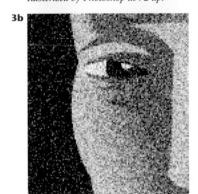

Gaussian Noise filter applied at an Amount of 50

---

want the image to be. Seabaugh accepted the size of the original Illustrator drawing and Photoshop's default CMYK Color mode and 72 dpi for a coarse texture, but you can change the size if you like and raise the resolution for a smoother look.

3 Modifying and printing the file. Make any changes you like to the rasterized art. For example, you can apply the Noise filter to add texture as Seabaugh did; he chose Filter, Noise, Add Noise, Gaussian and set the Amount at 50. Then print the artwork. 🙰

RASTERIZING OVERPRINTING

Normally, one object placed on top of another in a PostScript drawing program completely hides, or "knocks out," the color underneath. But with the Overprint feature, you can mix the two colors. Like the computer screen, film recorders and composite color printers (those that print color pages directly rather than printing from film separations) don't reproduce overprinting (near right). So printing an Illustrator or Corel Draw file on a desktop color printer will produce different results than printing from film separations. To make a desktop print that shows the overprinting, print from a copy of the file rasterized in Photoshop (far right).

Illustrator file with overprinting as printed on a composite color printer; overprint doesn't show.

As rendered in Photoshop and printed on a composite color printer; overprint shows.

CHECKING TRAP IN A POSTSCRIPT ILLUSTRATION

Photoshop can also be used to check trap, a slight overprinting of adjacent inks to ensure that no white space shows through if they become misaligned during printing. Checking traps in a PostScript drawing program can be a tedious, object-by-object examination. Instead you can open the EPS file in Photoshop and see the traps on-screen. Turn off Anti-alias PostScript under File, Preferences, General, and Open the file at a resolution that makes the trap at least 1 pixel wide. For instance, a file with 0.5-point traps should be rasterized at a resolution of at least 144 points.

Illustrator file with overprinted yellow stroke, as seen on-screen; trap is not visible.

As rendered in Photoshop and displayed on-screen; trap is visible.

Making a Montage with a PostScript Mask

Overview *Make the Photoshop files; draw a masking shape in Illustrator; place it in Photoshop; use it to select part of one image; feather the selection; paste this selection over the second image.*

an evening with
Peter Sprague and friends:
Peter Sprague: guitar,
Fred Benedetti: guitar,
Tripp Sprague: saxophone, flute,
performing jazz, classical,
and new music.
Sunday, April 26 7:00 pm,
Theatre East,
A Division of the
East County Performing Arts Center,
210 East Main Street, El Cajon.
$8 General, $6 Students/Seniors.
Box Office 440–2277 Noon–6 pm.
No service charge
for phone or mail orders.
Visa, MasterCard
and checks accepted.
Free parking.

Blurring the Edges

JOHN ODAM

1a **1b**

PHOTOSHOP'S PEN TOOL draws Bezier curves, but the program lacks the align-to-grid feature found in PostScript drawing programs. So if you need to create a mask with smooth, repeating curves, you can start in Illustrator or Corel Draw. Designer John Odam wanted a simple blurred transition for this poster for an evening of classical and jazz guitar music. So instead of "fooling around with alpha channels," says Odam, "I created a shape in Illustrator that I could use for a mask to blend the

2

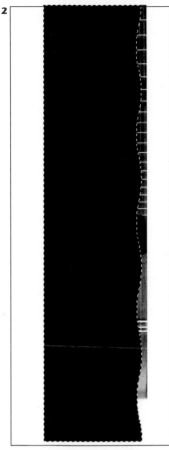

two guitar images." Then he used the shape again, adding a Gaussian blur, to create the border at the bottom of the page. The elements of the poster — montage, display type set in the Blur typeface from the FontShop, and border — were assembled in PageMaker, where the text type was added by setting a right-justified block and wrapping it around an invisible graphic by adjusting the wrapping border into the same wavy shape used in the Illustrator elements.

1 Preparing the two Photoshop files. Make two separate files, one with each part of the image. (In this case, each of the guitars was placed on a flatbed scanner and scanned. The scans were made to the final tabloid size of the poster at 300 dpi for printing on a thermal color printer. It took three scans to capture the full length of each instrument. Odam decided to keep the green iridescent sheen introduced by the scanner rather than correct it. Putting the three parts together was a fairly simple job of cut and paste; very little repair work was needed to hide the seams.) By opening both files at once, you can see how much to reduce the size of one of them if necessary to get the two parts to fit. Choose Image, Effects, Scale to change the size.

2 Drawing the mask in Illustrator and importing it. Use the pen tool to draw a shape in Illustrator that will be used for selecting the edge where the images will blend together. Give the shape a black fill and no line. Save the file in EPS format. Then open the first Photoshop file, choose File, Place, and carefully position the floating selection of the imported shape over the image so that the wavy edge falls where you want to blend the two images.

IMPORTING COREL DRAW FILES

To open or place a Corel Draw file in Photoshop, first save it in Adobe Illustrator format by using Corel Draw's Export To command. Keep in mind, though, that Corel Draw and Illustrator have different ways of dealing with some objects — such as patterned fills, composite paths, and masks. So the translation of a complex file from Corel Draw to Illustrator may not be completely accurate, and the Illustrator file may need adjusting before it's imported into Photoshop.

SCALING A PLACED IMAGE

Photoshop can interactively resize objects placed from Adobe Illustrator. Once the placed object appears on screen, drag one of the corner handles of the bounding box to resize the imported object. Resizing is automatically proportional; to change the proportions, hold down the Ctrl key while you drag. To move the object, drag on one of the sides or diagonals of the bounding box. Click inside the box with the gavel icon to finish the placing action.

3a

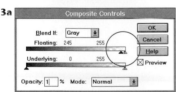

3b

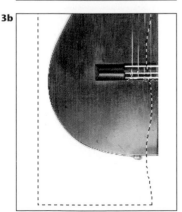

4a

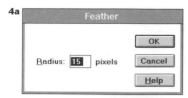

4b

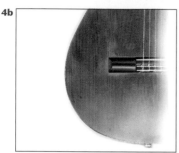

5

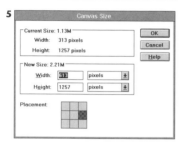

6

3 "Clearing" the mask. With the selection still floating, choose Edit, Composite Controls and move the black point of the Floating slider to the right. This clears all shades to the left of the slider's new position. (If Anti-alias PostScript is turned on in the General Preferences dialog box when a black object is imported from Illustrator, there will be several shades of gray along its edges, due to the antialiasing. Moving the black point slider as far to the right as it will go will prevent any of the gray from remaining in the mask.)

4 Blurring the edge and copying the selection. With the selection still floating, choose Select, Feather and set the Feather Radius at 15 pixels to blur the edges of the mask. Copy the selection to the clipboard (Ctrl-C). (This illustration shows what the selection would look like if it were pasted into a white background. Note the feathered edge.)

5 Making space for the other half. Open the second image. Choose Image, Canvas Size to add enough white space to the left of the image so the image stored in the clipboard can be pasted in.

6 Making the montage and saving the file. Paste in the image from the clipboard (Ctrl-V). While the image is still floating, position it over the second image. When it's positioned as you like it, click outside the selection to finalize the montage.

Using the mask again. To make the blurred border underneath the type at the bottom of the poster, Odam rotated the mask shape 90 degrees in Illustrator. Then he opened a New Photoshop file in Grayscale mode. The file was a little wider than he wanted the blurred edge to be. He placed the mask in the Photoshop file, and while it was still floating, he chose Filter, Blur, Gaussian Blur to blur the edge. He used the crop tool to crop the bottom and sides of the element, leaving the blur only on the top edge. The hybrid guitar and blurred edge were saved in TIFF format and assembled in PageMaker, where text type was set. Twenty copies of the 11 x 17-inch poster were output on a composite color printer.

CONVERTING RGB TO CMYK

If you've been working in RGB and want to print the file on a composite color printer, you can select Print In CMYK in Photoshop's Print dialog box to have Photoshop make a conversion from RGB to CMYK instead of letting the composite printer do it. This often gives a better result than letting the printer make the conversion, but you can try the print both ways to see which you like better.

Back and Forth Between Photoshop and Illustrator

Overview *Design the background art in Photoshop; draw PostScript elements; save each element as a separate file; place them in the Photoshop file; return to Illustrator to add the final type.*

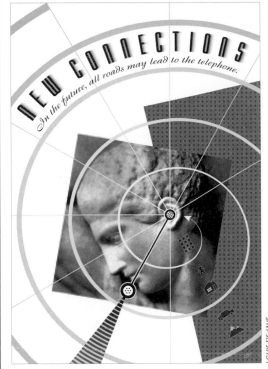

LOUIS FISHAUF

1

Background art in Photoshop

THERE ARE MANY WAYS to combine the "soft" effects that can be achieved in Photoshop with the precision of drawing and typesetting in a PostScript program. For instance, you can do what Louis Fishauf did to make this full-page black-and-white illustration for the *Wall Street Journal*. Import your Photoshop background art into Illustrator and create type and graphic objects in precise relation to it. Then import the PostScript artwork into the original Photoshop file and add special effects. The challenge at this step is to import individual type and graphic objects separately, so you can apply different effects to them as you bring them in, but also to keep all the objects exactly in position. The solution is to set up a bounding box in Illustrator. When you've finished importing Illustrator art and adding special effects, you may want to go back into Illustrator to add the final PostScript type so it will come out as smooth as possible when the file is output.

1 Creating the background. Paint or assemble a background in Photoshop and save it in EPS format so it can be placed in Illustrator. Fishauf assembled this background by opening a new file 500 points (about 7 inches) wide and 716 points high at 200 pixels per inch. He figured that with the 85-line screen that would be used to print the newspaper, 200 dpi

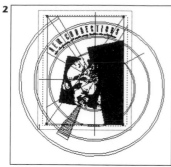

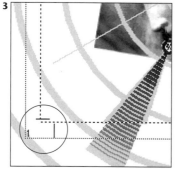

PostScript artwork added in Illustrator

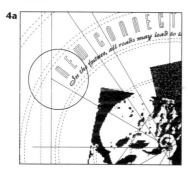

Bounding box set with Illustrator's crop marks

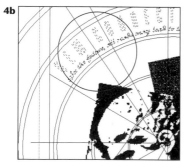

Illustrator elements made invisible as guidelines

at this size would provide more than enough resolution for good reproduction at the larger size. (For images with straight lines, resolution should be 2 times the halftone line screen: 2 x 85 = 170.) Fishauf created his background by selecting and pasting parts of two scans; one scan was a photo of a sculpture, to which he applied the Mosaic filter, and the other was a grid pattern to which he applied a Noise filter.

2 Creating elements in Illustrator. Open a New file in Illustrator and use the File, Place Art command to bring in the Photoshop art. Make sure the Show Placed Art option is selected in Illustrator's Preferences dialog box, accessed by choosing Edit, Preferences. Add type and graphic objects, using the imported artwork as a guide. Fishauf used the curve tool to draw the spiral, the line tool to draw spokes, and the blend function to create a series of equally spaced arcs of increasing line weight in the lower left corner of the image. He used the type-on-a-path tool to fit type to a curve and the Create Outlines command to turn the type into graphic objects, and he imported a series of small elements in the lower right corner by cutting and pasting from an Illustrator file of icons he had collected, drawn, or traced.

3 Defining a bounding box. Add a large rectangle exactly on top of the boundaries of the imported Photoshop artwork. Choose Arrange, Set Cropmarks to turn this rectangle into an invisible bounding box. The crop marks will "trim" the Illustrator artwork when it's brought back into Photoshop.

4 Separating the Illustrator elements. This step lets you import the Illustrator artwork in pieces so you can layer them and apply different Photoshop effects as they come in. The trick is to get all the pieces to land in their original positions.

For each piece he wanted to import, Fishauf selected all the other elements of the illustration and turned them into guidelines. This locked these elements in place in the file but made them invisible for the purpose of importing into Photoshop. (The importation is described in step 5.) After he had imported the first non-Guide piece, he went back to the Illustrator file. He released the guides, turning them back into objects; then he selected a new set of elements and turned these into guidelines, leaving a different set of non-Guide elements available for import to Photoshop. The result was several versions of the file: one with the large type (a), one with spiral and spokes (b), and others with various part of the communication imagery.

5 Importing an Illustrator element. To import an Illustrator element into Photoshop, first open the background art

5

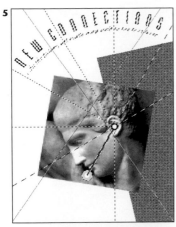

6

file in Photoshop. If you want
smooth outlines on the imported objects, be sure that
Anti-alias PostScript is selected
under File, Preferences, General. (Opening the Info palette

[Window, Show Info] will let you see whether imported objects
have to be scaled down to fit the Photoshop file.) Then choose
File, Place and select the illustrator file that you modified by
making guides. An "X" will appear in the Photoshop file to indicate the placed element. If you wait, the "X" will change
into an image of the imported object, whether or not you've
saved a preview with the Illustrator EPS file. The bounding box
of the Illustrator file will automatically trim the file to the size
indicated by the crop marks. The Info palette should show that
the object is being imported at 100 percent of its original
size. 🖎

SOME THINGS AREN'T IMPORTED

Some kinds of elements — patterns, certain kinds of text, and imported
artwork — are eliminated from an Illustrator file when it's opened or
placed in Photoshop. This is actually helpful when you are moving files
back and forth between Photoshop and Illustrator: You don't have to delete your Photoshop artwork from the Illustrator file before bringing the
Illustrator artwork into Photoshop because it will be deleted automatically in the import process. A dialog box will warn you that this is hap-
pening.

6 Modifying the PostScript elements. Each time you
import the Illustrator file, the non-Guide element comes in
selected. Before releasing the selection, you can correct its
color, apply filters, or make other changes. For example,
Fishauf applied a radial blend to the spiral and spokes, and
applied a radial blur to the large type using Filter, Blur, Radial
Blur with the Spin setting. He made the small icons in the
lower right quadrant of the composition semi-transparent with
the Opacity setting under Edit, Composite Controls.

Adding the final type in Illustrator. To make sure that
type looks as smooth possible, bring the Photoshop art back
into the Illustrator file and add the PostScript type (or type
converted to outlines) there. Fishauf opened the modified
Photoshop file in Illustrator and cut and pasted the curved lettering on top of its shadow (see the opening illustration). 🖎

■ To create *nUkeMan,* illustrator **Steve Lyons** started with a pencil sketch that he scanned and opened as a template in Adobe Illustrator. He used Illustrator's pen tool to draw the black-and-white background shapes, assigning them a fill but no line. Then he saved the file in EPS format and opened it in Photoshop, where he made feathered selections, applied Noise and Blur filters to add texture, and altered the color of some of the white areas. He saved the file in the EPS format appropriate for importing into Illustrator (Save As, EPS, Binary, 8 Bits/Pixel). Next, working in Illustrator again, with the same sketch used as a template, he drew the hard-edged PostScript artwork, selected it all, and grouped it so he could move all of it together. Three-dimensional elements were saved in EPS format and imported into Illustrator. To combine the soft and smooth layers, he imported the Photoshop art into Illustrator (File, Place Art) and sent it to the back (Edit, Send to Back). He saved the file in EPS format for separation in Adobe Separator.

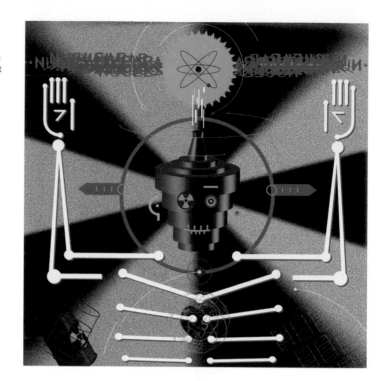

■ **Steve Lyons** created *nubART* by the same process he used for *nUkeMAN,* except that the background started out as a "checkerboard" design, to which he applied the Twirl filter before adding Noise. The nubby sphere in the center of the image was saved in EPS format and imported into Illustrator. But when imported, it proved unwieldy — "It seemed to take an hour-and-a-half just to preview it," says Lyons. So he placed it in the Photoshop background file instead. Then he completed the illustration as for *nUkeMAN.*

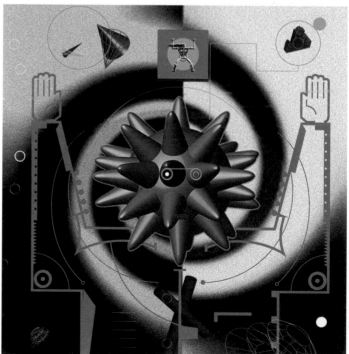

■ For this poster for the *Earth Summit in Rio*, **Louis Fishauf** used Adobe Illustrator to create precisely drawn elements, including the rays of the sun, set in place with the program's rotate-copy function. The elements were imported into Photoshop one by one (by the process described in "Back and Forth Between Photoshop and Illustrator") to add color, glow, and a softer look overall. When the artwork was complete, it was saved in EPS format and placed in Illustrator, where the final PostScript type was added.

■ **Louis Fishauf** created this illustration for the *1993 Macworld Expositions* in Adobe Illustrator, with the lettering on the globe built in Adobe Dimensions and brought back into Illustrator. But when he tried to output the file, he ran into PostScript errors related to the imported sphere, so he decided to rasterize the image in Photoshop. He opened the encapsulated PostScript file at a resolution of 250 pixels per inch at the dimensions at which it would be printed. When he examined the CMYK channels, he found banding of the black and one other color in some of the gradations. By selecting these areas, such as the two gradations above the eyes, he could apply the Blur filter to smooth the gradients. He found the Channels palette very helpful for this process, because he could view (by clicking in the eye icon column) all four color channels while running the Blur filter in only two of them (by clicking on the pencil icon in these channels only). The Photoshop trapping function (Image, Trap) allowed him to build trap into the image so that no white gaps would show if misregistration occurred during printing. Trapping is very often unnecessary in photo images because most individual pixels share one or more of the process printing colors (cyan, magenta, yellow, or black) with neighboring pixels. But Photoshop's trapping function can be helpful in images like this one, where there are smooth shapes and lines of contrasting colors.

■ To create the *Lost & Found Logo* for a CD-ROM title, **Kory Jones** prepared the line work in a black-and-white Adobe Illustrator file. He saved the file under three different names and then removed different elements from each of the three files, so that he had one file with the outlines of the puzzle pieces, one with the bodies of the letters, and one with the letter borders. He placed the three files into alpha channels in a Photoshop RGB file and created additional channels for the drop shadows and shading (creating masks for drop shadows and edge shading are described in the projects in Chapter 8, "Special Effects"). In a separate Photoshop file he created a color gradient by using the KPT Gradient Designer filter (see page 114) and copied this gradient to the clipboard. Then he loaded the letter-body mask as a selection in his original RGB file and pasted the gradient into the selection. Next he loaded the letter-edges mask as a selection and again pasted the gradient into it. With the selection still active, he chose Image, Map, Invert to change the color in the letter borders, so that the colors in each letter were bordered by their complementary colors.

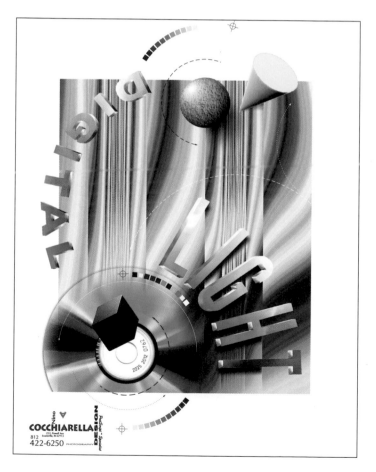

■ To make his *Digital Light* self-promo poster, **Nino Cocchiarella** started out in Corel Draw, producing the fractal background and fractal-filled 3D type, which he exported as a TIFF (the exporting process took 80 minutes) and opened in Photoshop. There he added a partially transparent scan of a compact disc, as well as the 3D cone, sphere, and cube. He Saved As to make an additional low-resolution version of the image, which he imported into Corel Draw as a template for adding line work and type. The line work and type assemblage was exported as a PostScript file, and final assembly of the Photoshop and PostScript components was done in QuarkXPress.

PICNIC
A Fresh Little Kitchen

James Simpson
Leslie Simpson

4325 Address
City, California
415-555-1212

■ **Kory Jones** created this *Business Card Comp for Picnic Restaurant* by combining two scans of clip art of ornamental woodcuts, filling parts of the scanned line work with color, and hand-painting the sun symbol with Photoshop's paintbrush tool. He set the black type in Adobe Illustrator and imported it into the Photoshop file by placing it in the main RGB channel.

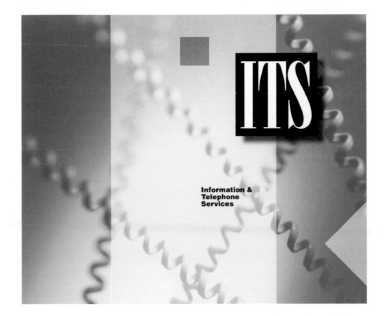

■ For the combined front and back covers of this *ITS Brochure* about telephone services, **Nino Cocchiarella** began with a dramatically lit photo of telephone cords, shot with a shallow depth of field and with green filters on the light. The line work that defined the rectangles and diamond was drawn in Corel Draw, and the Export To

command was used to convert it to Illustrator format so that it could be placed in an alpha channel in the Photoshop file that held the photo. To color the background, he loaded the mask into the main image channel as a selection, adjusted Hue/Saturation to produce the yellow color, and then inverted the mask and repeated the

adjustment process to refine the green. The black rectangle and its drop shadow were added (see page 150 for a quick way to make a drop shadow). The Photoshop file was then placed on a QuarkXPress page, where the type was added. The cover file was output, printed, and folded in half to enclose the booklet.

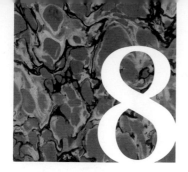

SPECIAL
EFFECTS

THE SPECIAL EFFECTS in this chapter are mostly simulations of the interaction between light and materials — from a simple drop shadow to the complex reflection and refraction that define chrome or crystal. Photoshop's channels, Calculate functions, and color and tonal manipulations comprise a powerful toolkit for creating photorealistic and superrealistic effects. The channels allow selections to be stored and loaded in precisely determined, repeatable positions. The Gaussian Blur filter plays a big part in softening edges and rounding curves, and the Emboss filter can add a dramatic sense of dimension. Through interaction with offset copies of identical masks, blurring and embossing also play an important role in modelling the play of light.

The ability to make "skinny" and "fat" versions of the same graphic by using Maximum, Minimum, and Stroke functions provides the basis for "cookie cutter" channels that can be used to sharpen certain of the rounded edges produced by blurring. The Calculate functions, particularly Difference, can capture interactions between modified graphics in alpha channels. Once the finished channels have been constructed and loaded into an image, the Levels and Color Balance functions from the Image, Adjust submenu and the Variations interface provide the subtle changes that differentiate the selection from the background to create an object — embossed, carved, metallic, glass, or crystal — where none existed before.

QUICK SHADOW

The following method provides a convincing drop shadow — it's quicker and easier than the method on pages 152 and 153, but you have to get it right the first time because there's no easy way to change it later. Place or paste a graphic object on your background image (or use the type tool) (A). While it's floating, copy it to the clipboard. Hold down the Ctrl and Alt keys and drag to offset the selection border (without the graphic itself) into position for the shadow (B). Choose Select, Feather and enter a Radius to soften the edges of the shadow. Then choose Image, Adjust, Levels and darken the shadow (C). Paste the clipboard contents on top of the shadow (Ctrl-V) and drag this selection back into place over the original (D) (if necessary, press Ctrl-+ for a closer view to do the alignment).

Dropping a Shadow

Overview *Create the object selection mask in an alpha channel; duplicate the channel and apply Gaussian Blur; view both channels while you work in one to offset the shadow mask; load the object mask into the shadow channel, invert the selection, and delete to white; invert the mask color; in the main channel load and fill the object selection; load and darken the mask.*

1 **2**

Object mask in "original" channel   *Duplicate blurred in "blur" channel*

3a **3b**

Viewing the effect with both "original" and "blur" channels visible (left) and with only one (right)

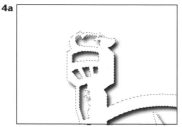

4a

"Original" channel loaded into "blur" channel; selection inverted and deleted

SOONER OR LATER, almost everyone who works in Photoshop needs to produce the proverbial drop shadow. And of course there's more than one way to do it (see page 150 and the Gallery at the end of this chapter for more shadow tips). The method described here provides the most flexibility for making changes later, because you end up with one alpha channel for selecting the shadowed object and one for selecting the shadow itself, completely independent of the object. That way you can later make changes to the shadow (such as darkening it or adding a color cast) without disturbing the rest of the image, or change the background and reapply the shadow.

1 Making the alpha channel for the art. Open a file and choose Window, Show Channels; then choose New Channel from the Channels pop-out menu, and type with the text tool or import the object you want to shadow by choosing File, Place. (In this case we turned a picture font character into an outline in Adobe Illustrator and placed it in a channel we called "original.")

2 Starting an alpha channel for the shadow. Choose Image, Calculate, Duplicate and designate the channel from step 1 as the Source and a New channel in the same file as the Destination; we called the channel "blur." Then choose Filter, Blur, Gaussian Blur to soften the edges of the mask. For this 850-pixel-wide image, we used a Gaussian Blur setting of 3 pixels.

3 Offsetting the shadow. Photoshop's default display color for alpha channels is red at 50% opacity. But if you change the display color for one of the alpha channels (by clicking the channel name in the Channels palette and choosing Channel

4b

"Blur" channel after Image, Map, Invert

5

Loading and filling the "original" channel selection with KPT Gradient Designer

6a

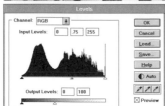

Loading the shadow selection from the "blur" channel

6b

Adjusting Levels to darken

Options) and view both alpha channels while you work, you'll be able to gauge the shadow effect as you offset the blurred channel from the sharp one. In this example, we left the "original" channel's settings at the default. But for the "blur" channel the mask was set to 50% green. To make "blur" both visible and active, we clicked on "blur" in the Channels palette. When we also clicked in the "eye" column for the "original" channel, both masks showed in color. (To position the object and its shadow precisely in relation to a background image that's already in place, you could also click in the eye column next to the main channel (in this case RGB).We selected the blurred mask (Ctrl-A, for Select, All) and dragged it down and to the right slightly until the overlapping red and green showed the shadow effect we wanted. Another click in the eye column of "original" turned off the mask colors and left only the "blur" channel visible.

4 Trimming the shadow mask. Now, working in "blur" only, load the selection from "original" (Select, Load Selection, original). Make sure the Background color icon in the toolbox is white (if not, click on the default colors icon to make the change). Then invert the selection (Select, Inverse) and press Backspace to fill the inverted selection with white. Check to see if this is the degree of shadow effect you want. If not, Undo (Ctrl-Z) and return to step 3 to adjust the offset. Then choose Image, Map, Invert to complete the selection mask for the shadow.

5 Creating the object. We chose Select, Load Selection, original to load the "original" channel mask into a background image that we had pasted into the RGB channel. We filled the selection with the KPT Gradient Designer.

6 Making the shadow. Now load the shadow mask (Select, Load Selection, blur); choose Image, Adjust, Levels, and darken.

Adding finishing touches. To add edge thickness to the graphic, we loaded the "original" mask as a selection in the RGB channel again and applied the Gallery Effects Emboss filter. Then we applied hue-protected Noise (see page 96) to get rid of the "too slick" look. 🎨

SHADOWING A CUT-OUT

To make the shadow mask for the image below, the "blur" mask shown in step 3b was inverted (Image, Map, Invert) before the "original" chan-

nel selection was loaded into it. When the selection was loaded, pressing Shift-Backspace filled the selection with black, trimming the outer edges of the white to produce this shadow mask.

Embossing & Stamping

Overview *Create an alpha channel; duplicate it to make a fat mask and a blur mask; emboss the blur mask; intensify highlights and shadows and separate them into two masks.*

1

Making the "skinny" mask

2a

Duplicating the mask

2b

Fattening the duplicate

3

Blurring a copy of the "fat" mask to make a "blur" mask

4a

Embossing the "blur" mask

4b

Increasing the contrast

EMBOSSING IS AN IMPRESSION PROCESS that produces a raised image on the surface of paper or other material. Embossing can either be overprinted or *blind* (impressed on blank material). Using Photoshop's Emboss filter (from the Filter, Stylize submenu) is only part of the process. The trick is to make masks for the flat surfaces and a mask for the edges. By combining these masks in various ways, you can produce highlight and shadow masks for different embossing effects. The one shown here is for a sharp-edged top surface with a gradual edge at the bottom of the embossing. Some other embossing variations are shown at the bottom of the next page.

1 Making the "skinny" mask. In an RGB file, open an alpha channel (Window, Show Channels, New Channel) and type (or Place graphics) into it. Then invert the color map (Ctrl-I) to produce a skinny mask for selecting the top surface.

2 Making the "fat" mask. Choose Image, Calculate, Duplicate to start a New channel (named "fat"). Apply the Maximum filter (from Filter, Other) to fatten the shapes. For this 1275-pixel-wide image, we used a Radius of 5 pixels.

3 Making the blur mask. Duplicate the "fat" channel to start a New channel ("blur"). Then apply the Gaussian Blur filter to soften the edges, using a blur Radius just a little larger than the Maximum setting you used. We used a Radius of 7 pixels for the Gaussian blur.

4 Embossing. Working in the "blur" channel, choose Filter, Stylize, Emboss and set the angle, distance, and opacity. We used –45 (light from the upper left), 3, and 100. Now choose Image, Adjust, Levels and click Auto to increase the contrast.

5 Creating the sharp-edged surface. Still working in the (now embossed) "blur" channel, load the "skinny" mask (Select, Load Selection, skinny). Use the eyedropper with the Alt key to click on the 50% gray of the mask and make it the Back-

5a *Loading the "skinny" mask and setting the background color to 50% gray*

5b

Filling with 50% gray

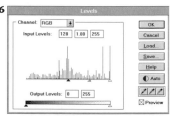

6

Isolating highlights

7

Isolating shadows

8

Lightening the surface

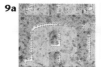

9a

Creating the highlight

9b

Creating the shadow

ground color. Release the Alt key and press Backspace to fill the selection with gray, sharpening the edge of the top surface.

6 Making the "highlights" mask. Now duplicate the "blur" channel (which has become the edges mask) into a new channel ("highlights"). Working in this new channel, choose Image, Adjust, Levels. Click the black-point eyedropper and then click somewhere on the 50% gray mask. The 50% gray and all darker shades will turn black, leaving a highlights mask.

7 Making the "shadows" mask. Again, copy the contents of the "blur"channel (the edges mask) into a new channel ("shadows"). This time, before you reset the black point, choose Image, Map, Invert. Now when you click with the black-point eyedropper, all but the shadow areas will turn black.

8 Lightening the embossed surface. Working in the main RGB channel, load the skinny mask (Select, Load Selection, skinny) and use Image, Adjust, Levels to lighten the surface.

9 Creating the edges. Next load the highlight mask (Select, Load Selection, highlights) and use Levels to lighten the selected areas. Then load the shadow mask (Select, Load Selection, shadows) and use Levels to darken.

Variations. With the masks created in steps 1 through 4 — "skinny," "fat," and "blur" (embossed but not yet trimmed), you can arrive at some interesting variations on the finished "blur"channel. Then follow steps 6 through 9 to make and apply highlights and shadows masks.

A *Blur mask embossed. This technique was used to create masks for the Embossed Paper effect on page 33.*

C *Start with A; load the "fat" mask; invert the selection and fill with 50% gray; then load the "skinny" mask, invert the selection, and choose Image, Map, Invert.*

B *Start with A; load the "fat" channel; invert the selection; fill with 50% gray; then load the "skinny" channel and fill with 50% gray. This produces hard edges at both top and bottom surfaces, a classic chiseled effect.*

D *For this License Plate effect, do the "stamping" with the highlights and shadows masks made in A; then load the "skinny" channel and fill with color or change the Color Balance.*

"Pillow" Embossing

Overview *Create a graphic in an alpha channel; duplicate the mask and use blurring, embossing, and Levels adjustments to make highlight and shadow masks; use the masks to modify the main image.*

JHD / PHOTO: FOLIO 1, D'PIX

"Original" mask

"Blur" mask

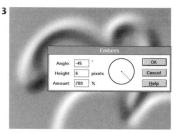

"Blur" mask, embossed

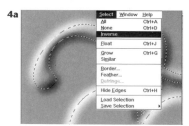

Loading "original" into "blur"

THE "PILLOW EFFECT" is a type of embossing that mimics quilted or heat-stamped fabric. Here we've embossed type on a photo of fabric and added "stitching."

1 Importing graphics to start the masks. Open an RGB file (File, New); we started with a photo of white satin. Add an alpha channel to it (Window, Show Channels, New Channel); we named the channel "original." Then type or import graphic elements. We had made an Adobe Illustrator document using Linoscript type and a dingbat from the Zapf Dingbats font and saved it as an EPS so we could place it (File, Place) in the "original" channel. Once it was placed, we dropped the selection (Ctrl-D) and inverted to white on black (Ctrl-I).

2 Blurring a mask. Use Image, Calculate, Duplicate (or Select All, Copy, New Channel, and Paste) to duplicate the graphics from step 1 in another channel ("blur"). Choose Filter, Blur, Gaussian Blur to soften the mask. For this 1100-pixel-wide image, we used a Radius of 6 pixels for the blur.

3 Embossing the mask. Choose Filter, Stylize, Emboss. In this case we used an angle setting that would simulate light coming from the upper left (Angle: –45), a Height of 6 pixels, and an Amount of 200%. (The Amount controls the contrast between the highlight and shadow edges and the 50% gray that the Emboss filter always applies to the flat surfaces.)

4 Making the shadows mask. To produce the crease for the quilted look, you will load "original" into "blur" as a selection and invert the color map within the selection: Working in channel 5, choose Select, Load, Selection, original; then choose Image, Map, Invert (Ctrl-I). Leave this file as it is and make a duplicate (Image, Calculate, Duplicate with "blur" as the source and a new channel called "shadows" as the Destination). To complete the mask for the embossing shadows, choose Image, Adjust, Levels, click on the black eyedropper

4b

Image map inverted within selection

4c

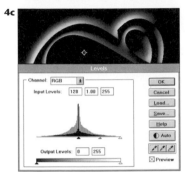

Finishing the "shadows" mask

5a

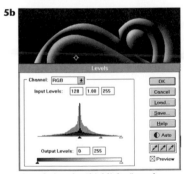

Starting the "highlights" mask

5b

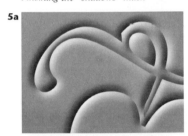

Completing the "highlights" mask

6

Applying color to the pillow embossing

button to select it, and then click this eyedropper on the 50% gray of the background. This and all darker shades turn black, leaving only the white and light gray.

5 Making the "highlights" mask. To produce a second version of the crease, activate the "blur" channel by clicking on its name in the channels palette. Choose Image, Map, Invert to reverse the tonality in the entire channel. To complete the mask that will isolate the areas you want to lighten, again click the black eyedropper button in the Levels box and click the eyedropper on 50% gray. This time everything but the highlights area turns black. Rename the mask "highlights."

6 Applying highlights and shadows and coloring the satin. With the "shadows" and "highlights" (formerly "blur" masks ready, load the "shadows" mask into the main RGB image (Select, Load Selection, shadows) and choose Image, Adjust, Levels. Move the black point of the Input or Output slider to make the shadows for the quilting. Then load the "highlights" mask (Select, Load Selection, highlights) and adjust the white point slider to lighten the highlight areas.

You can color the fabric by loading the original graphics mask (Select, Load Selection, original) and adjusting the color balance of the selected area: Choose Image, Adjust, Color Balance and experiment by moving the sliders. Then choose Select, Inverse to select the background instead of the graphics; adjust the color balance of this selection also.

Finishing. To add stitching, we imported a dashed-line version of the original Adobe Illustrator graphic into an alpha channel. We loaded the selection into the main image and Color Balanced. To enhance the "feel" of the fabric, we selected all and applied hue-protected noise (see page 96).

BORROWING A TEXTURE

You can develop a background with the texture of satin (or another material) by using alpha channels made from an image of the material you want to copy. To make channels for the soft highlights and shadows of satin fabric, for example, copy the image into two alpha channels. Invert one of the masks (Image, Map, Invert) to make the shadows channel. Use Image, Adjust, Levels on both channels to exaggerate the contrasts. Then load each mask into the background image and adjust Levels.

Original image

Highlights mask

Shadows mask

Aglow at the Edges

Overview *Save type or an imported graphic as a selection in an alpha channel; fatten and blur the selection to make a glow mask; combine the glow with the original mask; apply the mask to delete the shape from the background; adjust the color.*

"Original" mask created in an alpha channel

A GLOW EFFECT APPLIED TO TYPE or graphics can light up the page. Here are directions for adding a glow that extends both outward and inward from a bright edge. The technique can be applied to lettering or shapes created in Photoshop or to a graphic element imported from Adobe Illustrator, as in the example shown here.

1 Storing the graphic in an alpha channel. After opening or creating the graphic, copy it to an alpha channel to store it while you create a background for your glowing element: You can use Image, Calculate, Duplicate with the Invert box selected to make the new channel ("original"); you should end up with the graphic element in white and the background of the alpha channel in black.

2 Setting up the glow channel. Repeat the Image, Calculate, Duplicate function to copy the graphic, again in white, into another alpha channel (name it "glow"). To fatten the shape of the graphic or type, in the "glow" channel choose Filter, Other, Maximum and set the Radius value. The Maximum filter will extend the white areas farther into the black. The Radius setting will depend on the size and resolution of your image and how far outward and inward you want the glow to extend. For this example the resolution was 300 dpi, and the Ra-

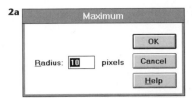

2a

dius was 10 pixels. (The lower the resolution, the lower the Radius setting would be to achieve the same effect; if the resolution had been 150 dpi, we would have used a Radius of 5 pixels to get an effect similar to the one shown here.) Loading a selection from the "original" channel and stroking it with a 10-pixel white line would produce a similar result.

3 Softening the glow mask. To soften the fattened shape, choose Filter, Blur, Gaussian and enter a Radius setting, again according to the size, resolution, and desired extent of the glow. For the example we used a Radius of 50 pixels.

4 Adding the original shape. To put the original shape into the glow to define the bright edge from which the glow emanates, load the selection from the "original" channel into the "glow" channel by choosing Select, Load Selection, original. Then choose Image, Map, Invert (Ctrl-I) to reverse the tonality of the selected interior of the bulb while leaving the unselected outside and center circle unchanged. You can now adjust Levels to change the brightness or contrast of the glow.

5 Putting the glow in place. To make a background for the glowing object, press Ctrl-0 (zero) or click on RGB in the Channels palette to open channel 0 (the RGB channel). Fill the background with a color, a texture, or an image. You can do this by selecting all and using the Fill command, for instance, or by opening another Photoshop file, copying it, and pasting

2b

Mask duplicated and "fattened" in the "glow" channel

3a

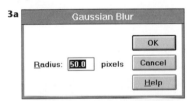

3b

"Glow" mask blurred

4a

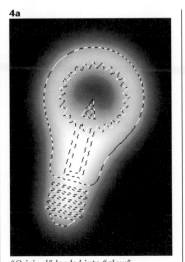

"Original" loaded into "glow"

4b

Brightness inverted within selection

5

"Glow" channel loaded into background in channel 0 and filled with white

6a

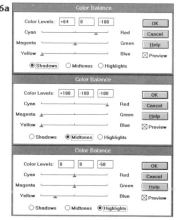

6b

Color balance of selection adjusted

it into channel 0. (We used a background copied from another Photoshop file.) In channel 0, choose Select, Load Selection, glow. With the background color in the toolbox set to white, (or any color you like) press Backspace to fill the selected area. This creates the glow.

6 Adjusting the colors of the glow. With the selection still active, feather it (Select, Feather, 10 in this case) to pick up some of the background image around the glow created by the Backspace. Then choose Image, Adjust, Color Balance to tone the shadows, midtones, and highlights. We used the settings shown here. We also chose Image, Adjust, Hue/Saturation and turned the Saturation up to 100 percent. You can Adjust the Levels (Ctrl-L) if necessary to create the glow you want. If you like this glow as a final effect, you can stop here.

Adjusting the colors of the internal glow. Now choose Select, Load Selection, original and color the graphic or type inside the edge of the glow by inverting the color of the selected area or by filling the selection with color, pattern, or image. To get the effect shown in the opening illustration, we chose Image, Map, Invert.

This variation on the light bulb was created by following steps 1 through 6 and then loading the "original" channel as a selection into the "glow" channel, copying the now-selected part of the "glow" channel to the clipboard, pasting it into channel 0, and while it was still selected, choosing Image, Map, Invert and using Image, Adjust, Color Balance to adjust the color.

This glow started with type set in Photoshop and saved as a mask in the "original" channel. The glow was built in the "glow" channel as described in steps 1 through 4. Then the "original" channel was loaded as a selection into channel 0 and a scanned rice paper texture was pasted into this selection. The "glow" channel was then loaded into channel 0 and filled with yellow.

REMOVING DEBRIS

When you paste a selected object into an image, use Ctrl-H to hide the selection border, and check for rough edges. Use Select, Defringe to clean up any debris before dropping the selection.

Carving in Stone

Overview *Import or create graphics or type; make five masks: "skinny," "fat," "bevel highlights," "bevel shadow," and "interior shadow"; apply the masks to a directionally lighted background.*

1a

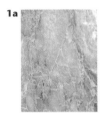
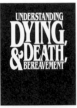

Background   *Importing lettering*

1b

"Skinny" mask

2

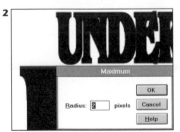

Making the "fat" mask

3a

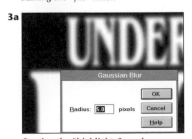

Starting the "highlights" mask

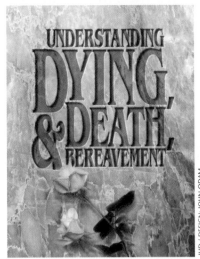

FOR THIS LOW-RESOLUTION BOOK COVER COMP, the type needed to be not only recessed but beveled. This beveling, along with some "hand work" on the shadows, adds realism to the carving.

1 Making the "skinny" mask. Start with an RGB image of a surface to be carved, open an alpha channel (Window, Show Channels, New Channel) and name it "skinny." Place the elements to be carved (File, Place); choose Select, Save Selection, skinny.

2 Making the "fat" mask. Use Image, Calculate, Duplicate with "skinny" as the Source and a New channel ("fat") as the Destination. Apply the Maximum filter (Filter, Other, Maximum); a value of 2 was used in the 750-pixel-wide image. Then choose Image, Map, Invert to save this fattened mask as black-on–white. The "skinny" and "fat" channels will be used to isolate the beveled edge.

3 Making an embossed mask. Choose Image, Calculate, Duplicate to make a copy of the "skinny" channel in a new channel ("highlights"). Apply a Gaussian Blur (Filter, Blur, Gaussian), and emboss the result (Filter, Stylize, Emboss). (We used a setting of 5 for the blur and 3 pixels for the emboss.)

4 Making masks for the highlighted and shaded parts of the bevel. At this point duplicate the "highlights" channel to make "shadows," a second embossed channel. Then to increase the contrast in the "highlights" channel mask, choose Image, Adjust, Levels and click the black point eyedropper on the 50 percent gray of the embossing background. In the "shadows" channel choose Image, Map, Invert to turn the shadows white. Increase contrast as you did for "highlights."

3b

Blurred "highlights" mask, embossed and ready for black point setting

4a

The result of loading the "fat" mask into the darkened "highlights" channel and filling with black

4b

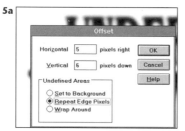

The result of loading the "skinny" mask into "highlights" and filling with black

5a

'Skinny" duplicated, blurred, and offset to start the "interior" channel

5b

"Skinny" loaded into "interior," selection inverted and filled with black

6a

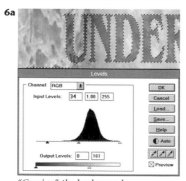

"Carving" the background

To turn the "highlights" and "shadows" channels into masks that will isolate the highlighted and shaded parts of the bevel, work first in the "highlights" channel and then in "shadows." In each of these channels, load the "fat" mask (Select, Load Selection, fat) and press Shift-Backspace (with black as the foreground color) to make a sharp edge for the embossing. Next load the "skinny" mask and again fill with black to trim away all but the bevel highlight or bevel shadow.

5 Making a mask for the interior shadows. Duplicate the "skinny" channel in another new channel ("interior") and invert the image map to produce black lettering on white. Gaussian Blur the channel (we used a setting of 5) and choose Filter, Other, Offset to move the mask down and to the right. Now load "skinny" as a selection, invert the selection (Select, Inverse) and fill with black.

6 Applying shadows and highlights. To make the bottom surface of the carving, activate the RGB channel (Ctrl-zero) and load the "skinny" channel. Choose Image, Adjust, Levels and darken the carved area. Then load "highlights" and "shadows" in the same way and use Levels to lighten or darken.

6b

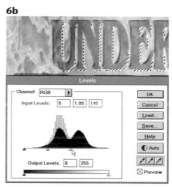

Making the bevel highlight

7a

Making the interior shadow

7 Finishing the shadows. Load the interior shadows mask (Select, Load Selection, interior) and darken. To anchor the carved points so they don't seem to be floating, use the dodge/burn tool in its burn (hand) mode to connect the interior shadows with the points. (Compare the point of the "Y" [already "burned"] with the point of the "N" [not yet done]).

7b

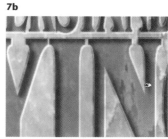

Retouching the shadow

Beveled Glass

Overview *Create or import a graphic; make masks to select all the surfaces, highlights, and shadows you want to manipulate; load these channels one at a time to select areas of the background image in the RGB channel; change the color or tone of each selection.*

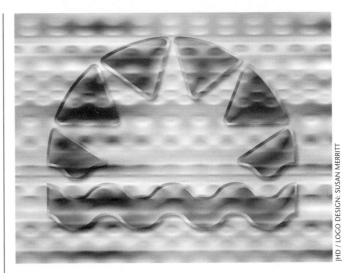

1 *Alpha channels*

2

Making the "master" channel

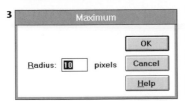

3

Making the "master big" channel

SIMULATING GLASS IN PHOTOSHOP is not for the faint-hearted. To create a convincing colored glass, you have to manufacture all these properties: transparency (you can see through it); refraction (it bends light so the surface behind it is distorted somewhat); an edge structure (in this case a bevel is used rather than a straight-cut edge); a diffuse highlight (light tends to be reflected internally in a complex interplay); and surface reflection (some light bounces off the surface of the glass instead of passing through it to the background beneath). The process of simulating glass involves making a series of channels so all these properties can be manipulated.

1 Planning the channels. In total you'll make seven alpha channels, some of which are early stages of others. Giving them names will make it easier to remember what each mask looks like. (To name a channel, double-click on its listing in the Channels palette, which opens the Channel Options dialog box, where you can enter the new name.) The "shadow" channel is made according to the procedure described on pages 152 and 153. The other masks are made according to the steps that follow here.

2 Defining the shape: the "master" channel. In the main RGB channel, use Photoshop's type tool or an anti-aliased, hard-edged selection tool to define a shape for your glass object. Or import a shape (choose File, Open, choose an EPS file, and respond to the EPS Rasterizer box). One way to copy this graphic into an alpha channel is to choose Image, Calculate, Duplicate and specify the same file but a New channel as the Destination. If your object is black-on-white rather than white-on-black, select Invert in the Duplicate dialog box before clicking OK. Name the channel "master."

4a

Making the "blur" channel

4b

Making the "blur offset" channel

4c

4d

Using Difference on "blur" and "blur offset"

5

Trimming the edges to start "highlight 2"

3 Making room for the bevel: the "master big" mask. Duplicate the "master" in another alpha channel (Image, Calculate, Duplicate, same file name, New). Then apply the Maximum filter (Filter, Other, Maximum). We used a setting of 10 pixels for this 1080-pixel-wide image. This setting determines bevel width.

4 Generating a basis for the highlights: the "blur," "blur offset," and "highlight" channels. Duplicate the "master" again in another alpha channel by the same Image, Calculate, Duplicate process used in step 3. Apply a Gaussian blur to the channel (Filter, Blur, Gaussian; we used a value of 20 pixels); you can name the channel "blur." Then duplicate "blur" into another channel by the same method. Apply the Offset filter (Filter, Other, Offset; we used 7 pixels right, 7 down; Wrap Around). Name this channel "blur offset." The offset amount determines how dramatic the light-and-shadow play in the glass will be.

To make the "highlight" channel, use Image, Calculate, Difference with the "blur" channel as Source 1, the "blur offset" as Source 2, and a New channel as the Destination. The Difference function compares the brightness of each pixel in Source 1 with each pixel in Source 2. The brightness of the pixel it puts in that spot in the Destination depends on how different the two source pixels are. If the two Source pixels are the same brightness, the Destination pixel will be black. If the Source 1 pixel is black and the Source 2 pixel is white (or vice versa), the Destination pixel will be white. Any other brightness values in Sources 1 and 2 will result in shades of gray, with lighter grays for big differences and darker grays for small differences. Name this new channel "highlight." Choose Image, Adjust, Levels and click Auto to pull out a full range of grays in the mask.

5 Starting the "highlight 2" mask. Load the "master big" mask into the "highlight" channel by choosing Select, Load Selection, master big. Then choose Select, Inverse to choose the spaces around and between the elements rather than the elements themselves. Press Shift-Backspace (with black as the foreground color) to trim the edges of the "highlight" mask.

6 Differentiating the bevel in "highlight 2." Load "master" into "highlight" by choosing Select, Load Selection master. Then choose Image, Map, Invert (Ctrl-I) to reverse the tonality of the selection. Now the surface and bevel will have distinctly different highlight characteristics. Choose Select, Save Selection and save the mask as "highlight 2."

7 "Bending" the background under the glass. This step sets up the refraction, the bending of light caused by the glass.

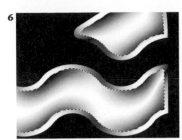

Completing the "highlight 2" channel

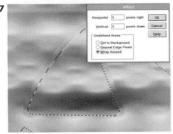

Using "master big" and "master" with the Offset filter to create the refraction

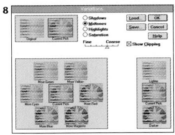

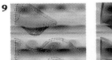

Loading "master big" and coloring the glass

Loading "highlight 2" and coloring the highlights

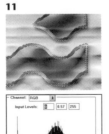

Loading the "shadow" mask

Return to the main RGB channel and replace its contents with a background. In this case we cleared the window and then generated a texture with the KPT Texture Explorer filter (see page 115), but you could fill with any pattern or paste in any image. When the background is in place, load the selection from the "master big" channel (Select, Load Selection, master big). Then choose Filter, Other, Offset and move the selected region, again using the Wrap Around option in the Offset dialog box. (For this image we used settings of 5 pixels right and down.) Next load the selection from the "master" channel, running the Offset filter at the same settings used for "master big." This offset creates the refraction, or "stairstep" effect.

8 Establishing the primary color of the glass. Load the "master big" channel again as in step 7 and use Image, Adjust, Variations to change the color of the selected area. Use the Fine-Coarse slider to control the amount of change as you experiment by clicking to select new color and lightness options.

9 Establishing the color of the highlights. Load the selection from the "highlight 2" channel (Select, Load Selection, highlight 2). (The "highlight 2" channel should look like figure 6.) Use Image, Adjust, Variations again to establish the highlight color. Experiment with the Highlights, Midtones, Shadows, Saturation, Lighter, and Darker options. The object is to establish a contrast between glass and background. If the background is light, you might want to try darkening the glass; if the background is dark, try lightening the glass.

10 Adding the shadow. Use the "master big" channel to make a "shadow" channel, as described on pages 152 and 153, duplicating, blurring, offsetting, and trimming. Load the selection from this channel (Select, Load Selection, shadow) and adjust the Input gamma and Output white point in the Levels dialog box to darken the selected area to make the shadow.

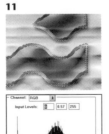

11 Highlighting the bevel: combining alpha channels. To select the beveled edge so you can lighten it, use Image, Calculate, Difference with "master" and "master big" as the two Source channels and Selection as the Destination. Use Image, Adjust, Levels to lighten the bevel.

Loading the "highlight 2" mask and lightening the bevel

Creating Chrome

Overview *Create a graphic in an alpha channel; create a fat mask and two offset blur masks; Calculate the Difference between blur masks; paste in a grayscale image at 50% opacity; use the fat mask to trim; copy the chrome, paste it into the RGB channel, and color.*

JHD / LOGO DESIGN: BETH VERNEK

1a

"Original" mask   "Stroked" mask

"Blur offset minus"   "Blur offset plus"

1b

"Chrome" channel

2

Blurring the reflected image

3a

Pasting the image into "chrome"

ONE GOAL IN SIMULATING CHROME is to achieve the organic, irregular look of reflections from a mirrored surface without having to paint them in by hand. The technique used for this rendering of the logo for an art gallery can also be used to add reflections to other special effects, such as glass and crystal.

1 Setting up the alpha channel for the reflections.
Open an alpha channel (Windows, Show Channels, New Channel) and import, type, or draw the graphics you want to turn into chrome. Invert the color map (Ctrl-I) if necessary. Duplicate this channel using Image, Calculate, Duplicate to make a "stroked" channel. Load the selection from "original" into "stroked"; with the selection active, choose Edit, Stroke, White, Center Line (we used 8 pixels for this 1100-pixel-wide image) to make the mask for the bolder graphic. This produces slightly rounded corners, rather than the square edges produced by Maximum. Then use Image, Calculate, Duplicate to produce two more alpha channels ("blur offset minus" and "blur offset plus") from "original." Choose Filter, Blur, Gaussian Blur (we used 10 pixels) in both channels. Offset the image in opposite directions in the two channels by using Filter, Other, Offset (we used settings of –5, –5 and +5, +5). Finally, choose Image, Calculate, Difference with "blur offset minus" and "blur offset plus" as the Sources and a New channel ("chrome") as the Destination. Use Image, Map, Invert to turn the mask mostly white, and choose Image, Adjust, Levels, Auto to increase contrast in the mask. This process makes the specular highlights on the corners that are characteristic of chrome.

2 Blurring the reflection source. Almost any photo can be used as the source of visual information for the reflection. Typically, a horizon line is used — mountains against the sky, for example — but for this piece, a candid backyard shot

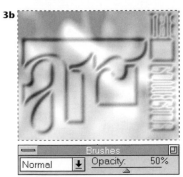

3b

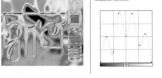

Image pasted, stretched, and transparent

4

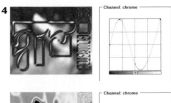

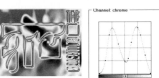

Experimenting with Image, Map

5

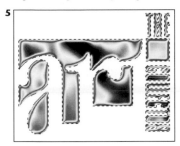

6

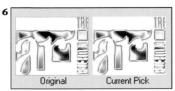

Original   Current Pick

Using variations

worked fine. Open this image file, convert it to grayscale (Mode, Grayscale), and choose Filter, Blur, Gaussian Blur. (We used a large enough blur Radius to eliminate the detail in the image. But to make a chrome that mirrors something specific in its surroundings, you can use a much less pronounced blur.) Finally, use Image, Adjust, Levels, Auto to increase contrast.

3 Applying the reflection to the alpha channel. In the blurred reflection image, Select All (Ctrl-A), and copy (Ctrl-C). Open the "chrome" channel and paste in the reflection image. Align the pasted image with a corner of the alpha channel. Then Choose Image, Effects, Scale and stretch the pasted image; there's no need to scale proportionally — just stretch to fit. Use the Brushes palette or Edit, Composite Controls (Normal mode) to set the Opacity of the pasted image to 50%.

4 Creating the mirrored look. To bring out the dramatic darks, lights, and edge details associated with a mirrored surface, choose Image, Adjust, Curves (Ctrl-M) and experiment with redrawing the curve. We chose a "double-hump" curve to get the light, dark, light effect as you see it.

5 Loading the chrome. The next step is to trim the chrome image and load it into the main RGB channel. In this case, unlike most others in this chapter, the alpha channel will be used to paste in the actual chrome texture, rather than to select part of the main image for modification. To trim the chrome, use the sharp-edged "stroked" mask to select from the "chrome" channel as follows: Load "stroked" (the stroked but not yet blurred version) into the "chrome" channel (choose Select, Load Selection, stroked). Copy the selection to the clipboard (Ctrl-C). Click on RGB in the Channels palette to open the main image. You'll see the marching ants of the selection you loaded; paste the image from the clipboard on top of this selection (Ctrl-V), and don't deselect.

6 Adding color. While the selection from step 5 is still active, use Image, Adjust, Variations to color the chrome. After selecting Highlights, Midtones, or Shadows in the dialog box, click on the color variations to arrive at the color you want. Adjust the Fine-Coarse slider as needed to see smaller or greater color changes in the variations. Adjust all three — highlights (we used yellow), midtones (cyan), and shadows (blue).

Adding detail. To add detail to the smaller type, we created a mask for the bevel (Image, Calculate, Difference, "original," "stroked"), loaded it, and inverted the color within this selection. We also added Noise and a slight shadow (see pages 152 and 153) to the entire graphic.

Creating Crystal

***Overview** Make a displacement map from type or a graphic and apply it to a background image using the Displace filter; make masks for coloring, shading, and creating highlights; load each mask in turn, adjusting color balance and Levels.*

RGB background   *"Original" mask*

"Blurred" mask   *"Trimmed" mask*

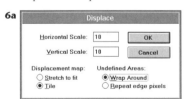

Displacement map

6a

Setting Scale values

6b

Loading a displacement map

PHOTOSHOP PROVIDES ANY NUMBER OF WAYS to distort an image. Some are controlled by hand, such as Image, Effects, Distort; others are formulaic and mechanical, such as the Ripple filter; and still others combine hand control with mechanical precision, such as Image, Effects, Perspective, for example. But there's one tool — the Distort, Displace filter — that can be used to control precisely how an image will be reshaped. Although the default displacement maps that come with Photoshop produce variations on random patterns like those that serve as the basis for a number of painterly filters produced by other software developers, a displacement map doesn't have to be a random pattern. If you use a recognizable image as a displacement map, you can get some very interesting results.

The Displace filter works by moving pixels of an image. The distance each pixel moves depends on the luminance (or brightness) of corresponding pixels in the displacement map. A displacement map can be any image in Photoshop 2.5 format except a bitmap. White pixels move their corresponding pixels in the filtered image the maximum positive (up or right) distance, black pixels produce the maximum negative (down or left) displacement, with 50% brightness producing no displacement at all. Scale factors determine how large the maximum will be. If the displacement map has two channels, the first controls horizontal displacement and the second controls vertical. If there is only one channel, it's applied for both horizontal and vertical displacement. The maps can be wrapping patterns (like the Widgets on the Wow disk) or graphics, like the ampersand used for this crystal effect.

1 Making a background. Create the background that will be displaced to create the crystal effect. If you use an image with lines or a grid, the effect will be easier to see. We used a background created with the KPT Texture Explorer filter.

6c

Displaced image

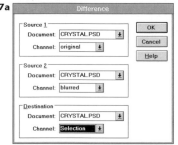

7a

Creating a mask to darken the edges

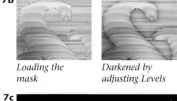

7b

Loading the mask   *Darkened by adjusting Levels*

7c

A highlights mask (based on #15 on page 33)

7d

Loading the highlights mask to adjust Levels

2 Making an alpha channel. Open a new channel (Window, Show Channels, New Channel) and set type or import a graphic into this channel ("original"). Use Ctrl-I, if necessary, to arrive at white on black.

3 Blurring a mask. Use Image, Calculate, Duplicate with "original" as Source and a New channel ("blurred") as Destination. Then choose Filter, Blur, Gaussian Blur to make soft edges on this mask. We used 10 pixels for this 500-pixel-wide file.

4 Trimming a blurred mask. Duplicate "blurred" into a new channel ("trimmed"). Choose Select, Load Selection, original to load the original mask into this new channel. Then choose Select, Inverse to select the background. With black as the foreground color, press Shift-Backspace to fill the selection with black and trim away the outer part of the blur.

5 Saving the displacement map. Use Image, Calculate, Duplicate to copy "trimmed" into a new Grayscale file, and save this file in Photoshop 2.5 format.

6 Applying the displacement. Working in the main channel of the background file, choose Filter, Distort, Displace. When the Displace dialog box appears, set the amounts for scaling. This setting will depend on the amount of distortion you want and on the contrast in the displacement map. For an effect like this one and a displacement map with pure black and white as well as light grays, a setting between 2 and 10 seems to work well. (Since in this case the displacement map is exactly the same size as the background file, the Stretch To Fit/ Tile setting was irrelevant. However, whenever a displacement map is tiled or stretched, edge problems require some cleanup.) When you click OK after making the settings in the Displace dialog box, select the displacement map file you created.

7 Coloring and enhancing. At this point the Displace filter has shifted the background image to create the refraction effect. To complete the illusion, you"ll change the color at least slightly and adjust the lighting. To change the color, load the "original" mask (Select, Load Selection, original) and use Image, Adjust, Variations or Color Balance. To adjust lighting, we combined the "original" and "blurred" masks with Image, Calculate, Difference to make a mask through which we could adjust Levels to darken the edges; then we created another alpha channel (based on #15 on page 33, with black point adjusted and background darkened by loading "original," inverting the selection, and filling with black). Through this mask we could adjust Levels to lighten edges and create highlights.

Working with "Widgets"

Overview *Apply the Displace filter using "dropdisp.psd"; make patterns and then masks from the highlights, shadows, and surface channels; apply the masks.*

JHD

1a

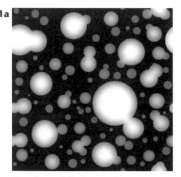

Dropdisp.psd displacement map

1b

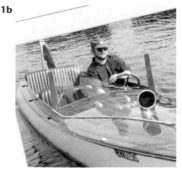

Original image

1c

Applying the Distort, Displace filter

THE WOW WIDGETS DISPLACEMENT MAPS on the Wow disk are seamlessly wrapping patterns. Like the crystal ampersand (see pages 168 and 169 for more about making and using displacement maps), the water drops map shown here was made by producing a blurred mask whose edges were given a sharp trim. The displacement map is a single-channel grayscale file (dropdisp.psd), and additional masks for selecting the surface of the drops, the shadow, and the reflections are provided in a multichannel file (liteshad.psd).

1 Applying the displacement map. Open the image to which you want to add drops; duplicate it (Image, Calculate, Duplicate) so that you have a file to work on and another (the original) that will stay intact so you can use it later (at step 3). In this new file choose Filter, Distort, Displace and enter settings of 2, 2, Tile, Wrap. Select dropdisp.psd.

2 Applying highlights. Now you'll open the liteshad.psd file and turn each channel of this multichannel file into a wrapping pattern; the spacing in the pattern will automatically match the wrapping of the displacement effect. Working in the highlights channel, choose Select, All; then choose Edit, Define Pattern. Then, back in the RGB illustration file, open a new alpha channel (Window, Show Channels, New Channel). Working in that channel (which we named "highlights"), choose Select, All and Edit, Fill, Pattern so the channel fills with the highlights pattern. Working in the main RGB channel, load the new pattern-filled alpha (Select, Load Selection, highlights) and choose Image, Adjust, Levels to lighten; or, as we did here, fill the selection with the foreground color (light blue) by pressing Shift-Backspace.

Make and apply shadow mask: Working in the multichannel file again, in the shadows channel choose Select All; then choose Edit, Define Pattern. Back in the RGB illustration once again, open another new alpha channel "shadows"), and

1d

Choosing the displacement map

1e

The Displace filter applied

2a

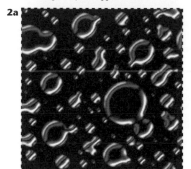

Making the highlights channel into a pattern

2b

Filling an alpha channel with the pattern to make the highlights mask

choose Select, All and then Edit, Fill, Pattern to fill this new channel with the shadows Pattern. Then work in the main RGB channel; choose Select, Load Selection, shadows, and choose Image, Adjust, Levels and darken the selected areas.

Repeat the process of defining a pattern, filling an alpha channel with it, and loading this mask in the RGB channel once more, this time starting with the "surface" channel of the multichannel file. When the surface mask is loaded as a selection in the main RGB image, use Image, Adjust, Levels to lighten the tops of the drops, but not as light as the highlights.

3 Tailoring the effect. To limit the effect to only part of the image, lasso an area that includes drops that you want to keep. Then use the Ctrl key with the lasso to delete any drops within that area that you don't want to keep. And use lasso and Shift to add drops to the selection. Then open the original RGB image, Select All, and Copy. In the image to which you've added the drops, choose Edit, Paste Behind, and move the pasted image about the same amount and direction as the displacement map moved it. This will put back the original image except in the areas where you have selected the drops. 🐌

2c

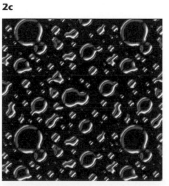

Highlights mask

2d

The highlights mask applied

3

Some of the drops removed

■ For this experimental *Chiseled Monogram,* **Jack Davis** began by drawing the letterforms in Adobe Illustrator, assigning colors to the faces; the background was set at 50% black. He opened the file in Photoshop's Grayscale mode and copied the entire image to an alpha channel (#2). Working in channel 2, he selected individual faces of the letterforms using the magic wand with antialiasing turned on and with the Tolerance set at 0. To develop the mask, the individually selected sides were "lighted" with the gradient tool's linear fills. Then the Stylize, Crystallize filter was run on the alpha channel (with a cell size of 3 in this 505-pixel-wide image) to roughen the edges of the letters to match the background, which was a scan of a textured wall that was pasted into the Black (main) channel of the file. The selection was loaded into this background, and Image, Adjust, Levels was used to darken the shaded sides of the chiseled letters. Then Select, Inverse was chosen and Levels was used again, this time to lighten the remaining faces. Because the background was 50% black, it was darkened with the first Levels adjustment and then lightened again with the second. (The darkening and lightening process changed the background somewhat. To set up shadow and highlight masks that will leave the background unaffected, see "Embossing & Stamping" on pages 154 and 155.) The finished image was converted to Duotone mode and assigned a set of custom-color-and-black duotone curves.

■ For this *HiRez Audio* CD ROM Cover, **Jack Davis** began by manufacturing a background: He started in an RGB file with a random noise pattern (Filter, Noise, Add Noise) and applied the Motion Blur filter to make multicolored streaks. After adjusting Levels (Ctrl-L) to get the color and contrast he wanted, he imported the lettering from Adobe Illustrator and used the "Quick Shadow" method described on page 150 to make the shadows. Before adding the lettering itself, he selected the top half of the background with the rectangular marquee and inverted the color map (Ctrl-I). The letters were pasted from the clipboard and also saved in an alpha channel for future use. The chrome texture was assigned with a beta version of the Gallery Effects Chrome filter. A bevel mask was made by loading the "skinny" mask (the original alpha channel of the imported lettering) into a "fat" one created with the Maximum filter, and then filling with black (Shift-Backspace). The resulting edge mask was saved and loaded as a selection, and the color map was inverted to make the bevel. The gradient tool was used in Quick Mask mode to make a mask for lightening the upper left corner of the letters and for recoloring this region using Image, Adjust, Color Balance.

■ For his images for the award-winning *Industrial Strength Eyewear catalog*, **Jeff McCord** constructed the transparency and reflectivity of the clear lenses, and the drop shadow beneath the glasses, in Photoshop. McCord started with product shots of glasses with different colored lenses that Tom Collicott had photographed on glass against a neutral backdrop. McCord opened Scitex scans of the images in Photoshop in CMYK mode. He worked with prepress consultant Doug Peltonen to select the gray background with the magic wand and delete it, leaving the glasses on white. For the clear-lens glasses shown on this page, he started with a photo of glasses of the same models but with yellow lenses. After using the magic wand tool to select the background and Select, Inverse to select the

glasses, the first step was to make the drop shadow. For each pair of glasses, he copied the glasses to the clipboard. Before pasting the glasses into the main image, which was another scanned and modified photo, he pasted them into an alpha channel and saved the selection. He applied a Gaussian Blur and the Offset filter to the channel to make a shadow mask he could use to darken the image in the shadow area.

With the shadow in place, McCord pasted the glasses from the clipboard into the the main CMYK channel of the image (#0). While the pasted glasses were still floating, he adjusted the Opacity in the Composite Controls dialog box to 60% to let the background and shadow show through. With the pasted selection still

active, McCord pasted again, bringing in another copy of the glasses exactly on top of the first paste, and subtracted (lasso with Ctrl key) the lenses from this new floating selection so that only the frames were pasted in at full opacity.

To restore the highlight that had been lost in making the lenses transparent, McCord pasted the glasses once again, this time setting the mode to Lighten in the Composite Controls dialog box. Then he used Image, Adjust, Levels to increase the contrast until he achieved the specular highlights he wanted. McCord saved the file in EPS/DCS format and imported it into QuarkXPress, where type was added. (Art direction for the catalog was by Seattle ad agency Matthaeus, Donahoe, Halverson.)

■ To make the *San Diego Comic Convention Logo*, **Jack Davis** used displacement techniques like those applied in "Working with Widgets" in this chapter. After running the KPT Texture Explorer to generate a background in an RGB file, he imported lettering from Adobe Illustrator into an alpha channel. He used the same lettering to create an alpha channel for the lettering itself and one for making specular highlights ("Creating Chrome" and "Creating Crystal" in this chapter tell how to create a mask for specular highlights). He also used the lettering to make a displacement map file.

He applied the Distort, Displace filter, loading the map he had made from the lettering. Then he loaded the highlights mask into the main RGB channel and adjusted Levels. He loaded the mask for the lettering itself, used Select, Inverse to select the background instead of the lettering, and pressed Backspace to turn the background white. He cut the lettering to the clipboard and loaded the alpha channel for the lettering again. He moved the selection border for the lettering downward and to the left slightly, feathered the selection, and adjusted Levels to make a shadow. Then he loaded the selection from the alpha channel again and pasted in the lettering from the clipboard. He used the Ctrl key to delete the "ComiCon" lettering from the selection and used Color Balance to change "San Diego1994." Shown here are the displacement map (left), the background after Displace, and the highlights mask.

■ To make the layered lettering in the *Hybrid Logo* for an interactive television application, **Steve Lomas** set the "HYBRID" type in two alpha channels, and then created two additional offset and blurred channels that could be used to select areas to be darkened for the shadows; a larger offset and softer blur was used for the "H," "B," and "I," so that these letters seem to float higher above the gray paper texture of the background. The

paper texture was copied to the clipboard. Then the Y,R,D shadow channel was loaded into the RGB channel and Image, Adjust, Levels was used to darken the background. Then the Y,R,D lettering channel was loaded as a selection and the paper texture was pasted into it and colored. The Select, Border command was used to add a white edge. Then the H,B,I shadow was applied, the H,B,I lettering channel was loaded as a selection, the

texture was pasted into it, and the lettering was colored and edged. The bar at the top of the logo was imported from a 3D program, where it had been created by Kory Jones as part of the Hybrid interface.

Lomas used the logo in making a series of "luggage tag"cards for members of the Hybrid Applications Team. He used Image, Image Size to resize the logo to fit the card.

■ **Stephen King** imported PostScript line work to serve as the basis for the neon profile in this *ImagiTrek Ad*. The line work was first placed in an alpha channel (#4) of the background image file, rather than in the main RGB channel. Then this alpha channel was duplicated to another alpha channel (Image, Calculate, Duplicate, same file, New channel) and a Gaussian blur was applied to make a selection for the glow around the neon. This blur channel was loaded into the main RGB channel as a selection (Select, Load Selection) and was filled (Shift-Backspace) with a bright blue that had been designated as the foreground color. Then the linework channel was loaded and filled (Shift-Backspace). More color elements were added by using the paintbrush tool and a Wacom tablet with pressure-sensitive stylus. "Glow spots" were added with the airbrush tool and a fairly large brush tip. King painted highlights on the neon squiggles with a small paintbrush and lighter tints of paint. This illustration could also have been done using a different approach. The initial Bezier curves could have been drawn with the pen tool rather than imported, and then Stroke Path (from the pop-out menu in the Paths palette) could have been used to add the diffuse airbrush glow first and then the neon tube with a smaller, more compact paintbrush tip.

■ For the *Revealer* cassette cover design, **Jack Davis** set type and saved it in three alpha channels. After creating the spotlight and background with the feathered lasso and Image, Adjust, Levels, he distorted the type in one of the three channels (Image, Effects, Skew and then Rotate). He loaded the selection and filled it with black (Shift-Backspace) to make the shadow. In the next channel he fattened the type with Filter, Other, Maximum. He loaded this selection and filled it with a diagonal Linear gradient from dark gray at the upper left to light gray at the lower right. Then he loaded the last of the three channels as a selection and filled it with a diagonal gradient in the opposite direction. Also shown here is an alternative treatment, with variations on the gradient contrast and directions and the glow.

■ For the *Bow Down* Album Cover showing the rainbow around the heavenly throne of God, **Jack Davis** scanned a Doré woodcut and selected the background with the lasso. He applied a rainbow gradient fill from a white foreground color (chosen from a blue range of the spectrum) to a red background color. He added Noise, which contributed texture to the image. When the background was complete, he used the airbrush in Darken mode to add rainbow highlights to the robes.

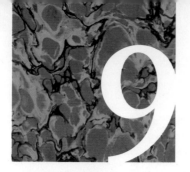

3D/4D – ADDING DEPTH AND MOTION

IN ADDITION TO LENGTH AND WIDTH, a third dimension — depth — is implied in almost all photographs and in many illustrations. Rather than looking like a collection of flat lines and color-filled shapes, most Photoshop images provide a view into or onto a scene.

To enhance the dimensionality of an image, the Levels command, applied to selected areas, provides the ability to create shadows and highlights that add depth to a scene. In addition, three of Photoshop's Image, Effects functions (Skew, Perspective, and Distort) allow you to select part or all of an image and telescope or "bend" it to exaggerate perspective, and the Spherize filter also creates depth illusions.

Filters supplied by other developers, such as the KPT Glass Lens (described in Chapter 5), can also add dimensionality. But only a 3D program can extrude or rotate a two-dimensional object to model a component of an image, or stage an entire scene from such models and then quickly and easily change the viewpoint or lighting to produce a new image.

Photoshop can work with the models designed in 3D programs in two ways. It can serve as the recipient of an object modeled in three dimensions, or it can serve as a source for images that can be used as surface maps to add color, pattern, and detail to a 3D rendering. This chapter includes examples of both.

177

Taking a 3D View

Overview *Prepare artwork in a PostScript illustration program; import it into Photoshop and add perspective; incorporate other elements; create shading, shadows, and reflections to complete the 3D illusion.*

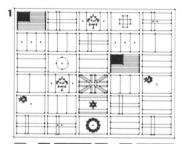

Vertical surface flags created in Illustrator, shown in Artwork mode (top) and Preview mode

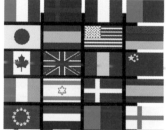

The two flags files assembled in Photoshop, with Perspective applied to the second (Placed) image

PHOTOSHOP'S PERSPECTIVE FUNCTION (found under Image, Effects) can be used to create true perspective distortion, the result you get isn't as smooth and trouble-free as what you can achieve by doing the distortion in some 3D programs and importing the result into Photoshop. This illustration for the cover of a book about health issues in foreign traveling includes a horizontal surface in perspective, made from an assemblage of flags and a backdrop that blends the original vertical version of the flags into an image of international currency. Adobe Illustrator provided the precise, crisp lines and shapes needed to trace the flags from a scan. Then the Adobe Dimensions program (on the Macintosh) was used to "lay it flat." Since a Windows version of Adobe Dimensions does not exist as this book is being completed, an alternative method of creating the flags in perstpective is presented here.

1 Drawing and saving the artwork in Illustrator. Create two pieces of artwork in Adobe Illustrator, one for the vertical part of the backdrop and another for the horizontal surface. We started with two rectangular assemblages of flags like the one shown here. Group each illustration before saving it in EPS format.

2 Importing the artwork into Photoshop. Make sure that Anti-alias PostScript is selected under File, Preferences,

3

Flags imported into Photoshop; gradient Quick Mask created

4

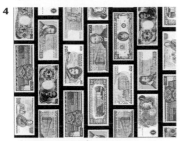

Currency scanned

5

Currency Pasted Into gradient selection; top darkened

6

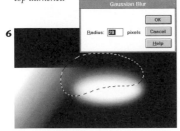

Creating a shadow mask

General. Then open the Illustrator EPS file for the vertical surface in Photoshop, choosing the size and resolution you want in the EPS Rasterizing dialog box. The resolution for this image (at a final size of 7-1/2 x 9-1/4-inches) was 200 pixels per inch, making it 1500 pixels wide altogether. Use Image, Canvas Size to add space at the bottom and sides of the image. Then use File, Place to bring in the Illustrator EPS file for the horizontal assemblage. Place it so that its top edge meets the bottom edge of the vertical surface, but enlarge it proportionally so its bottom edge fills the width of the canvas. While the placed image is still selected, choose Image, Effects, Perspective and drag one of the top corner handles inward to meet the corresponding bottom corner of the vertical surface; then drag one of the bottom handles up. This will make the image appear to be extending toward you on a horizontal plane. (By reducing rather than expanding edges, you'll cut down on the amount of "stairstepping," blurring, and other distortion introduced by the application of Perspective. Even so, you may need to do some work at high magnification with the pencil or a small paintbrush to clean up edges within your image.)

3 Making a gradient in Quick Mask mode. Click the Quick Mask mode icon in the toolbox. Then use the gradient tool to draw a gradation, which will appear as a mask in the color you've chosen for Quick Mask. (Double-click the gradient tool to open the Gradient dialog box to set specifications to control the gradation.) In this case a Linear setting was used with a 50% Midpoint Skew to make a balanced gradation, and the gradient tool was dragged diagonally over a short distance near the middle of the window; this would make a fairly quick transition from full-opacity flags to full-opacity currency.

4 Preparing the second image. In another Photoshop file, scan, paint, or import the second image you want to combine, making the file the same resolution as the first and an appropriate size to blend with the first image. The background file used here was produced by scanning bills on a desktop flatbed scanner. The scan was retouched and scaled to create a "money grid" that would align with the flags. When the image is complete, select it and copy it to the clipboard.

5 Blending the images. Working in the first image again (the flags in this case), click the Standard mode icon to convert the Quick Mask to a selection. Then choose Edit, Paste Into to blend the clipboard contents into the file. After the currency image was pasted into the flags file, the top part of the image was darkened by making another graduated Quick Mask selection so Image, Adjust, Levels could be applied across a gradient.

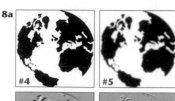

#4   #5

#6   #7

Masks for "emobssing" the continents using the "Satin Pillow" effect described on pages 156 and 157

8b

Embossed and highlighted

8d

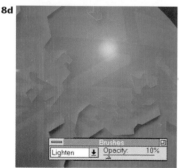

Controlling opacity to add a reflected image

6 Adding to the depth effect. You can use shading and shadows to add to the 3D illusion you created with the perspective effect. In this case, another Quick Mask gradient was used to create a selection for the left side of the flag floor. This was saved as an alpha channel (Select, Save Selection) so it could later be loaded to create a shadow that would darken a corner of the room. A feathered selection was made with the elliptical selection marquee (double-clicked to set the feather). This selection was added to the shadow channel (#4) by setting all the channels to be viewed but only channel 4 to be edited, and then pressing Backspace. Then, to soften the transition of this shadow into the background, a lasso with a 50-pixel feather was used to select the trailing edge and a Gaussian blur (Filter, Blur, Gaussian, 20 pixels) was applied. This mask was then loaded and Levels were adjusted to darken the shadow areas.

7 Adding a 3D object. To complete the illustration, create or import a 3D foreground object. The globe for this illustration started out in black-and-white. This file was opened in Photoshop and given a "satin pillow" treatment, as described on pages 156 and 157. To get the masks needed for this effect, a copy of the image, saved as a mask in channel 4 was blurred (channel 5) and embossed (channel 6). Then the mask from channel 4 was loaded as a selection in channel 6; Image, Map, Invert was chosen, and the result was saved in channel 7.

   To get the basic globe on which to run the satin pillow effect, a circle was drawn to fit the globe image by Shift-selecting with the elliptical selection marquee. The foreground color was set to lime green and the background color to dark green, and a radial fill with its center offset was applied by using the gradient tool within the circular selection. Additonal radial fills were used on selected areas, such as the white highlight. Then channel 4 was loaded as a selection (Select, Load Selection, #4) to coincide with the green circle, and Image, Adjust, Hue/Saturation was used to change the color of the water to blue.

   After the satin-pillow effect was applied, a pseudo-reflection was created by selecting a part of the original flag image with the rectangular marquee, floating a copy (Ctrl-J), spherizing it (Filter, Distort, Spherize), cutting the copy to the clipboard (Ctrl-X), and Pasting Into the selected globe, where opacity was controlled with the Brushes palette. The still selected globe was copied and pasted onto the main file, and Select, Defringe was applied to clean up the montage.

Animating a Logo

Overview *Import QuickTime movies and images from Photoshop into Premiere; animate the still images with the roll filter; use Photoshop alpha channels to mask the animations in Premiere; assemble the animations; use Photoshop to composite still images into the animation.*

ANIMATION: GREG UHLER / LOGO: JHD

1a

Video clips

1b

Still images

PHOTOSHOP HAS BECOME AN ESSENTIAL TOOL for developing desktop animation. It can provide image editing, color conversion functions that surpass those of most desktop animation programs, and alpha channels that can be imported into Adobe Premiere and used for masking. To create an animation based on the original Presto Studios logo by Jack Davis, Greg Uhler used Adobe Premiere, MacroMind Director 3.1.1 on the Macintosh, and Photoshop. To start, he divided the logo into a foreground and a background. The foreground layer, consisting of the hat and glowing pearl, would remain motionless. The background, where all of the motion would take place, was divided into four areas: Earth, Air, Fire, and Water. He decided to animate each of the background areas separately, bring them all together, and then add the foreground layer.

1 Using "clip animations" and animating still images. Use Adobe Premiere to create seamlessly looping movies. Uhler was able to find video clips for the Air and Fire animations. So he cropped them to the right size. Since he had no video for Earth or Water, he created them from still images. To animate each still image, he imported it from Photoshop into Premiere and applied the roll filter. Uhler animated the Earth to roll from left to right and the Water from top to bottom.

2 Importing alpha channels. To create two levels of animation in the background, import black-and-white alpha channels from Photoshop. These can serve as masks that allow one animation to run in the white part of the mask and another in the black. Use Premiere's Transparency function to load the alpha channel into the right track.

2a

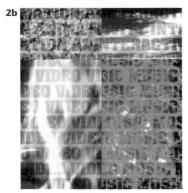

Photoshop alpha channels

2b

Assembled background animation exported from Director

3

Elements and alpha channels for compositing in Photoshop

Uhler scaled Davis' original alpha channels used in creating the logo and imported a mask for each of the four background areas. For each of his four animations he used both the A video track and the Super video track in Premiere. The A track held the image that would be inside the lettering in the alpha channel. The Super video track held the part of the image outside the lettering, so he assigned the alpha channel, with its black lettering on white background, to the Super video channel. To make the text readable, he had used a darker version of each animated image or movie in the A track (for inside the lettering) and a lighter version in the Super track (outside).

3 Combining the animations. Uhler wanted to arrange the animations into a single background. For this he used MacroMind Director on the Macintosh, although it could have been done in Premiere.

Adding the foreground elements. Composite the foreground elements onto each frame of the animated background. In Photoshop Uhler used an alpha channel to hold the position of the hat and pearl in each frame so that these elements could be pasted precisely in the same position in each image file of the animation. For each image he opened the image file, loaded the alpha channel, pasted the hat and pearl from the clipboard, loaded the edge alpha channel, adjusted Levels to darken the edge, closed the file, opened the next, and so on.

Producing the final animation. When the images had been composited and color-converted, Uhler imported them back into MacroMind Director, synchronized them to music, and ported them over to the Windows platform with Director's Windows Player. 🎩

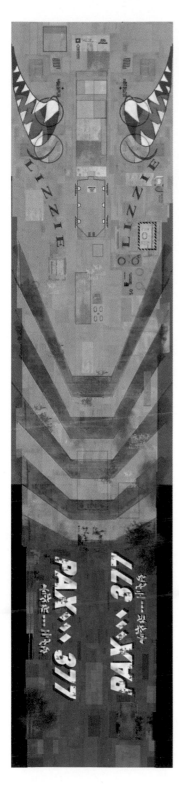

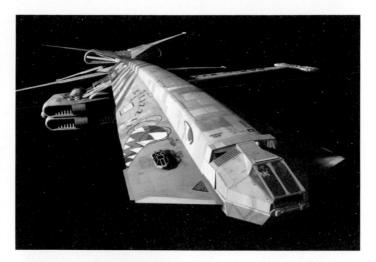

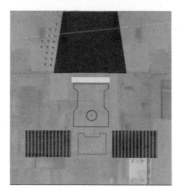

■ To design the *Sling Ship* for the science-fiction television series *Space Rangers*, **John Knoll** of Industrial Light & Magic, and a co-developer of Photoshop, used a 3D program to translate ILM art director Ty Ellingson's sketches into a 3D model. Then he used Photoshop to create texture maps (the flat artwork to be applied to the surfaces of the model to make it look like it's made of real materials) to turn the vehicle into a beat-up spaceship for chasing criminals for this futuristic show about an understaffed, underfunded police outpost. Knoll scanned several photos of the side panels of military aircraft and cut and pasted these elements, turning them into the "paint" he needed to assemble a patchwork image of dull gray metal with rivets, small doors, and scuff marks from which to build the more than 2000-pixel-long texture map for the fuselage. Because he knew that the front end of the ship would be used in several close-up shots, Knoll created the fuselage at a higher resolution than the wings and back of the plane. The shark's teeth that "personalized" the ship were scanned directly from sketches by Ellingson. Knoll rendered the ship (that is, applied the texture maps to the model) and animated its motion in a 3D program.

■ *Mars Canyon* was created on the Macintosh by **Jack Davis** and **Michel Kripalani** for an animated fly-through for *The Journeyman Project,* the world's first photorealistic interactive adventure game on CD ROM. It began as a grayscale topographic view of the canyon created in Photoshop on the Macintosh and exported in the CyberSave format (via a Photoshop plug-in provided with the Electric Image software). The file was opened in Electric Image's Transporter module, which used the grayscale values of the image to create a 3D mesh of polygons; the light portions of the grayscale image were extruded up,

and the dark portions down. The arrow in the grayscale image indicates the camera viewpoint used to produce the rendering above. Textures and bump maps were applied to the model in Electric Image. A sky image was wrapped on the inside of a cylinder that was built to enclose the canyon model, so that the sky changes during the flight around the environment. The lens flare filter was used to put the final touches on the scene. It was applied to frames in which the sun appears from behind some feature of the landscape during flight.

■ *The Mine Transport* was created for *The Journeyman Project* by **Phil Saunders, José Albañil, Eric Hook,** and **Jack Davis.** After the transport was modeled and rendered in a 3D program, the shading was added by hand in Photoshop. Shadows for most of the other environments for the game were also added in Photoshop to provide more control than could be accomplished with a 3D program. A feathered lasso was used to select the shadow areas, and Image, Adjust, Levels (Output) was used to lower the contrast and darken the image. Details (such as the screen dump on the clipboard) were created separately and added to the scene.

■ **Phil Saunders, José Albañil, Michel Kripalani, Geno Andrews,** and **Jack Davis** created the *NORAD Control Room* for *The Journeyman Project*. Davis combined 16 different images and a wall texture of "greeblies" into one large image that was exported to a 3D program and mapped onto the inside of the cylinder that enclosed the control room. The final animation of the scene, with walls, globe, and furniture, was rendered as a series of 36 images with the globe at a different degree of rotation in each image. A glow was added to each image by a method similar to that described on page 81, and each was composited with a Photoshop painting of unconscious workers and saved.

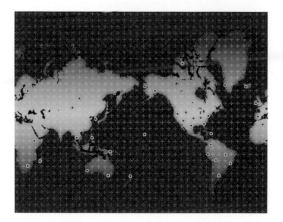

■ **Jack Davis** worked in Photoshop to create the images for a *Holographic Globe* that was animated as part of the underwater, futuristic NORAD Control Room. Shown here are three of the five textures used for the globe animation. The five elements were applied to transparent spheres of slightly different sizes to produce a layering effect.

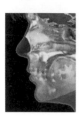

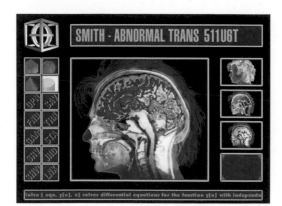

■ Designing interfaces for interactive multimedia and simulating the tactile space of their navigational systems makes use of virtually all the pieces of Photoshop's building set. For the interfaces on these two pages, **Jack Davis** used everything but the kitchen sink. For example, to make the computer read-out of the boosted brain activity of the "innocent villain" Jobe for the interface of the bad guys' *Virtual Space Industries* in the movie *Lawnmower Man,* he used a half-dozen photographs, from monkey brains to Polaroid prints of the actor. The skull and brain were made to follow the contour of the actor's profile by using feathered lasso selections, the Image, Effects, Scale function, and the rubber stamp tool.

■ The interface for *A Radius Rocket Home Companion,* a corporate informational CD ROM, involves a background of textured stucco wall (imported PostScript art that was treated with Noise and embossed). It was lighted with a spotlight created as a feathered selection and lightened by adjusting Levels. The embossed color-coded buttons provide the navigational interface.

■ The interface for Linnea Dayton's *"Look & Feel"* column about the role of computers and multimedia in education in *Verbum Interactive 1.0, CD ROM Multimedia Magazine* involved the use of imported PostScript graphics, simulated textures, alpha-channel-based glows, embossing, bevels, and drop shadows. Photoshop was essential for creating and processing the thousands of images and animations needed for this ambitious project.

■ The interface for the *HiRez Audio* CD ROM demonstrates a way of meeting one of the primary challenges of interface design: having as many of the relevant options on-screen as possible so the user doesn't have to spend a lot of CD access time searching for them. The "Pillow Embossing" technique (see pages 156 and 157) was used to make some of the buttons. Motion-blurred Noise was used for the background.

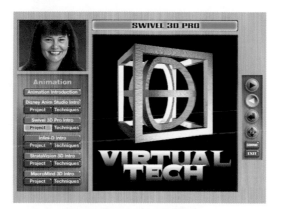

■ In this rough comp for the companion CD ROM for *Verbum's Multimedia Power Tools* book, the layout and buttons were generated in Adobe Illustrator (as were most of the other interfaces on these two pages). Since the highlighted edges and specular highlights were built of layers in the PostScript program, hundreds of text and color variations could be created quickly by importing the artwork with text already in place and color assigned. The buttons were based on a technique developed by Tztom Toda, who originated his elements in Aldus FreeHand.

■ The virtual-reality-like interface for *Seemis,* a safety training program for offshore oil rig workers, was presented as an all-day Saturday TV session, with a TV programming guide that lets the student choose selections, the TV screen that enlarges to show the text and illustrations of the lessons, a changing drinking vessel (juice glass, milk glass, and Coke bottle) that empties to show progress through the syllabus, and a phone that rings to quiz the student on lessons learned. After the patterns and fabrics were created in Photoshop, the furniture and other elements were modeled in a 3D program. These were then brought back into Photoshop, where the lighting changes (for morning, afternoon, and evening) were added primarily with feathered selections and Levels adjustments. The Image, Effects, Distort command was used with rectangular selections to make the folds of the drapes.

■ To make this *3D Logotype*, **Jack Davis** set type around a circle in Adobe Illustrator and imported the result into a 3D program, where he extruded it and established lighting and perspective. He saved the 3D type in EPS format and opened it in Photoshop. There, he used Image, Adjust, Color Balance to turn it gold, exaggerating yellow in the highlights, magenta in the shadows. He duplicated this file (Image, Calculate, Duplicate) and applied the Photocopy filter from Gallery Effects Vol. 2 to the duplicate. This filter exaggerates areas of contrast in the same way that a photocopy machine does, so that in this image with pure white faces on the type and relatively flat shading, it exaggerated the edge definition. The original color-balanced version of the image was then copied and pasted on top of the filtered image, with Multiply chosen in the Brushes palette and with a slight reduction in Opacity, to arrive at an Art Deco airbrush effect.

■ To create the *TBN Nameplate* for a magazine cover, **Jack Davis** recycled a "poly earth" illustration created several years ago in a 3D program. He also rendered the earth with cloud reflection maps in a 3D application and then opened it in Photoshop. He selected two of the four quadrants in turn and chose Image, Map, Invert to create a positive-negative grid. Then he made a rough selection of the illustration with the lasso, with a Feather of 30 in this 885-pixel-wide image. He stroked the selection path with the Gradient on Paths filter from Kai's Power Tools, which creates an effect based on the degree of feather. Finally, each quadrant was selected again and colored using the Hue slider under Image, Adjust, Hue/Saturation.

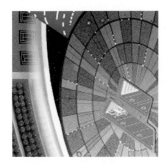

© Bert Monroy 1993

■ In *Orbital World* **Bert Monroy** achieved a 3D look without using a 3D program. He started with shapes drawn in Adobe Illustrator, saved them in encapsulated PostScript (EPS) format, and opened the file in Photoshop. There he filled the shapes with color and then went to work with the paintbrush and airbrush in tiny sizes to create the minute detail characteristic of his work. Monroy often works at relatively low resolution to do most of the work on an image, then uses Image Size to increase the resolution before adding the finest details.

■ **Jack Davis** modified a scan of a Doré woodcut in Photoshop by applying the Blur filter and adjusting Levels to achieve a stereoscopic 3D effect. (The techniques he used can also be applied to add depth to a photo.) He isolated four separate groups of background figures with the lasso and then applied the Gaussian Blur filter. The filter was applied one, two, three, or four times, with the smallest (farthest back) figures being blurred the most. He also differentially lightened the figures with Image, Adjust, Levels.

Appendix A
Image
Collections

Addresses and phone numbers of the publishers of these images on CD are listed on page 201. Image sizes are for open RGB files. Letter codes refer to the rights conferred on the buyer of the disk; the codes are explained below.

Letter codes* *used in disc descriptions in Appendix A:*

A *Unlimited or nearly unlimited reproduction rights*

B *Unlimited or nearly unlimited rights with credit to the photographer*

C *Some size and distribution limits on reproduction with credit to the photographer*

D *Some size, distribution, and usage limits on reproduction with credit to the photographer and special copyright information*

E *For use on screen and in design presentations; other rights by negotiation*

* The codes used here are general indications of license agreements; confirm all rights with the image publisher. Usage agreements vary greatly from one supplier to another. Some license agreements have unusual or even unique restrictions; be sure you understand the limitations on photos you want to use.

Island Designs *(2 disks)*
200 island batik fabric prints and old Hawaiian shirt prints; to 900K; 150 audio clips and sound effects; D; Aris Entertainment

Deep Voyage
100 underwater photographic images of fish and other sealife; to 900K; 100 original audio and sound effects; 25 video clips; D; Aris Entertainment

Jets and Props *(2 disks)*
200 color photos of planes; to 900K; 50 Mac/MPL movies; 200 audio clips and sound effects; D; Aris Entertainment

Business Backgrounds
100 photos; to 900K; 100 audio clips and sound effects; D; Aris Entertainment

Full Bloom
100 photos of beautiful and exotic flowers from around the world; to 900K; 25 video clips of flowers in motion; 100 classical audio clips; D; Aris Entertainment

Majestic Places
100 photos of nature — famous spots to general views; to 900K; 100 audio clips and sound effects; D; Aris Entertainment

Money, Money, Money
100 photos of coins and paper money; to 900K; 25 Mac/MPL movies; 100 audio clips and sound effects; D; Aris Entertainment

Tropical Rainforest
100 photos of rainforest birds and scenery in South America; to 900K; 100 clips of Andean pan flute music; 25 video clips; D; Aris Entertainment

Wild Places
100 photos of North America; to 900K; 50 audio clips and sound effects; D; Aris Entertainment

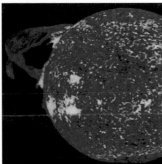

Worldview
100 photos of earth and other astronomical features from space; to 900K; 25 Mac/MPL movies of blast-offs; 100 audio clips; D; Aris Entertainment

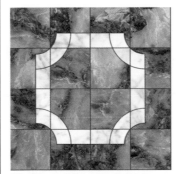

Marble and Granite *(2 disks)*
40 high-resolution scans of exotic marbles; also a collection of buttons, mortises and tiles for 3D rendering and multimedia; to 25 MB; A; Artbeats

Marbled Paper Textures *(2 disks)*
40 high-resolution scans of pages of marbelized paper; most to 26 MB, with two double-page images at 49 MB; A; Artbeats

Digital Sampler: Cliff Hollenbeck
50 images of natural sites in Kodak Photo CD format; one in a series from famous photographers; B; to 18 MB; Digital Zone

Digital Sampler: Kevin Morris
50 images of natural sites; Kodak Photo CD format; one in a series from famous photographers; B; to 18 MB. Digital Zone

Wraptures One
130 seamless, tiling photographic textures and backgrounds; to 900K; D; Form and Function

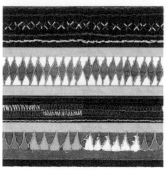

Wraptures Two
130 seamless, tiling photographic textures and backgrounds; to 900K; D; Form and Function

African Wildlife
200 photos by Carl and Ann Purcell; to 2.2 MB; C; Gazelle Technologies, Inc.

Antique Toys
150 historical images of antique toys; to 2.1 MB; A; Gazelle Technologies, Inc.

Aquatic Art
200 images of Hawaiian and Caribbean marine life; to 1.8 MB; A; Gazelle Technologies, Inc.

Aviation
200 photos of military and civilian aircraft from 1940 to present; to 2 MB; C; Gazelle Technologies, Inc.

Creative Backgrounds and Textures
200 photos of textures, sunsets, skylines, bridges, desert, and sky; to 2.3 MB or to 18 MB in Kodak Photo CD format; D; Gazelle Technologies, Inc.

Kids
200 images; to 2.1 MB; C; Gazelle Technologies, Inc.

Male Models
25 photos of men in casual settings and classic portraiture; to 500K; on five 800K floppy disks; Gazelle Technologies, Inc.

Nature's Way
196 images of natural scenery; to 2.3 MB; B; Gazelle Technologies, Inc.

Ocean Imagery
Boats, ocean life, seascapes, surfing,
waterskiing, windsurfing; 2.5 MB; B;
Gazelle Technologies, Inc.

Ocean Magic
160 color images of ocean life and
coral; to 2.5 MB; A; Gazelle
Technologies, Inc.

People at Leisure
200 photos; to 2.2 MB; A; Gazelle
Technologies, Inc.

People in Business
200 photos; to 1.8 MB; A; Gazelle
Technologies, Inc.

People of the World
200 photos; to 2.1 MB; A; Gazelle
Technologies, Inc.

**Professional Photography
Collection**
100 photos of business, leisure,
government, travel, food; Photo CD
format; A; DiscImagery; Gazelle
Technologies, Inc.

Swimsuit Volumes 1 and 2
200 color images of women in
swimsuits; to 2.2 MB; C; Gazelle
Technologies, Inc.

World Travel Europe
240 stock photos by Carl and Ann
Purcell; to 2.3 MB; C; Gazelle
Technologies, Inc.

World Travel Far East and Asia
200 images of temples, landscape, and
clothing by Carl and Ann Purcell; to
2.20 MB; C; Gazelle Technologies, Inc.

PhotoTone-Fontek
More than 500 images for use as backgrounds, including industrial, natural, paper/textiles, and food; E; Letraset USA

Vol. 1 – Business and Industry
408 images of business people and work scenes; to 7.1 MB; A; PhotoDisc

Vol. 2 – People and Lifestyles
409 images of families, teens, kids, and seniors in action; to 8.5 MB; A; PhotoDisc

Vol. 3 – Full-Page Backgrounds
111 studio stills and photos of natural backgrounds; to 17.2 MB; A; PhotoDisc

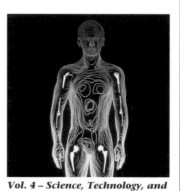

Vol. 4 – Science, Technology, and Medicine
220 images of computers, health care settings, lab equipment, and people; to 8.4 MB; A; PhotoDisc

Vol. 5 – World Commerce and Travel
350 images of native peoples and business scenes in Europe, Asia, Africa, and the Americas; to 8.4 MB; A; PhotoDisc

One Twenty-Eight
128 seamlessly tiling digital photographic textures; 512 X 512 pixels; Pixar

Mosaic Album 2
300 photos of people, nature, structures, vehicles, animals, and plants; to 12 MB; A; Vintage

Photo Pro Volume 1: Patterns in Nature
100 photo images of nature scenes; to 4 MB; B; Wayzata Technology, Inc.

Active Lifestyles
100 images of sports and activities; to 18 MB in Kodak Photo CD format; A; Digital Stock, Inc.

Animals
100 images of birds, mammals, reptiles, amphibians, butterflies and other insects; to 18 MB in Kodak Photo CD format; A; Digital Stock, Inc.

Babies & Children
100 images of children to early teens, individually and in small groups, portraits and active shots; to 18 MB in Kodak Photo CD format; A; Digital Stock, Inc.

Buildings & Structures
100 images of landmark buildings (ancient and modern, worldwide), bridges, architectural structure, and cityscapes; to 18 MB in Kodak Photo CD format; A; Digital Stock, Inc.

Business & Industry
100 images of factories, small businesses, offices, high-tech/ laboratories, and money; to 18 MB in Kodak Photo CD format; A; Digital Stock, Inc.

Flowers
100 images of flowers, from extremely close-up to vistas of flower fields; to 18 MB in Kodak Photo CD format; A; Digital Stock, Inc.

Indigenous Peoples
100 images of people in New Guinea, Bali, India, Thailand, Burma, Borneo, Ecuador, and Tanzania; to 18 MB in Kodak Photo CD format; A; Digital Stock, Inc.

Landscapes
100 images of landscapes of the western United States (including Hawaii), Mexico, New Zealand, and France; to 18 MB in Kodak Photo CD format; A; Digital Stock, Inc.

Men, Women & Romance
100 images of individuals and couples; to 18 MB in Kodak Photo CD format; A; Digital Stock, Inc.

Mountains & Waterfalls
100 images of mountains and falls of the western United States, Canada, Austria, Switzerland, Mexico, Ecuador, and Tibet; to 18 MB in Kodak Photo CD format; A; Digital Stock, Inc.

Oceans & Coasts
100 images with and without people; to 18 MB in Kodak Photo CD format; A; Digital Stock, Inc.

Space & Spaceflight
100 images of earth, other planets, astronomical features, blast-offs, and space walks, most from NASA, JPL, and NOAO; to 18 MB in Kodak Photo CD format; B; Digital Stock, Inc.

Sunsets, Skies & Weather
100 images, many with clouds or silhouetted trees; to 18 MB in Kodak Photo CD format; A; Digital Stock, Inc.

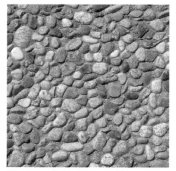

Textures & Backgrounds
100 images of natural and manmade textures; to 18 MB in Kodak Photo CD format; A; Digital Stock, Inc.

Transportation
100 images of planes, trains, roads, traffic, cars, and boats; to 18 MB in Kodak Photo CD format; A; Digital Stock, Inc.

Trees
100 images of trees, forests, fall foliage, winter scenes, and cactus, including some sunsets; to 18 MB in Kodak Photo CD format; A; Digital Stock, Inc.

Undersea Life
100 images of fishes, coral, sponges, squid, octopus, other invertebrates, kelp forests, sea mammals, and divers; to 18 MB in Kodak Photo CD format; A; Digital Stock, Inc.

Image Samples (3 discs)
100, 100, and 20 professional photos of backgrounds and textures, nature and scenics, wildlife, travel, business and industry, architecture, sports, environment and pollution; to 18 MB; D; ColorBytes.

The World Bank
3000 images from 38 countries on 30 discs; color-corrected CMYK TIFFs; to 5.5 MB; A; Aztech/New Media Corp.

Sky (Vol. 1)
100 sky images, from dawn to blue to stormy to crisp to dusk; to 15 MB; A; CD Folios

Electric Iris (Vol. 1, No. 1)
60 images of children, family, nature, leisure activity, and people; to 10.3 MB; A; Digital Knowledge

Contact information for the photo disks listed in Appendix A.

Aris Entertainment, Inc.
4444 Via Marina
Suite 811
Marina Del Rey, CA 90292
310-821-0234
310-821-6463 fax

Artbeats
P.O. Box 1287
Myrtle Creek, OR 97457
503-863-4429
503-863-4547 fax

Aztech/New Media Corp.
2255 Markham Rd.
Scarsborough, Ontario
Canada M1B 2W3
800-361-0669

CD Folios
22647 Ventura Blvd.
Suite 199
Woodland Hills, CA 91364
805-527-9227

The Classic Archives Company
3 West Rocks Road
Norwalk, CT 06851
203-847-0930
203-845-0679 fax

ColorBytes, Inc.
2525 South Wadsworth Blvd.
Suite 308
Denver, CO 80227
800-825-2656
303-989-9205

Digital Knowledge Corp.
8100 Wayzata Blvd.
Golden Valley, MN 55426
800-279-6099

Digital Stock, Inc.
400 S. Sierra Ave.
Solana Beach, CA 92075
619-794-4040
619-794-4041 fax

Digital Zone Inc.
P.O. Box 5562
Bellevue, WA 98006
800-538-3113
206-623-3456

D'Pix, Inc.
929 Harrison Avenue
Suite 205
Columbus, OH 43215
800-238-3749

Form and Function
San Francisco, CA
800-843-9497

Gazelle Technologies, Inc.
7434 Trade Street
San Diego, CA 92121
619-536-9999

Letraset USA
40 Eisenhower Drive
Paramus, NJ 07653
201-845-6100
201-845-7539 fax

PhotoDisc, Inc.
2013 Fourth Avenue
Suite 200
Seattle, WA 98121
206-441-9355
206-441-9379 fax

Pixar
1001 West Cutting Blvd.
Richmond, CA 94804
800-888-9856
510-236-4000
510-236-0388 fax

Vintage
422 4th Avenue SE
Pacific, WA 98047
800-995-9777
206-833-3995

Wayzata Technology Inc.
P.O. Box 807
Grand Rapids, MI 55744
800-735-7321
218-326-0597
218-326-0598 fax

Appendix B
Software Information

Software of potential interest to readers of The Photoshop Wow! Book

Adobe Systems, Inc.
P.O. Box 7900
Mountain View, CA 94039-7900
800-833-6687

Illustrator: Design tool with powerful illustration and text handling capabilities.

Premiere: Digital video editing software.

Separator: Utility for color separation; ships with Illustrator.

Type Manager (ATM): Generates type for both displays and printers from high quality PostScript outline fonts.

Aldus Corporation
411 First Avenue South
Suite 200
Seattle, WA 98104-2871
206-622-5500
800-685-3537

FreeHand: Design and illustration tool for graphics professionals. Combines easy-to-use interface with exceptional power.

Gallery Effects (Vols. 1, 2, and 3): Plug-in filters; special effects transform color, grayscale, and bitmapped images into sophisticated art.

PageMaker: Desktop publishing software. Integrates text and graphics, allowing users to write, design, and produce professional-quality printed communications.

Andromeda Software Inc.
849 Old Farm Road
Thousand Oaks, CA 91360
800-547-0055
805-379-4109 fax

Series 1 Photography Filters: Optical Lens Effects

Art Parts
P.O. Box2926
Orange, CA 92669-0926
714-633-9617 fax

Clip art of animals, people, dingbats, holiday, business/travel.

HSC Software
1661 Lincoln Blvd.
Suite 101
Santa Monica, CA 90404
310-392-8441
310-392-6015 fax

Kai's Power Tools (KPT): Plug-in filters for special effects, designed by Kai Krause.

Quark, Inc.
1800 Grant Street
Denver, CO 80203
303-894-8888
303-894-3399 fax

XPress: Desktop publishing software. Integrates text and graphics, allowing users to write, design, and produce professional-quality printed communications.

Symantec Corporation, Peter Norton Group
2500 Broadway
Suite 200
Santa Monica, CA 90404

Norton Utilities: A set of applications for system maintenance

Appendix C
Publications

Books and other publications of
potential interest to readers of
The Photoshop Wow! Book

Adobe Systems, Inc.
P.O. Box 7900
Mountain View, CA 94039-7900
800-833-6687

Adobe Technical Notes: Free by fax or
mail, on such Photoshop-related topics
as The Lab Color Mode; Scanning
Basics; Working with Type in Adobe
Photoshop, Creating predictable
Separations, Maximizing Performance,
The Adobe Photoshop Raw File
Format, Questions to Ask Your Printer,
Adobe Photoshop Tips, Using
Separation Tables, and many more.

**Agfa Prepress Education
Resources**
P.O. Box 7917
Mt. Prospect, IL
800-395-7007

An Introduction to Digital Color Prepress
and *Digital Color Prepress Volume 2:*
Short, colorful technical publications
on digital color prepress; also available
as 35mm slide shows.

Peachpit Press
2414 Sixth Street
Berkeley, CA 94710
800-283-9444

Photoshop in Black and White by Jim
Rich and Sandy Bozek: Coverage of
tonal adjustment and other topics
specific to achieving consistently good
qualtiy in reproducing Black-and-white
images.

Four Colors/One Image by Mattias
Nyman: Coverage of scanning,
calibration, separations, tonal value
changes, image compression, screen
angles, output resolution, and other
topics as they relate to Photoshop
QuarkXPress, and Cachet.

Step-By-Step Publishing
111 Oakwood Road
E. Peoria, IL 61611
800-255-8800

Step-By-Step Electronic Design: Monthly
newsletter covering Photoshop,
Illustrator, FreeHand, PageMaker,
QuarkXPress, and other programs and
topics of interest to graphic designers
using computers

Step-By-Step Graphics: Bimonthly
magazine covering traditional; and
electronic design

Verbum
P.O. Box 12564
San Diego, CA 92112
619-944-9977

The Desktop Color Book: A small,
colorful, friendly book on color
systems, color reproduction, desktop
tools for color, PostScript illustration,
bitmapped artwork, and input,
storage, and output options

The Photo CD Book: A short
introduction to Photo CD products
and how to use them.

Appendix D
Artists and Photographers

Michel Kripalani 184, 185
Presto Studios, Inc.
P.O. Box 262535
San Diego, CA 92196-2535
619-689-4895

Steve Lomas 174
GTE Interactive Media
2385 Via Roble
Carlsbad, CA 92009
619-431-8801

Steve Lyons 146
136 Scenic Road
Fairfax, CA 94930
415-459-7560

Craig McClain 34
619-469-9599

Jeff McCord 55, 173
Free-Lancelot
1932 First Avenue, Suite 819
Seattle, WA 98101
206-443-1965

Susan Merritt 163
CWA, Inc.
4015 Ibis Street
San Diego, CA 92103
619-299-0431, 619-299-0451 fax

Bert Monroy 135, 189
1052 Curtis Street
Albany, CA 94706
510-524-9412

John Odam 140
John Odam Design Associates
2163 Cordero Road
Del Mar, CA 92014
619-259-8230

Doug Peltonen 173
Pre-Press Associates
1722 32nd Avenue
Seattle, WA 98122
206-325-3031

Phil Saunders 184, 185
Presto Studios, Inc.
P.O. Box 262535
San Diego, CA 92196-2535
619-689-4895

Max Seabaugh 138
246 First Street, Suite 310
San Francisco, CA 94105
415-543-7775

Russell Sparkman 73, 87
Seiwa Commons, Apt. D
2-100 Issha
Meito-ku
Nagoya
Japan 465
052-703-6305
052-703-6986

Cher Threinen 72, 130
475 San Gorgonio Street
San Diego, CA 92106
619-226-6050

Greg Uhler 181
Presto Studios, Inc.
P.O. Box 262535
San Diego, CA 92196-2535
619-689-4895

Sharon Varley 120
1043 University Ave. #248
San Diego, CA 92103

Beth Vernek 166
CWA, Inc.
4015 Ibis Street
San Diego, CA 92103
619-299-0431, 619-299-0451 fax

Tommy Yun 132, 135
Ursus Studios
P.O.Box 4858
Cerritos, CA 90703-4858

PHOTOGRAPHERS

Tom Collicott 173

Ellen Grossnickle 66

Susan Heller 68

Grant Heilman 76

Brant Hemingway 44

Douglas Kirkland 56

Mary Kristen 72

Craig McClain 30, 45, 47, cover

Kazuo Nogi 40

Carl and Ann Purcell 38, 102

Roy Robinson 61

Yuji Sado 102

Taizo Tashiro 99

Index

More from Peachpit Press...

CorelDRAW 4: Visual QuickStart Guide
Webster & Associates
Our popular quick-reference guide to Corel.
(350 pages)

Four Colors/One Image
Mattias Nyman
Explains how to manipulate and reproduce color using Photoshop, QuarkXPress, and Cachet.
(96 pages)

Jargon
Robin Williams
Useful, insightful, and eminently readable—this guide to commonly used computer terminology is a good resource for computer users of all levels. *(688 pages)*

The Little PC Book
Larry Magid
This bestseller, recommended by the *Wall Street Journal*, is a "gentle" introduction to the PC. Destined to be a classic. *(400 pages)*

The Little Windows Book, 3.1 Edition
Kay Yarborough Nelson
Includes handy summary charts of keyboard shortcuts and quick tips. *(144 pages)*

Mastering CorelDRAW 4
Chris Dickman
A comprehensive guide, written by a Corel master. Comes with a handy disk of fonts and utilities. *(776 pages)*

PageMaker 5 for Windows: Visual QuickStart Guide
Webster & Associates
A quick introduction to this widely used, powerful desktop-publishing tool. *(254 pages)*

The PC is not a typewriter
Robin Williams
PC users can now learn the secrets of creating beautiful type. *(96 pages)*

Photoshop 2.5 for Windows: Visual QuickStart Guide
Elaine Weinmann and Peter Lourekas
A quick, visual introduction to the basics of using Photoshop features and filters. *(264 pages)*

Photoshop in Black and White
Jim Rich and Sandy Bozek
A guide to manipulating black and white images in Photoshop. *(44 pages)*

The QuarkXPress Book, 2nd Edition for Windows
David Blatner and Bob Weibel
The Mac version of this book has been a bestseller for two years—so useful that Quark's own support staff uses it. *(542 pages)*

Real World Scanning and Halftones
David Blatner and Steve Roth
Learn how to master the digital halftone process, from scanning images to tweaking them on your computer to imagesetting. *(296 pages)*

The Windows 3.1 Bible
Fred Davis
A wall-to-wall compendium of useful information about Windows. Comes with an index so thorough it will make you weep with pleasure. *(1,154 pages)*

The Windows Bible CD-ROM
Fred Davis
Over 500 MB of reference material, tools, fonts, games, music, and video.

Word 6 for Windows: Visual QuickStart Guide
Webster & Associates
A highly visual guide to Word 6. *(208 pages)*

WordPerfect 6 for Windows: Visual QuickStart Guide
Webster and Associates
A quick and easy visual guide. *(272 pages)*

Order Form

to order, call: (800) 283-9444 or (510) 548-4393 or (510) 548-5991 (fax)

#	Title	Price	Total
	CorelDRAW 4: Visual QuickStart Guide	15.00	
	Four Colors/One Image	18.00	
	Jargon	22.00	
	The Little PC Book	17.95	
	The Little Windows Book, 3.1 Edition	12.95	
	Mastering CorelDRAW 4 (with disk)	34.95	
	PageMaker 5 for Windows: Visual QuickStart Guide	14.00	
	The PC is not a typewriter	9.95	
	Photoshop for Windows: Visual QuickStart Guide	18.95	
	Photoshop in Black & White	18.00	
	The Photoshop Wow! Book, Windows Edition (with disk)	34.95	
	The QuarkXPress Book, 2nd Edition for Windows	24.95	
	Real World Scanning and Halftones	24.95	
	The Windows 3.1 Bible	28.00	
	The Windows Bible CD-ROM	34.95	
	Word 6 for Windows: Visual QuickStart Guide	15.95	
	WordPerfect 6 for Windows: Visual QuickStart Guide	14.95	

SHIPPING:	First Item	Each Additional	Subtotal		
UPS Ground	$4	$1			
UPS Blue	$8	$2	8.25% Tax (CA only)		
Canada	$6	$4	Shipping		
Overseas	$14	$14	**TOTAL**		

Name

Company

Address

City   State   Zip

Phone   Fax

☐ Check enclosed   ☐ Visa   ☐ MasterCard

Company purchase order #

Credit card #   Expiration Date

Peachpit Press, Inc. • 2414 Sixth Street • Berkeley, CA • 94710
Your satisfaction is guaranteed or your money will be cheerfully refunded!